Secret Squadrons of the Eighth

Secret Squadrons of the Eighth

LONDON

IAN ALLAN LTD

First published 1990
Reprinted 2000

ISBN 0 7110 1881 2

Published by Ian Allan Publishing

an imprint of Ian Allan Publishing Ltd, Terminal House, Shepperton, Surrey TW17 8AS

Printed by Ian Allan Printing Ltd, Riverdene Business Park, Hersham, Surrey KT12 4RG.

Code: 0010/3

CONTENTS

ACKNOWLEDGEMENTS

There are so many people without whose invaluable assistance this book could not have been written. In particular there are those members of the Cheddington (STN 113) Association, who served with units of the United States 8th Air Force (US 8th AF) during World War 2. It is, however, impossible for me to express my gratitude to each and every one individually. I therefore hope that they will forgive me.

During the many years of research that have culminated in the publication of this book, a number of units and institutions have been contacted or visited. In America they include the USAF Historical Research Center, Maxwell AFB, Alabama; the Inspection & Flight Safety Center, Norton AFB, California; the National Archives & Record Center; and the American Battle Monuments Commission, Washington DC. In England, the Air Historical Branch of the MOD and the Public Record Office, Kew; the Royal Signals & Radar Establishment, Malvern; and both the Imperial War Museum, Lambeth, and the RAF Museum, Hendon. I am indebted to the staff involved who assisted with my many requests for help and information.

A number of private individuals also contributed in more ways than they could possibly know: 'Willy' Donald kept my spirits up when the postman failed to arrive, and fellow 'Bud' drinker Steve Pigott, due to his criticism, gave me the determination to continue. Likewise so did Simon Waite, but in his case it was praise that kept me going. Ann-Marie Mitchell moved the commas and my sister Marie Harris exchanged the 'dones' for 'dids'.

Last but not least, if it had not been for the discomfort my wife Shirley and two children Peter and Marie suffered from the continuous buzz of my printer, then this book would never have been completed.

To all of you I say 'thank you'.

Pat Carty
England 1989

'What will become of this little section of England that has been our life for the last year or two? Will the runways and hardstands lay abandoned and untouched in mute tribute to the men who worked, lived and sweated out the planes during the years of war and restriction? What will become of the dogs once fed so well around the mess halls — the legion of station mascots? Will they walk through deserted kitchens wondering where the chow lines and their GI pals have gone? What impression have we Americans made in our frequent contacts with the English people who have been our neighbours, and companions, during these long monotonous war-weary years? Probably, these questions which probe into the future will not be answered for many years.'

American GI, Cheddington 1943

Right:
For the many American servicemen stationed at the nearby base, Cheddington railway station spelled journey's end after the arduous Atlantic crossing and wearying train ride from Liverpool Docks. Here men from the 1077th Signal Company arrive at Cheddington in June 1943. *B. Downs/113 Association*

406 BOMB SQDN. (H)

I
THE HOME

Cheddington

Set in a triangle of countryside bounded by the tranquil villages of Long Marston, Cheddington and Marsworth, is an area of farmland reminiscent of the kind of setting seen in a John Constable painting. However, this is not what it turned out to be, for some 40 years ago this area became home to units of the United States Army Air Force (USAAF) whose missions were some of the best kept secrets of World War 2.

This area, 30 miles northwest of London and shared by the Home Counties of Buckinghamshire and Hertfordshire, had for many years been a quiet spot in the English countryside. Events in other parts of the country, however, were far from quiet. In response to the increasing threat of war — on 26 May 1939 — and as a result of the RAF's expansion plan — an 'Aerodrome Board' was formed by the Air Ministry. The Board members were instructed to seek sites for the building of airfields with the requirement that they be at least three to five miles apart and at least 50ft above sea level (ASL). This was to eliminate the risk of flooding, but the sites could be no more than 650ft ASL due to the problems this would engender from mist and fog. When such a site was found, and if it were free from obstructions, it would be marked off on an Ordnance Survey map within a 1,000yd circle.

This circle would then be inspected for any minor obstructions and the proposed runways 'walked out'. Finally, a geological map (if one was available) was used to study the structure of the subsoil.

When two Long Marston farmers, and Arthur Reeve the tenant farmer of Church Farm, Marsworth, found out that a Mr Phipps from the 'Board' would be touring their area looking to requisition such land, they had no worries — or so they thought! What a shock however, when, soon after the visit and its ensuing meetings, they found out that their land, with two large hills to the northeast, Dunstable Downs to the southeast, and Marsworth Church to the southwest, had been one of 4,000 inspected sites and that it was now required! Arthur Reeve, who had farmed the area for many years, like his parents before him, not only had a shock, but could not believe his eyes when, within a few days of the visit, he received a letter instructing him not to plough his soil any more. If what he read in the letter was correct, and he forfeited his land, it would mean he would stand to lose his farmhouse; and if he lost that, he would lose his livelihood. For a man with a wife and young family, the future indeed looked bleak!

The area in question was soon requisitioned, trees removed and the surface levelled by gangs of workmen who had been

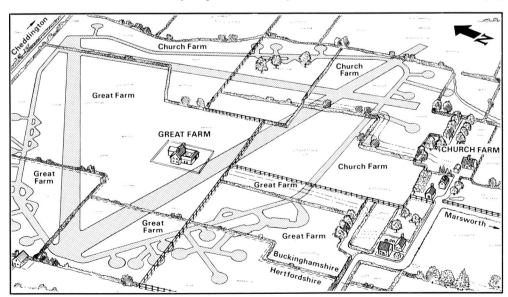

Left:
Church Farm, Marsworth in 1940. Arthur Reeve who farmed Church Farm had all his land requisitioned to enable Cheddington airfield to be built.

7

hired by a local government contractor, B. Sunley Ltd. However, progress was slow, so in June 1941 the Government brought in the well known construction firm of George Wimpey to take over the contract and finish the earth moving, cutting-out and laying of the runways, and erection of the main buildings. For the electrical installations, two firms — Malcome & Allen and Crompton Parkinson — were used. This left just the living sites to be constructed by G. Walker & Slater and Lansdown's. To improve the bricklaying time, an automatic bricklayer was used and put to work on the control tower. The bricklayer consisted of a box structure into which bricks and mortar were placed. This removed the need to line up each row. This 'quick' bricklaying method was of little benefit for after the brick walls had reached 3ft high, they were out of true by 3in. As the control tower was designed to be some 30ft in height, it would have been out of true by 30in on completion! This of course was not acceptable, so the whole construction was pulled down and rebuilt by hand, the finished article being a Type 13079/41 control tower.

The Royal Air Force

When all building work had been completed and the new airfield named 'Cheddington' after the nearest railway station, the Royal Air Force took command. As it had already been decided by the Air Ministry that the airfield was to be used as a bomber training airfield, and because the building of the runways on the nearby airfield at Wing in Buckinghamshire had not been concluded, it was agreed to move the Headquarters of No 26 Operational Training Unit (OTU), which was due to use Wing, into Cheddington. The date selected was 9 March 1942. On 15 March, 121 officers and other ranks of the OTU Servicing Squadron followed, and made preparations for the arrival of their aircraft. This did not take long as four Avro Ansons arrived on 22 March, followed the next day by the first of the unit's Vickers Wellington bombers. The first flight out was made on the 26th, when an Anson left conveying an instructor on liaison duties.

Within a month the number of aircraft assigned to the OTU was 17 Wellingtons and six Ansons. One of the Ansons, Mk I DJ124, had the distinction of being the unit's first aircraft to be damaged when it was involved in a ground accident on 3 April. Accidents, however, went hand-in-hand with training, as No 2 Squadron from RAF Sawbridgeworth could verify. Soon after it had set up a temporary camp at Cheddington on 27 April for Exercise 'Sapper', Curtiss Tomahawk Mk I, AH934 XV-0, flown by Plt Off Vaughan, damaged a wing. The purpose of the squadron exercise was for three Tomahawk aircraft to perform artillery reconnaissance (ARTY/R), tactical reconnaissance (TAC/R) and message dropping sorties in support of British Army units. The squadron must have taken a liking to Cheddington, as it returned for

Below:
Cheddington — General arrangement.

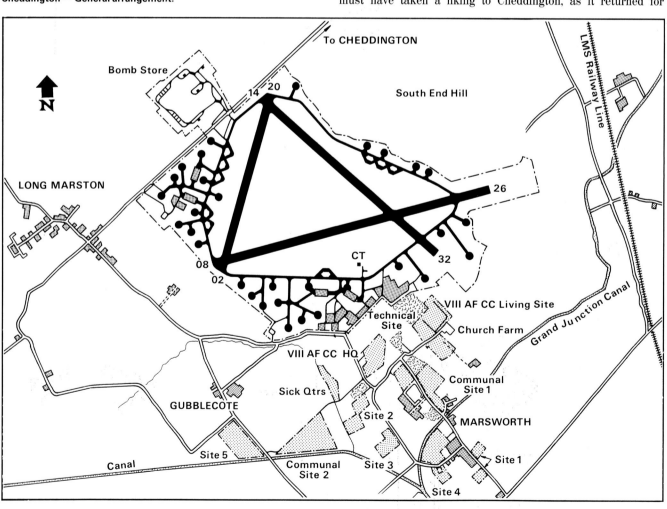

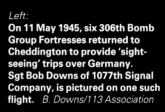

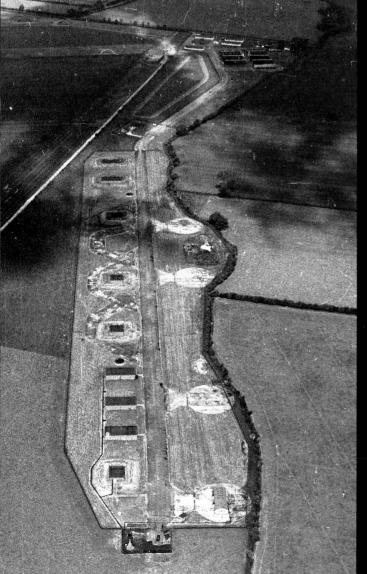

Exercise 'Sledgehammer' the following November with its Mustang Is.

The month of May brought bad news when the first aircraft loss was reported on the 31st. Wellington Mk IC DV707 EU-D was reported 'missing in action' (MIA), following the historic 1,000-bomber raid to Cologne. August was also a bad month, as three other Wellingtons were also struck off charge. On the 5th, X9675 caught fire and the crew had to abandon it over Burton Coggles near Grantham. On the 12th, DV868 EU-E, whilst landing one side of the flarepath, retracted the undercarriage to go round again. Air speed could not be maintained, and she stalled and burned out in the crash that followed. There were no injuries to the crew, however. This was not the case when, on the 30th, DV825 EU-U also burned out. She took off at 15.45hrs for circuits and landings, but lost speed, bounced, then swung round and stalled trying to clear the hill to the south of Cheddington airfield. The pilot, Sgt McDougall, and one of the gunners, Sgt Hendricksen, both died from burns despite being pulled from the flaming wreckage by Gordon Miller and his cowman Dan Millins of Manor Farm, Marsworth. These two rescuers received the British Empire Medal from the King for their brave actions.

The Mighty Eighth

When the construction of RAF Wing had been accomplished, it could not have been a day too soon for the men of the OTU to move in, and away from the hills and obstructions that were to be found around Cheddington airfield. Reports were soon submitted claiming that the airfield was unsuitable for RAF training purposes. Four days later, on 7 September 1942, the empty airfield was handed over to the United States 8th Army Air Force (8th AF). The intention was for it to become an administration satellite for nearby Bovingdon. The Americans during this time were deficient in the number of airfields available to meet their requirements, and wasted no time in accepting the airfield — not for administrative use, but as a base for their fast-growing air armada.

The period from March 1942, whilst the airfield at Cheddington had been experiencing growing pains, was also a time of great change for many units of the 8th AF. Far across the wide Atlantic in America, the 44th Bomb Group had been struggling to form itself into a fighting unit. The Group had been activated and trained at Barksdale Field, Louisiana, and were almost fully

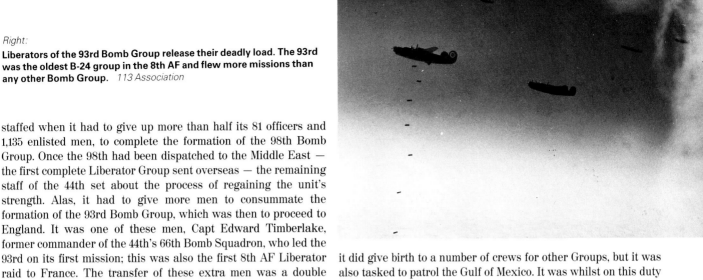

Right:
Liberators of the 93rd Bomb Group release their deadly load. The 93rd was the oldest B-24 group in the 8th AF and flew more missions than any other Bomb Group. *113 Association*

staffed when it had to give up more than half its 81 officers and 1,135 enlisted men, to complete the formation of the 98th Bomb Group. Once the 98th had been dispatched to the Middle East — the first complete Liberator Group sent overseas — the remaining staff of the 44th set about the process of regaining the unit's strength. Alas, it had to give more men to consummate the formation of the 93rd Bomb Group, which was then to proceed to England. It was one of these men, Capt Edward Timberlake, former commander of the 44th's 66th Bomb Squadron, who led the 93rd on its first mission; this was also the first 8th AF Liberator raid to France. The transfer of these extra men was a double blow, for in the same month the Group forfeited additional men to complete the formation of the 90th Bomb Group, destined for duty in Australia. It was a task that almost made the unit's staff officers 'throw in the towel'. All hope was not abandoned in the 44th, however, as the 8th AF 'Selective Service' machinery was functioning at full speed and during April more replacements poured in from Induction Centres all over the United States. By May, the 44th had a full complement, but then had to give up more officers and men (10 trained crews) to fill gaps in a number of other bomb groups. There was a further blow, for it had also to send a crew on a secret mapping expedition into the cold of the Arctic, the concept being to make the ever-increasing airways from North America to Europe a safer route to travel. This task they accomplished and, was a result, many fliers now owe their gratitude to that intrepid crew.

Do not be deceived however, as the stay for the 44th at Barksdale was more than a rest period at a maternity home. True,

it did give birth to a number of crews for other Groups, but it was also tasked to patrol the Gulf of Mexico. It was whilst on this duty that it first engaged the enemy in combat and sunk one of his submarines!

The sweltering days of July 1942 came, and the 44th proceeded to Will Rogers Field, Oklahoma City, to continue training, but with more vigour as the unit had been informed to prepare for overseas duty within three months. War does not wait, for within 30 days it was on its way overseas. The ground echelon was transported by three trains to Fort Dix, New Jersey where there was a mad scramble to procure extra equipment. On 3 September the officers and men piled on to special trains for Jersey City, and from there were ferried up the Hudson River to Cunard Dock where the liner *Queen Mary* was waiting. She set sail the next afternoon in brilliant sunshine down the Hudson, and out by the Statue of Liberty. Up past Coney Island, until the shores of America passed out of view, then nosed her way out into the cold Atlantic. Five mornings later she sailed down the Irish Sea, with a view of the green fields of Ireland to starboard and the rolling

Below:
Training Record
Prior to service in England with the Night Leaflet Squadron, Gunner Jake Sandoval spent many hours training at Yuma and March AFB in America.

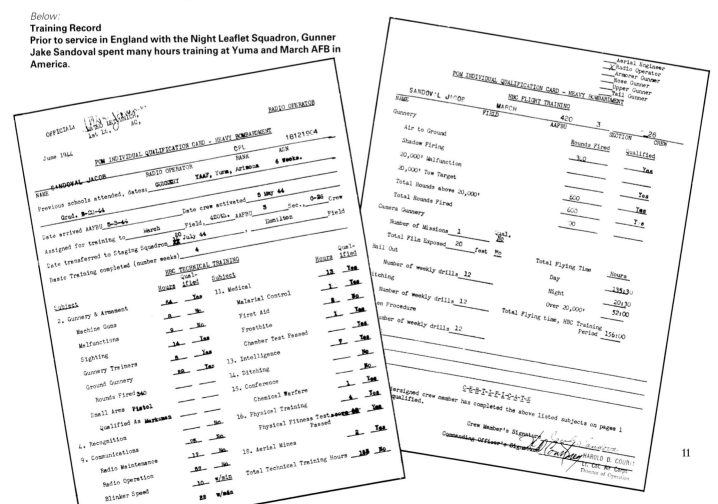

11

hills of Scotland to port. She dropped anchor in the Clyde, her men disembarked, then boarded trains for their new English home at Cheddington.

Back in America, the air echelon of the 44th was fighting the 'Battle of Camp Grenier', to obtain as much equipment as possible. When the battle had been won and the intensive training programme completed, it too left the beloved homeland. The echelon made the difficult North Atlantic crossing not by sea, but in 27 of its trusty B-24D Liberators. The first nine crews, from the 66th Squadron, arrived at Cheddington on 1 October and, once reunited, the officers and men of the air and ground echelons set out to firmly establish Anglo-American relationships whilst off-duty. When on duty there was an intensive programme of conditioning for the new climate and the environment. The men soon learned to say 'three ha'pennies', 'chairs', 'you cahn't miss it' and many other quaint old English figures of speech that were new to their ears. These soon became part of their everyday vocabulary. The men were also initiated into the English joys of drinking non-intoxicating warm beer, and the difficult task of hardening a certain part of their anatomy for a new mode of transport — the bicycle. This required learning to ride, for them, on the 'wrong' side of the road!

The stay at Cheddington for the 44th was short, for in less than a month the unit, together with its equipment and all but one Liberator, set off for another new home — Shipdham in Norfolk. The reason for leaving Cheddington was that the airfield was again found to be too small and the runway not long enough or hard enough to take the pounding of heavy bombers day after day. This change of station for the 44th changed its whole future, for had it remained at Cheddington on the training task intended, it would not have suffered 153 aircraft missing in action, or endured the tragic loss of life that resulted.

Meanwhile, the resident Clerk of Works for the Air Ministry was informed about the airfield's problems and he in turn informed his area office. As a result it was agreed that the 8th AF would move out and that extra construction would take place to enlarge the living, technical and recreation sites. On 26 October, with the exception of three officers and six enlisted men who remained on a 'care and maintenance' basis, the 8th AF departed. During the next four months the enlarging of the airfield was

accomplished, but not without mishap. Whilst the runway was being resurfaced with the aid of a bitumen layer (which took only 252 man-hours), two members of an American Army Engineering Unit under the Officer Commanding, Capt Patton, fell into the boiling pitch. The accident was only noticed when their bones were reportedly spread over the runway and mixed in the solution.

On 18 November at 06.30hrs, Avro Anson Mk I, N5004, from No 10 OTU, RAF Abingdon, also came to grief. Whilst on a cross-country training flight from its base in Oxfordshire, its pilot, Sgt Lockhart, became lost in 10/10th cloud. He asked his wireless operator to call for assistance but, despite the wireless set being in good working order, he could not receive the control tower at Cheddington. Lockhart brought the Anson lower and circled the airfield beacon, but could not see a 'T' displayed to indicate the direction of the runway in use. He came lower but then saw red flares being fired from the control tower. Having no idea of the aircraft's location, and short of fuel, he ordered his crew to bale out, which they did without injury. Sgt Lockhart then crash-landed the Anson in an orchard at Hawkings Farm, Pitstone, just outside the 'Closed' airfield boundary.

By January 1943 the construction had been completed and the airfield was by then ready for operations, so the RAF transferred to No 2 Gliding School for Exercise 'Spartan'. This consisted of 15 officers and 120 other ranks who, despite bad weather, achieved 1,182 day-tows and 287 night-tows in the unit's Hotspur gliders, towed by their Miles Master Mk II tugs. Once the exercise had been completed, on 20 March 1943, the school moved to Weston-on-the-Green in Oxfordshire, and left the airfield vacant for its next occupants to move in.

———

Below:
A RAF pilot signs the obligatory Form 700 before taking a pupil up for a training flight in a Hotspur II training glider. The Hotspur was used primarily as an operational trainer with the Airborne Division.
IWM CH7883

Left:
Men of the 2901st CCRC Group sit around the stove that provided the warmth. The boxes on the floor provided heat in another form: chilli con carne. These men were the first Americans to arrive at Cheddington.
R. Dennison/113 Association

Far away in America, it had been a clear, crisp, blue sky that greeted five enlisted men from the US Army when they reported for duty at MacDill Field, Florida, in late October 1942. The privates, George Sweeny, Arny Van Heuvelen, Bill Weintraab, Henry Woolf and Johnny Wildman, were all fresh from Army Administration School and had been posted to MacDill to form the nucleus of a new Bomb Wing. Its Table of Organisation (TO) for staffing and rank structuring called for 45 officers and 130 enlisted men (EM), plus a signal company for communications. The Wing would be attached to the 3rd AF but was soon due to be reassigned to the 8th AF.

The first day of November saw the men in the new Bomb Wing treated, if one can use that term, to yet another parade. This one was more formal for it was the appointment of their Commanding Officer, Capt Garret C. Houseman. Within a few days of his appointment Capt Houseman received an influx of personnel and from them appointed 2Lt Robert Waite as Wing Adjutant, 2Lt Robert Moore as Commanding Officer Headquarters Squadron, and 2Lt Ira Reimer as Supply Officer. On 18 December Capt William McCaslin was appointed Assistant A-2, and two days later Maj Joseph Nate was posted in to take over command of the Wing from Capt Houseman. Maj Nate had been appointed CO several weeks earlier but had been on temporary duty at the Harrisburgh Intelligence School.

Maj Nate's wife, a 2Lt in the WACs, also arrived to spend Christmas with her husband. Christmas came, and despite the war all present had a marvellous time. The Major, who was expecting a posting for his unit at any moment, took full advantage of the interval. When the visit came to an end, he appointed an aircraft and crew from the Station Flight to fly his wife back to her unit, and accompanied her on the aircraft so as to be together for the extra few hours. The aircraft took-off and made for the Gulf of Mexico but, along with its crew and passengers, disappeared without trace. As a result of this loss, Capt Houseman became CO once more, but only for the short period to 10 March 1943, when Maj Oscar Steely arrived and assumed command.

For the Wing it was now time to enter the basic phase of overseas training, and the men were sent to specialist schools to prepare them for their subsequent work in the organisation. The majority of men had already attended training school once and were therefore engaged in an elaborate course of basic training with ample opportunities to apply all the knowledge they had previously acquired from their initial training. This included such subjects as chemical, desert and jungle warfare, map reading, extended and close order drill, commando tactics, protection against all methods of attack, field problems, first aid, field sanitation and general body conditioning, and forced marches both day and night in full pack. All this was quite unrelated to aviation, but it must be remembered that at this time the men were not attached to the Army Air Corps. During this training period more changes were made against staff officers; it was even reported that cash exchanged hands on a day-to-day basis as the enlisted men made bets on 'who would be boss today'. By the first week of May the constant changes had come to an end and had resulted in Capt McCaslin becoming Wing Adjutant; Lt Moore, Squadron Adjutant; Capt Hende, Squadron Commanding Officer; and Capt Houseman was back in command of the Wing.

The staff changes and completion of overseas training were just in time, for on 8 May 1943, having been alerted a week earlier, the Wing left by train for Camp Shanks, New York, on the initial stage of its long overseas journey. It arrived on the 10th and set up camp. In the days that followed, latrine rumours began to flow thick and fast: the men had no idea of their final overseas destination, even on the 23rd when they marched up the gang-plank of the liner *Mariposa*, which was berthed at Staten Island. Where were they going? Some said the South Pacific, others said Iceland, a few thought China, and one or two put forward England. The rest had no idea, but would not have been surprised if it had been Texas! However, Headquarters Army Air Corps had no doubt about the destination for the Wing, which by now had taken on the full title of the 20th Bomb Wing (Heavy), and its destination was to be England — in support of the daylight bombing of Germany.

On 1 June the *Mariposa* docked at Liverpool after her long Atlantic crossing. The officers and men of the 20th disembarked and boarded trains for their first English base at Headquarters VIII Bomber Command, High Wycombe. 'Pinetree' as the base was known, had taken over a girl's school and was set in a tree-shrouded area not far from the centre of town. This location,

30 miles from London was only four miles from RAF High Wycombe, Headquarters of RAF Bomber Command. The next few days were spent unloading bags, setting up home and being briefed about England and what to expect. The one thing the men were not told to expect was that Pinetree would be their home for just a week, for within seven days of arriving, 200 officers and men departed by truck convoy for a second change of base — the airfield at Cheddington.

Whilst the 20th Bomb Wing had been disembarking at Liverpool, the famous liner *Queen Mary*, which had previously brought over the 44th Bomb Group, was again crossing the 'Big Pond'. On board was another cargo of men and machines, including **Sgt Bob Downs**. He remembers that crossing very well:

'Whilst on the voyage we were only given fresh water for drinking. For washing or bathing, we had to use salt water which was terrible. As a result, few if any of us did wash, and so it was with much relief that, on June 6th 1944, we berthed in Scotland. Orders were given to wash, then dress in our "first class" uniforms and heavy wool coats. After what seemed hours, further orders were given to board a small boat which took us ashore. As we landed, we were greeted by the sound of bagpipes and the sight of Red Cross girls giving out coffee and cakes. It was then time to board a train and we were off. Whilst the beautiful countryside passed by, the men became very boisterous with singing and gambling taking place. At about midnight, we arrived at a station and off-loaded. We were then told by a group of officers who had come to meet us that we were at Cheddington, England, and it would be our home. They sounded as though they liked the place, since they mentioned an abundance of girls! We collected our packs and barrack bags and lined up on the platform, to wait for transport to arrive from the motor pool. The bags were heavy and put a strain on our backs. To relieve it, some of us leaned back against the ticket office. Private Hoskins leaned too far and, as he went through the window bum first, became our unit's first casualty.'

Above:
B-24s attempt to evade accurate and heavy flak. Note the bizarre patterns traced in the foreground, presumably caught through the use of a fast camera shutter speed. *113 Association*

Once driven to the airfield, all the men who were from the 379th Service Squadron, 9th Station Complement Squadron, 1077th Signal Company and the 39th Service Group, set up home alongside those from the 20th Bomb Wing. There was now at Cheddington, for the first time, a complete structure to staff and run a combat airfield. The delay in this formation may well have caused frustration in many of the officers and men, and together with their uncertain future, may have cast a shadow of doubt on the ability of their Commanding General and his advisors. This lack of confidence was unfounded, for these moves were just one small part in the build-up and formation of what was to be the biggest air force ever assembled — 'The Mighty Eighth'.

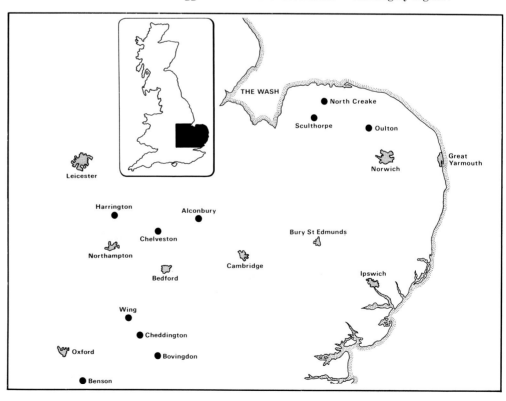

Right:
Airfields referred to in the text.

14

II
TRAINING

B-17 Flying Fortress

From the early days of operations by the 8th AF in England it was accepted by the American commanders that there would be a requirement for American crews to adopt many of the British military procedures. This was to ensure the safety and effectiveness of those units which would be involved in combat. It was therefore an early priority for Gen Eaker, Commander General, US 8th AF, to establish a training programme in England, so a request was made via Washington for a Table of Organisation (TO) to form Combat Crew Replacement Centres (CCRC). At the same time, the British Government was asked for any available airfields on which to base these centres, the idea being to run them on the same lines as RAF OTUs. Whilst this TO was being formulated and the airfield request assessed, the role of Bovingdon airfield in Hertfordshire was changed from combat

to Fortress crew training. Bovingdon had been home for American combat crews from the 92nd Bomb Group, whose 325th, 326th, 327th and 407th Bomb Squadrons were known as 'Fame's Favoured Few'. These squadrons had all flown B-17Fs, but with the activation of the new CCRC they were exchanged for older B-17Es that had been used by the 97th Bomb Group at Polebrook. The 'E' models were then used by the 92nd staff to train all future Fortress crews for combat in Europe.

B-24 Liberator

During the winter period of 1942 and into early 1943, bomber crew training had been for Fortress crews in the main — this was only natural, as there were many Fortress Groups arriving in England, but only one Liberator Group. A second was due, but had been sent to North Africa on temporary duty. It did not take much foresight to see Liberator replacement crews would soon be

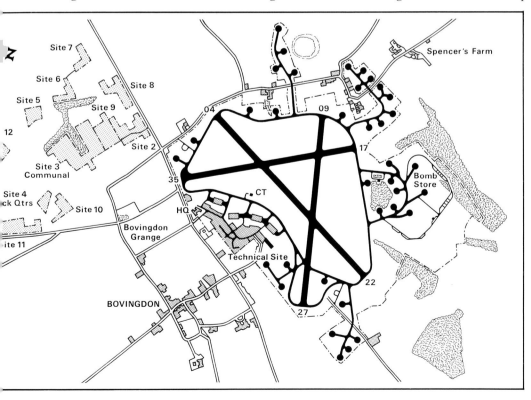

Left:
Bovingdon – General arrangement.

required, and so the June gathering of units at Cheddington was an ideal time and place to form the first Liberator CCRC. In less than a month, staff from the Ordnance, Quartermaster, Signal Company, Service Squadron, Station Complement Squadron and Headquarters Squadron, reported for duty and 12 CCRC was activated. Maj Robert Grandmontagne, who had been at Bovingdon, was appointed Director of Training, and Maj 'Podge' Reed was appointed as the Base Commander. Maj Reed became ill and was admitted to hospital and, as a temporary measure Maj Grandmontagne assumed command of the Base, as well as keeping his other duties. He acted in this role until 21 August, when a Col Taylor, who was also from Bovingdon, arrived and assumed command.

At 12.00hrs on 16 August 1943, the RAF Ensign was lowered and replaced by the American 'Stars and Stripes' when the airfield handover service took place and the USAAF took control of the airfield. Everyone on the station had given what assistance they could to help get the school underway, with the result that when classes began on 13 July, the 19 crews present had a varied and intensive curriculum, which was divided into six subjects which covered: air & tactics, take-off checks, bombardment, gunnery, radio and intelligence.

The school instructors were former combat crew members, most of whom had completed a tour of 25 missions, and were well informed from personal experience of the latest developments in combat operations in the European Theatre of Operations (ETO). For the trainee crews who had just completed their basic training, the direct contact with men who had experienced what they themselves would soon be facing, and who knew most of the answers to their questions, was without doubt a bonus. As a result, 32 crews passed through in the first month of the school's operation.

On 4 September 1943 the TO designed for the operation of the school came through and was put into effect. The school designation was changed to the 2901st CCRC and had attached the 2904th Replacement & Training Squadron (RTS). Maj William Todd was appointed CO and Maj Grandmontagne appointed his Director of Training. The school designation changed again on 15 November, to the 2nd CCRC, with the 2nd RTS attached. The school was well equipped with an intelligence library, radio facilities, bombardment and navigational equipment, and a left-over from the 44th Bomb Group — one of its old B-24D Liberators. This was mounted on concrete plinths and used as a crew trainer.

Personnel

For pilots and co-pilots the course in air & tactics was divided into 15 subjects: Pre-op checks, briefing procedure, air-sea rescue, interphone control, enemy tactics, ditching equipment, bale-out/ crashes, flying control, W/T facilities, weather, lost procedure, crew co-ordination, formation flying, aerodrome lighting and engine operations.

Above:
The crew of a 392nd Bomb Group Liberator returns to Cheddington, the station where they were trained for combat.
N. Senter/113 Association

Right:
Liberators of the 453rd Bomb Group stream contrails in the cold upper atmosphere en route to the target. Hollywood film star James Stewart was the Group's Executive Officer.
113 Association

Radio operators arriving at the school from America were faced with the problems of familiarising themselves with British systems, ie: High Frequency and Direction Finding (HF/DF) for obtaining homings, fixes and bearings. Also the use of Wireless Telegraphy (W/T), Beacons and Beams for the same purpose, and the use of the Bomber Code, 'Q' Signals, and Aircraft-to-Ground Challenging Procedure.

For the navigators the course covered navigation in the UK, hazards, weather balloons, and also delineated the duties of the combat navigator, lead navigator and wing position navigator. Map reading, co-ordination between bombardier and navigator, visual aids, radio aids to navigation and the use of the 'flimsy'. This contained all the signal information including code letters, the ground challenge and reply, the colours of the day for flare signals over England, navigational radio beacons, direction-finding stations and airfield signals, and the night's codes for use between a bomber and its home station.

Bombardiers were trained for missions in an atmosphere that re-created the actual one that would shortly become a part of their daily lives. Orders would arrive, followed by reveille and breakfast, briefing and pre-take-off duties, forming up over England, the trip in over the target, the trip back and finally the interrogation. All rehearsed and dramatised in conditions approaching as near as possible the actual combat situation. Combat bombing problems were also discussed and ironed out, and so, too, was the use of computers. Target identification was explained and last but not least, the use of the bomb fuses described.

All crew members attended the intelligence lectures that comprised of simulated briefing and interrogation scenes. Subjects covered included enemy shipping recognition, the various types of anti-aircraft fire, railway flak, flak ships, flak towers and the evasive action to be taken if it was encountered. Lectures were also given on the Luftwaffe and its strength before the war and up to the present time; a comparison of Luftwaffe aircraft types used against Allied forces, and also aircraft recognition using the five principal types of enemy fighters used in combat; defences and camouflage; the procedure for escape in Germany, France and the Low Countries, including evasion techniques with the aid of escape kits and foreign currency. Finally, dangerous avenues of escape were described together with suggested alternatives.

If subjects for the training courses were not in short supply there was one thing that certainly was — aircraft! It was true that a L-4B Piper Cub had been in use from the first few weeks in June but, as for heavy bombers, there were none. None that is until 15 August when out of the clear blue sky came a sight to warm most hearts on the field: an ex-381st Bomb Group B-17E that was war-weary and surplus to requirements. It had been named

Above:
Men from the 9th Station Complement Squadron swing the prop of a L-4B Piper Cub. This was the first American aircraft assigned to Cheddington.
N. Senter/113 Association

Right:
Jack Wrenn and four of his crew pose for the camera dressed overall in flying kit during early combat training. All five men wear Type B-7 flying goggles. The crew man on the far right wears the Type B-8 winter flying helmet whilst the man at second left wears what appears to be the Type B-3. All the others wear what appears to be rare Type B-7 helmets. Each man wears a Type B-3 shearling flying jacket and Type A-3 trousers, weatherproofed with brown polyacrylate leather die and lacquer as a top finish. Intended for use with the shearling winter flying clothing was the A-6 shearling flying shoe — as worn by Jack Wrenn's crew — one of the best known types of footwear ever used by the Army. However, the A-6 shoe proved to be cumbersome and bulky for ball turret gunners.
M. Wrenn/113 Association

Above:
Annie Freeze, a B-17E, was the first bomber assigned to the 2901st CCRC Group. 41-24500 was the 160th 'E' model to be built.
R. Burri/113 Association

Right:
From an old converted Fortress nose-cone the runway control van 'Hillside One' was born. Cpl Millard Bloxham is the controller.
N. Senter/113 Association

Below right:
An interior view of Cheddington's Pilot Briefing Room in February 1944. *N. Senter/113 Association*

Annie Freeze due to a glycol problem in the engine coolant system and bore the serial number 41-24500. Old she may have been, but she was put to use straight away and used not only by the trainee Liberator crews, but as an experimental radio aircraft and a transitioning ship.

Technically the airfield was closed for flying, but this did not deter either the Cub or Fortress, or stop the many RAF and USAAF aircraft that landed for fuel or directions. The correct paperwork was soon obtained for the airfield to be officially opened, and on 17 October, it was given the airfield code 'CZ' and the Army Air Force number 113. All that was now required was more aircraft. These duly arrived on the morning of 20 December in the form of 10 B-24D Liberators, and they were immediately put into operation, providing combat crews with actual flight training during their course. However, with the arrival of the aircraft came a new problem — the servicing. When the school had opened its doors to combat crews in July, there had been present the 379th Servicing Squadron. This unit had coped with all the resident aircraft, all visiting aircraft and an Oxford which had replaced the Cub on 16 December — but a flight of 10 B-24s was another problem. It was soon solved, for in America the 465th Servicing Squadron had been preparing for overseas duty, and was now ready to follow the well-trodden path of the many units

18

Above:
The reason why Cheddington's callsign was 'Hillside'. The main 08/26 runway ran from right to left. *N. Senter/113 Association*

Right:
The Pilot Briefing Room at Cheddington as seen in February 1944. In the background is the airfield lighting panel and station interphone. *N. Senter/113 Association*

Below:
'Last one up closes the door' — the 465th Service Squadron, 331st Service Group crack a collective smile for the camera. *D. Goss/113 Association*

on their way to England. The training of the 465th had taken place at a number of bases in America including Pendleton Field, Oregon, a place best left to the description contained in a letter home from one of the 465th engine mechanics, **John Wilkins:**

'Dear Folks, so this is Pendleton Air Base. It reminds me of the valley of the dead. It's a wonderful place for people to go to who don't want to be anywhere!

'The dust here is so deep and thick, that it goes over the top of your head while you are walking. When the wind blows, you think that there is an eclipse on, as the dust blots out the sun. The nights are so cold, that it takes the rest of the following day for the blood to start circulating again.

'Ah, but Pendleton is a wonderful city. Population is three thousand including sheep, goats and pigs, but that is OK though, because there are only a few soldiers here — only 50 to every

citizen! We don't mind that, because every week or so, if we are watching close enough, we can get a glimpse of a female in the distance. I am lucky though, and all the fellows envy me. Last Saturday night after careful manipulation I was able to come within 20ft of one of these creatures! Yes these native girls have two legs and the fellows are all thanking me for my invaluable information.

'Here the airfield is situated on top of a high mountain. This place is the first time in history that planes have to fly up to land. It is a remarkable sensation to watch a squadron of planes, hundreds of feet below you, struggling and straining to gain enough height to land! The planes here do not take off, they have a fine roller-coaster system to conserve gasoline and the wear and tear on the aircraft. The planes are placed on a declining runway and shoot out over the brink of our mountain paradise. It is only in a matter of a short few moments that they gain enough

speed, when they then cut in their ignition, and we watch them gracefully sailing through the air, into the blue sky below us.

'One gains the terrible habit in this high altitude, of attempting to eat, on rare occasions. The mess halls here are really something to talk about. I don't mind falling in line for chow, but gad, when you can't even see the end of the line you just forget about being hungry. Last week I was lucky enough and managed to get inside the mess hall, but when my turn came to be served, the food was all gone!

'When you can't eat, you look for something else to do, to pass the time — like go to bed! We sleep stacked in threes on bunks. It is very irritating. Once I got to sleep on the top however, it still took me 20min to take a breath without my stomach and chest coming in close contact with the roof. I fixed that though, by setting fire to my mattress and burning half of it away, thereby giving me room to breathe.

'Pay call here is fine. Every few months they manage to get up enough ambition to slip us a few dollars. That makes it very nice as the money they give sometimes lasts us a few days. Being with money over five percent of the time would not make us feel like soldiers anyway. I also love the way our mail is so efficiently and reliably handled. They have now got it down to a system where the mail we get is only post-marked a month old. That makes you feel good, as there is no feeling grand as to keep in close contact with our close ones!

'Everyone here is happy and contented, and we are going to keep it that way, as good morale is the backbone of our

organisation. They have tried to ship me out of the unit a few times. Once they went so far as to ship my records to another organisation. I don't know where they are now — nobody does either, so I guess that makes it OK. The last time the Major said he could not get along without me, so I am still here. I will probably die here. Love from your Soldier Son, John.'

Once in England, the 465th under the command of Maj Joseph D. Wager-Smith, moved in to AAF Station 120, Attlebridge, and was assigned to fatigue detail and exempted from work on the flight line. This involved laying concrete, constructing Nissen huts, wood-chopping and trash details. After that they were then given kitchen, police, coal and quartermaster duties. It was with great relief to one and all when on 24 December 1943 they moved by truck to Cheddington and set up their new home. Whilst most of the 465th men were enjoying Christmas, it was a sad time for others at the new base and far, far from home. John Wilkins recalls that he unpacked his kit, had a meal and, because he had the rest of the night off, set out on a borrowed bicycle to find a town. He came across a canal and followed it, and soon found Tring. As it was Christmas Eve, he started to look for a church to attend Mass, but whilst passing a house, he heard singing. He paused, not for long, but long enough for tears to form in his eyes and a lump to form in his throat. He then gave up the idea of a happy Christmas and made his way back to camp and slept off his sadness. The morning came, Christmas Day, and he was back at work on the flight line. As for that house in Tring where he had heard the singing, he did go back: as a result he married the owner's daughter!

No time was lost before the squadron was given the CCRC's 10 Liberator aircraft to service. This task, for the first few days, was more of a training exercise as it was a new job for the unit to actually get its hands dirty on aircraft. It was therefore their claim to fame that their unit had the unique distinction of being the only known service squadron in existence which, at that time, was not only capable of — but which actually did — provide groundcrews to work on aircraft. The work included as much maintenance as equipment would allow. It was carried out in the open and with the aid of mobile workshops containing the tools, and it could undertake mechanical, electrical or sheet-metal repairs, a task in cold weather that took the men some time to get used to.

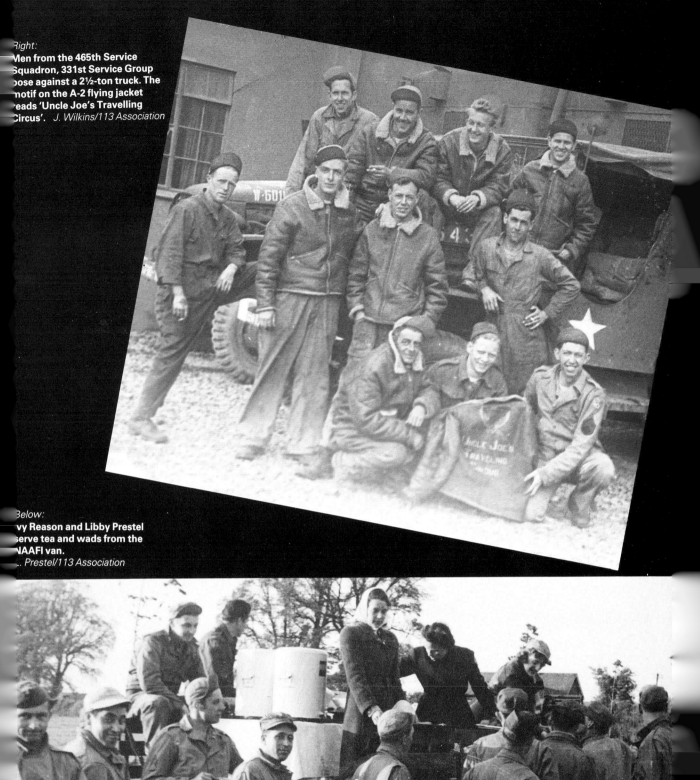

Right:
Men from the 465th Service
Squadron, 331st Service Group
pose against a 2½-ton truck. The
motif on the A-2 flying jacket
reads 'Uncle Joe's Travelling
Circus'. *J. Wilkins/113 Association*

Below:
Ivy Reason and Libby Prestel
serve tea and wads from the
NAAFI van.
L. Prestel/113 Association

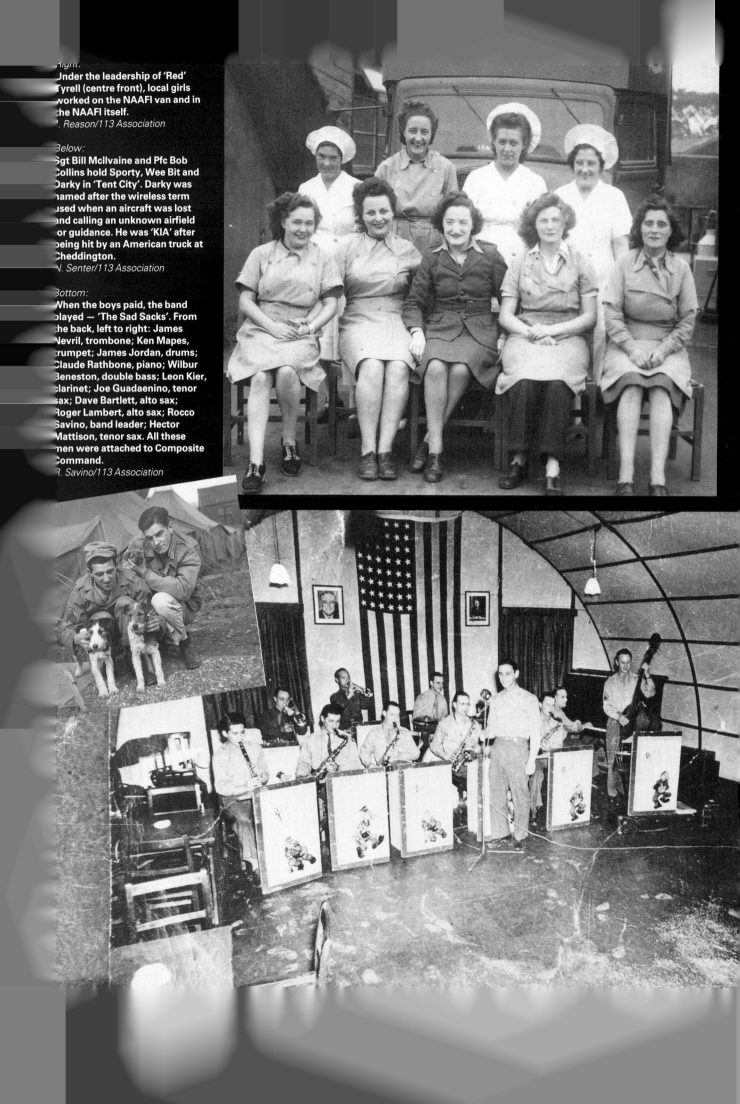

Right:
Under the leadership of 'Red' Tyrell (centre front), local girls worked on the NAAFI van and in the NAAFI itself.
R. Reason/113 Association

Below:
Sgt Bill McIlvaine and Pfc Bob Collins hold Sporty, Wee Bit and Darky in 'Tent City'. Darky was named after the wireless term used when an aircraft was lost and calling an unknown airfield for guidance. He was 'KIA' after being hit by an American truck at Cheddington.
N. Senter/113 Association

Bottom:
When the boys paid, the band played — 'The Sad Sacks'. From the back, left to right: James Nevril, trombone; Ken Mapes, trumpet; James Jordan, drums; Claude Rathbone, piano; Wilbur Beneston, double bass; Leon Kier, clarinet; Joe Guadaenino, tenor sax; Dave Bartlett, alto sax; Roger Lambert, alto sax; Rocco Savino, band leader; Hector Mattison, tenor sax. All these men were attached to Composite Command.
R. Savino/113 Association

Whilst in America, the squadron had adopted a mascot, a Spaniel puppy called Rex. Wherever the unit went, so too did Rex. When it came time for the squadron to board ship for England, Rex was doped so as to get him up the gang-plank and past the MPs. The trick worked and Rex became well known around the living and technical sites at Cheddington. He was only one of a number of pets on the base, the others being two more dogs named Darky and Sporty, and a mouse called Monty. Monty lived in Flying Control, under the care of TSgt Nick Senter. As well as being used to remove any discarded food, Staff Officers awaiting the return of their squadron aircraft would place bets on the time he would 'show'. Incidentally, it was Nick who, whilst on Control Tower duty one day, half asleep and with his cap over his eyes, heard the sound of an aircraft approaching. As the runway at Cheddington was clear, he fired a 'green' to give the clearance for it to land. As a result, he became the first American airman to give a German V-1 Flying Bomb permission to land, which it did — near the village of Tring!

For the officers and men it appeared that at long last they were assisting in the war effort, and finally had a purpose. It is true to say that many were unhappy they were not firing bullets at the enemy or bombing them out of existence, but at least they consoled themselves with the thought that they were making such action possible. As for out-of-hours activities, the men had plenty to do. There was the Aero Club run by John Martin, who was the Base Red Cross Director, and his assistant Miss Elizabeth Hainer. They held many dances when the station band 'The Sad Sacks', under the direction of Rocco Savino, entertained. For company and to dance with, the men had the choice of WRENs or WAAFs from RAF Stanmore, local Land Army girls and ATS girls from

Below:
'Dirty Rat' film star James Cagney meets the officers from Composite Command during a March 1944 USO visit. *113 Association*

Left:
He kept them steamed and he kept them cleaned — the base tailor in his shop. *113 Association*

Above:
**The crew of B-17F *The Bad Penny* 41-24480 and some VIP passengers.
This B-17 was attached to AFCC for VIP duties.** *M. Hunt/113 Association*

Left:
**Brig-Gen Hill commanded Composite Command from December 1943.
Today, his uniform can be seen on display at Duxford Air Museum.**
M. Hunt/113 Association

Luton. Local girls not in uniform also attended, as they were brought in by trucks driven by men from the motor pool. For the officers there was the Officers' Mess where one could get a good breakfast of oranges, sausage and fresh egg — on the first day it opened! From then on the choice was not so good! The building used was a long Nissen hut that had been rebuilt after RAF use. It boasted a bar consisting of a curved counter that had been built by the enlisted men. Behind the counter were three mirrors mounted on walls painted in different shades of blue. As well as the bar there were two other rooms: the central one was used as a lounge and furnished with comfortable chairs, magazines and a wireless. The second room on the other side was used for dancing. Also on the station was the Special Service Section which organised entertainment in the form of live shows and regular movies. There were even educational activities including language classes in French and German, with an instructor who had a linguaphone.

It had taken from early 1942 for the units to form in America, complete their basic training, travel overseas to England and to work up to strength. Now time could be spent making them more efficient, more at home, and ready for combat — or could it? Headquarters 8th AF and a new Command whose jurisdiction the units at Cheddington now came under had other ideas.

III
THE COMMAND

Formation

On American Independence Day, 4 July 1942, the 8th AF activated a new Command in America. It was known as Composite Command (AFCC) and was tasked to oversee all 16 airfields that had been earmarked for training crews for both Fighter and Bomber Commands of the 8th AF in England. These airfields, where possible, were in Northern Ireland to conserve those on the mainland of England for operational purposes. To be in the midst of this action AFCC arrived in Ireland on 12 September 1942, and was based at RAF Long Kesh. This was just a temporary home and in November it moved to Kircassock House, Lurgan — codename 'Nyack'. Once set up at Nyack AFCC set out to plan for future training requirements and to solve any problems that were then present. One large problem was that the Irish Republic (Eire) had a government separate to that of Great Britain. Therefore none of Ireland, with the exception of Ulster and its six counties in the northeast, were subject to British civil or military control. From the beginning of hostilities, the Eire Government had been determined to pursue a policy of neutrality in respect of territory adjoining the European Theatre of Operations, ie: Ulster — and this presented problems for the British and American Forces. The chief problem, as far as American forces were concerned, was that crews accidentally or wilfully entering Eire territory would be interned for the duration of the war. There was also the possibility that any forced-landing of a US aircraft would result in the internment of the crew and seizure of the aircraft by the Eire Government under international law. The 8th AF had foreseen this possibility and had liaised with the Air Ministry and RAF in Northern Ireland for their co-operation in the recovery of aircraft wherever possible. The US Minister to Eire, Col John Reynolds, who was also the Military Attaché, had also initiated talks on the problem between the US State Department, the US War Department, and the Eire Legation in Washington. This was the situation when Brig-Gen Edmund W. Hill assumed control of Composite Command on 10 December 1942.

On 29 December an official message was received by AFCC informally announcing that the Eire Government would release aircraft and crews who had landed by mistake, but only whilst on non-combatant missions, and that such crews should notify local Irish authorities that their mission was non-combatant and that they wished to leave as soon as possible. It was also stated that no publicity should be given to such incidents. Following this message, on 14 January Brig Hill wrote a letter to the Commanding General, 8th AF, and requested his authority to visit Eire, accompanied by his Assistant Chief-of-Staff. The reason for this visit was that he wished to liaise with the American Legation

in Dublin to co-ordinate special plans and procedures to effect the rescue of ALL US crews in Eire. This request was approved and a conference was set up that included Brig Hill, Col Simon Robineau, Assistant Chief-of-Staff, and from the Eire Government, Minister Gray and Col James Hathaway. The meeting was held from 3-5 February in the offices of the US Legation at Dublin and a plan was agreed which, if officially approved, would initiate definite diplomatic channels to end the problem. This plan was accepted and implemented. Today there is no doubt that the personal efforts of Brig Hill in maintaining good relations with the Irish people, as well as his foresight and skill in seeking to implement the proper channels to deal with this delicate diplomatic and military problem, resulted in great benefit to the Allied cause. It was also a fine example of international goodwill.

The agreement between AFCC and Eire was terminated on 4 April 1944, but continued by the 8th AF which took over as the responsible body. On its termination, a report was compiled showing the results of the agreement, from 8 December 1942 up to and including 5 March 1944. It reported that during the period in question that:

● Twenty-six USAAF aircraft had landed in Eire comprising of 12 B-17s, three B-24s, three B-26s, one P-38 and one P-39 — a total of 20 combat aircraft and 172 US military personnel. Five C-47s and one Miles Mentor, carrying in total 39 US military personnel. These, in the main, were ATC pilots and crew.

● The total number of US personnel involved was 211, of which 93 were Officers, Flying Officers or Warrant Officers, the balance of 118 being enlisted crew members. Of that total, casualties were 15 of which eight were killed. All casualties resulted from the crash-landing of two aircraft: Ten casualties were the combat crew of a B-17, and five the crew and passengers of a C-47 which was totally destroyed.

● Twenty-six aircraft force-landed. Of these 13 were flown out and resulted in 100% recovery of aircraft and crew. Twelve

aircraft were salvaged in varying extents from 15% to 90%, and one aircraft (the C-47) was a total loss. It was estimated that the 13 aircraft flown out had a value of salvaged material in excess of $1 million!

● During this period NO American crews were interned, but secret statistics obtained from the Commanding General of the Eire forces indicated that from the beginning of war to January 1944, the British suffered 75 aircraft crashes or forced landings. They had obtained the release of 19 aircraft and 167 personnel. Fourteen aircraft had been salvaged, 45 personnel had been interned, 11 of whom subsequently escaped, and 23 were eventually released. Fifteen German aircraft had been involved in crashes or forced landings, and 53 German personnel were interned — one was released and one escaped!

Another point of interest that came out of the agreement was that to assist US crews with navigation, shore markers were placed along the entire coast of Eire. By June 1943, 6ft high letters spelling 'EIRE' had been erected on at least 83 points. The size was subsequently enlarged to 30ft.

During the whole period of the agreement it was policy to interrogate very thoroughly the members of all crews on their eventual return. Repatriated crews were also required to sign a

Top:
Weather Flight Fortress 42-39871 was 'bent' after a mishap at St Eval, Cornwall in 1944.
R. Chappel/113 Association

Above left:
When the day's work for the men had finished, there was time to get a closer look at a 'Hun' Ju88.
B. Downs/113 Association

Left:
The Flight also brought a Bf-110c-5 'AX772' for inspection, flown by Flt Lt Lewendon.
B. Downs/113 Association

written pledge of secrecy regarding the details of their release from Eire. At all stages the utmost caution was taken to guard the security of the arrangements, and at no time did any official disclose by any source, either the events that had taken place, or the agreement. Whilst AFCC had been busy in Northern Ireland, Cheddington had not been dormant. As 1943 drew to a close, the 8th AF Weather Flight moved in on 20 December with its B-17s; the runways at Bovingdon, where the Flight was based, were being resurfaced. The purpose of the Flight's existence was to provide HQ 8th AF with weather data 12 to 18hr prior to each mission. There was information already available covering the Atlantic approaches, from where most weather fronts originated, but this was inadequate. Therefore, it was agreed that the USAAF would form a unit with B-17s and cover the Eastern Atlantic under RAF guidance as **Maj Arthur Gordon** of the Weather Flight recalls:

'We made some of the longest operational flights on record, up to 2,000 land miles. Land miles was a figure of speech, as most of the 14 to 15hr flight was spent over the cold waters of the Atlantic. That cold it would — and did — freeze downed crews in a matter of minutes. Our flights would carry a crew of seven or eight, a full complement of armour plate, 0.5in machine guns and plenty of ammunition, but no bombs, as the bomb-bay was full of tanks to supplement the regular wing tanks, and Tokyo tanks. The total aircraft weight was more than that of a combat Fortress. If an engine failed under the strain of take-off it was just too bad. This happened at Bovingdon on 9 December at 18.56hrs, when B-17 42-37744 crashed, and the following crew died:

temperatures at the lowest of altitudes. This required the aircraft to swoop down so low that the waist gunner could taste the salt spray from the ocean on his lips. Sometimes the sea was less than 50ft below! There was no trick in this type of low flying in daylight, but on a wet dark night it called for more than just good faith in your instruments!'

Low flying was the cause of the unit's second accident although it was not on a Weather Mission. Five days after moving into Cheddington the flight sent Fortress 42-37869 with its crew of eight, including Sgt Basil Brown RAF the met observer, on a weather sortie. Because the airfield at Cheddington was closed due to adverse weather, the Fort put down at St Eval in Cornwall on completion of the sortie. When the all-clear at Cheddington was given, the aircraft took off for its flight home. The weather in the West of England had been reported as having a cloud base of 2,500ft and visibility of 2-4 miles. Near Bridestow the aircraft entered mist in the hilly area of Okehampton Moor, skimmed over the first hill which was 1,430ft above sea level and then entered an area of heavy mist. The pilot went on to instruments and started to climb, but the Fortress's engines did not have the power. It struck the next hill which was 1,750ft high, and the aircraft bounced along for ¾-mile, split open, then caught fire. The pilot and co-pilot managed to escape from the wrecked Fort when it

Lt Laverne Rissinger	Pilot
Lt Bill Holcomb	Co-Pilot
Lt Otto Ahlers	Navigator
MSgt John Buchanan	Radio Engineer
TSgt Peter Costello	Engineer
SSgt Bernard Cohen	Gunner
Sgt Ralph Harding	Gunner
Cpl Matthew Ekes	Assistant Engineer
Sqn Ldr Jack Osborne	Met Observer (RAF)
Flt Lt Harry Leigh-Clare	Met Observer (RAF)

'The take-off, however, was not the only hazard, for weather observation called for periodic sampling of air pressure and

came to rest, and two other bodies were thrown clear. A total of five crew were killed.

The New Year was ushered in and on 11 January 1944 the Weather Flight left Cheddington and returned to Bovingdon. On the 27th there came dull, damp, dreary weather, but it brought some new visitors to the airfield: the circus! The Station Headquarters was informed and the Station Weather Flight was asked for details of the weather conditions; and the staff in the know were eager to knock off work early and get a front seat. But for this show there would be no seats, for it was a circus with a difference! It was also to be a day with a difference for the circus staff, who had woken that morning at RAF Steeple Morden. This circus did not include clowns, lions or tigers — but aircraft. It was the RAF Flying Circus — better known as No 1426 Enemy Aircraft Flight from RAF Collyweston.

After the morning show the Flight's Junkers Ju88 and Messerschmitt Bf110 left Steeple Morden en route for Cheddington, escorted by six USAAF P-47 Thunderbolt fighters. Missing was the Flight's Bf109F which was delayed because of engine trouble, but due to follow later in the day. On arrival at Cheddington the Ju88 and Bf110 both gave a short display, then landed in order to show those on the ground the captured German aircraft in close-up. As the P-47 fighter escort returned to its base it was passed by other P-47s escorting the Bf109 to Cheddington. Its flight, however, was not so simple for, en route, the airscrew motor drive sheared, causing excessive rpm. Flg Off Lee-White throttled back and carried on at reduced manifold pressure, and at 2,500rpm. But all was not well with the engine and, as the aircraft reached Cheddington, Flying Control reported smoke and glycol streaming in excessive amounts from the disabled aircraft. Upon landing, the engine was examined and it was confirmed the oil level had dropped to almost nil, but the cause of the problem could not be located. All three aircraft were then parked for inspection by the station personnel and were also well photographed. The Flight's FW190, like the Bf109, also had engine trouble, but had been left at Poddington for repairs.

The next day two RAF Lockheed Hudson aircraft arrived to take air-to-air photographs. They soon departed when they found out that only morning and afternoon ground displays of the enemy aircraft would be put on. There was no flying scheduled due to the Bf109's engine problem, and the fact that both the other aircraft required wheel tyres. These were fitted the following morning, along with a new port tyre and pitch motor for the Bf109. Its engine was test-run, but then white metal and bronze was found in the oil filters, so it was agreed to dismantle the aircraft and transport it back to base at Collyweston by road. A phone call was made, the transport laid on, then the Ju88 and Bf110 took to the air, buzzed the field and with their new escort of Polish Spitfires from RAF Northolt (for protection against Allied guns) left for Collyweston. The Flight's lone Airspeed Oxford followed behind. Next day the Bf109 departed on a 60ft Queen Mary transporter along with the staff in their trusty Leyland bus, and so ended tour No 11 of the RAF Flying Circus. A tour that gave many more 8th AF men and women a chance to see what the enemy had in store for them.

The pilots and aircraft on the tour were as follows: Flt Lt Lewendon — Bf110C-5 serial number AX 772; Flg Off Gough — Ju88 A-5 serial number HM509; Flg Offs, Lee-White and Staples, who could fly both the Bf109F, serial number NN644, and the FW190. Flg Off Staples was killed in the 190 when, in October 1944 he crashed on landing.

The Enemy Aircraft Flight was not the only visitors to create attention at Cheddington during January. On the 26th a Douglas C-47 landed. This in itself was not an unusual occurrence, but due

Top left:
Another task included truck driving. This WAAC is at the wheel of a 2½-tonner . . .   *M. Hunt/113 Association*

Centre left:
. . . and assisting the Adjutant General, Lt Hyland.
M. Hunt/113 Association

Bottom left:
The girls were issued with firearms and had to know how to use them. In the background is the ex-44th Bomb Group Liberator mounted on concrete plinths.   *M. Hunt/113 Association*

Right:
The sign on the gym wall reads 'THRU THESE PORTALS PASS THE BEST DAMNED ATHLETES AND PENCIL PUSHERS IN THE WORLD!' and the girls from AFCC proved it.   *M. Hunt/113 Association*

Below:
Composite Command Officers (from left to right): Maj Bob Chestnutt, Capt Marj Hunt, Lt John Culhane, Lt Art Larson, Lt Bob Senn and Lt Robert Sandburg.   *A. Larson/113 Association*

Left:
The crew of 'Hillside Two', the airfield red and white checkered jeep which was crewed by men from the 9th Station Complement Squadron.
N. Senter/113 Association

to a series of strange events that took place, the landing attracted more attention than usual. Flying Control was the first to be informed that there would be an unexpected landing and told it was due to Bovingdon being 'closed' by fog. Then, along with Base Operations, it was told NOT to ask who would be on board and NOT to send any member of staff to find out. Had that order not been given, it would just have been another day and another flight, with the aircraft almost ignored! However, the whole section now was poised and waiting for the big event.

Just prior to the aircraft's touchdown, a number of cars drove up to the visiting aircraft ramp. As the C-47 landed and parked, the reception party left the comfort of their vehicles and stood to attention. The C-47's door opened and down the steps came a General. First to greet him was Maj-Gen John Clifford Hodges Lee, Eisenhower's deputy Supreme Commander, and with him, Cdr Butcher, Eisenhower's Naval Aide. The secret visitor, along with his party, entered the waiting cars and drove off into the Cheddington mist, and towards London for a meeting with Eisenhower.

Who was that visitor? It was Gen 'Blood and Guts' Patton and it was the sight of his two ivory-handled Colt .45 pistols that had given the secret away. But all was not lost, for his secret arrival in England was a secret that the British Government wanted the enemy to know, and in doing so deceive him into false beliefs.

At a Commanders' meeting held at the start of February 1944, it was announced that Composite Command would undergo some major changes. The main result of these would be the move of its Headquarters to Cheddington, and No 2 CCRC at Cheddington would move to Ireland. On Monday 7 February, the change came into effect. Two aircraft left Station 597 at Langford Lodge in Northern Ireland with an advance party on board to commence the move to Cheddington, arriving at noon. The rest of the staff were kept busy for the next six days whilst equipment was collected and loaded into their 37 Army trucks and attached trailers. On the 13th, at 07.00hrs, the convoy — which included staff cars, two British utility cars and two ambulances — moved off for Larne and the sea crossing to Stranraer. At 07.45hrs the remaining staff left for Station 239 to board a group of waiting B-17s for the flight to Cheddington, but the weather on arrival at the airfield prevented take-off. On the 15th they did manage to get airborne, however; as the flight was fairly short, all but one aircraft landed at 13.30hrs. The remaining B-17 had become lost

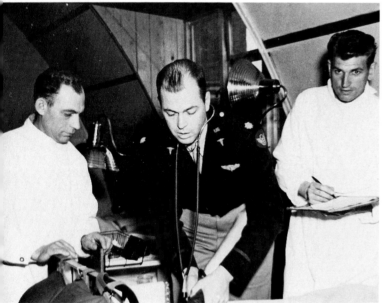

Top:
An interior view of one of the barrack huts used by the 9th Complement Squadron during one of the periods they were not accommodated in tents.
N. Senter/113 Association

Above:
Medical Section, from left to right: Sgt John Mazaceck, Col James Tilden and Sgt George Presinger.
L. Walck/113 Association

Right:
The men from the airfield's Crash Crew. *N. Senter/113 Association*

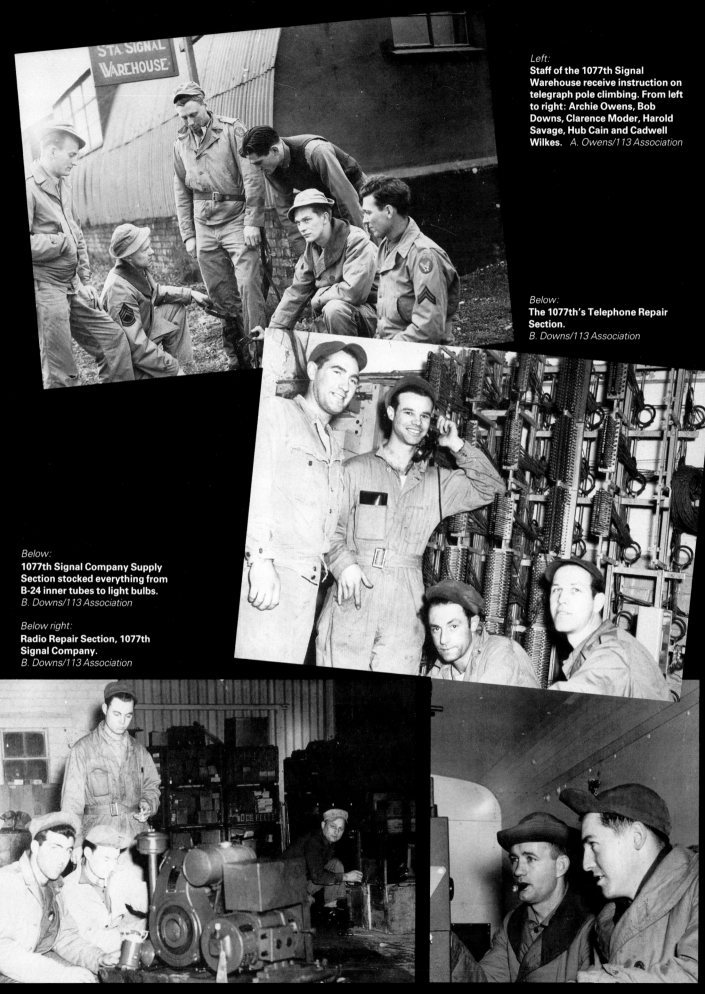

Left:
**Staff of the 1077th Signal
Warehouse receive instruction on
telegraph pole climbing. From left
to right: Archie Owens, Bob
Downs, Clarence Moder, Harold
Savage, Hub Cain and Cadwell
Wilkes.** *A. Owens/113 Association*

Below:
**The 1077th's Telephone Repair
Section.**
B. Downs/113 Association

Below:
**1077th Signal Company Supply
Section stocked everything from
B-24 inner tubes to light bulbs.**
B. Downs/113 Association

Below right:
**Radio Repair Section, 1077th
Signal Company.**
B. Downs/113 Association

and landed at Bovingdon — from where its passengers were trucked to Cheddington, arriving at 15.30hrs. For the convoy, its journey was longer. After the crossing to Stranraer, it was a tiring trek to Cheddington via Carlisle, Preston and Lutterworth. It was escorted by MPs and each night stopped at a transit camp. The convoy arrived at its new home at noon on the 17th. As for the move of the CCRC to Ireland, this had taken place on 14 February when the staff, along with their 10 B-24Ds, left for Station 238 Cluntoe.

Responsibilities

When established on Site 4 at Cheddington, the staff of Composite Command set out to do their best with what they had. A Directive from 8th AF Headquarters and addressed to the Commanding General, outlined his Command responsibilities as follows: control of all Heavy Bombardment CCRC Groups for the 8th AF; operation and control of pre-combat training centres for fighter pilots for the 8th AF; pre-combat training of crews and personnel for the 9th AF; operation and maintenance of Gunnery Training Establishments for aerial gunners, and gunners to man defensive ground gun positions; administrative control and general court-martial jurisdiction over all ·units and establishments assigned to the 8th AF Composite Command — to sort out the bad boys! Supervision and control of off-station discipline by Military Police District 'B'; research, development, experimentation, and training on H2X radar; and operation and control of the 492nd Bomb Group at Alconbury in Huntingdonshire, who were on 'Pathfinder' operations.

The Command had also been instructed to make plans to absorb the operation and control of all Rest and Recuperative homes (R&R); to operate and supervise all units and functions which were not suitable for direct Air Force supervision, or assignment to either Fighter or Bomber Command. As if that was not enough, it was required to provide accommodation at Cheddington from time to time for any Bombardment Group that required revitalising, or a home whilst forming. It did not take long for this provision to be required, not by a Bomb Group, but a new Wing that would be commanded by a Very Important Person!

On 20 February 1944, orders were given by HQ 8th AF for a number of unit changes to take place. In the main these required

the staff from the 5th and 6th CCRC at Station 240 Mullaghmore, Northern Ireland, to be transferred to the 77th Station Complement Squadron. The unit designations were then transferred to Cheddington with the equipment trucked first to Station 237, then flown over to Cheddington on the 29th. What was the purpose of these moves? Answer: the formation at Cheddington on the 23rd, of the 8th Reconnaissance Wing (P), commanded by Elliott Roosevelt, son of the American President.

On 4 March, three provisional squadrons were formed under the Wing. The 8th Weather Squadron (Heavy), the 8th Weather Squadron (Light) and the 8th Courier Reconnaissance Squadron (Special). Within a few days 10 B-17Fs moved in, followed by P-38 Lightnings from the 50th Fighter Squadron (Twin Engine), from Iceland. The crews were then trained on British de Havilland Mosquito Mk XVIs by de Havilland staff and RAF personnel, a task that, due to the strange system of foot-operated brakes and steering, caused many unusual landing sights! After a few more weeks, the 8th Reconnaissance Squadron (Special) with B-17Fs, three Vultee L-5B Sentinel and six Noorduyn UC-64 Norseman aircraft, took over the work of the Courier Squadron, which was then disbanded. As these squadrons were now floating and in need of a Group Headquarters, the 8th Reconnaissance Group (Special) was formed on 22 March. Shortly thereafter the name was changed to that of the 802nd Reconnaissance Group (Special) (P), and in April the Group with its provisional squadrons and aircraft moved to Watton in Norfolk. The Wing HQ moved to 8th AF Headquarters, High Wycombe. In August, the Wing became the 325th Photo Wing (Reconnaissance), and the 802nd Reconnaissance Group (P) became the 25th Bomb Group. As for its squadrons, they became:

8th Weather Reconnaissance Sqn (H) (P) = 652nd Bomb Squadron (H)
8th Weather Reconnaissance Sqn (L) (P) = 653rd Bomb Squadron (L)
8th Reconnaissance Squadron (Special) = 654th Bomb Squadron (L)

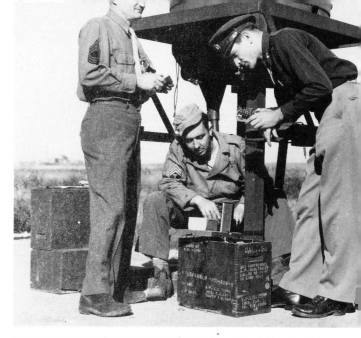

Assigned Units

The next few months at Cheddington, in more ways than one, were a short hiatus in its development. Composite Command was well and truly dug-in. The men on the airfield could reaffirm the term 'dug', for digging became the order of the day. Whether it had been trenches for cables, trenches for gun or blast shelters, or just plain trenches, it was dig, dig, dig. Col Crisp, the new Station Commander, set about a station beautification programme which involved members of the Base performing pick and shovel details, clearing up areas, and laying down concrete walks. In order to accomplish this work, staff were confined to the Base, and performed these tasks for two to three hours in the evenings. This was after their regular duties had been completed! In conjunction with the beautification programme, a basic training programme was inaugurated which featured close-order drill, the manual of arms, firing on the range and lectures on chemical warfare. The beautification details came to an end when it became clear that the laying of paths had made the airfield more obvious to the enemy from the air. As for the lectures on explosives, they came to an abrupt end for the two instructors, Lt Louis Sherman and Sgt William Daugherty, when they were killed demonstrating to a class the method of handling incendiary bombs on 4 April 1944. Both men were from the 9th Station Complement Squadron. The 9th had also provided personnel to man the Motor Pool, Flying Control, Chemical Warfare, Fire and Crash Crew Sections, plus the Radio Direction-Finder (RDF) stations which were located just outside the base in Wilstone village.

The one thing the base did not have was women. This situation was improved on 23 May when, following a visit by two Womens Army Corps (WAC) officers from HQ 8th AF, a detachment of 56 enlisted women and two officers arrived. The detachment was commanded by Capt Marjorie Hunt, and took over the duties of some of the men in the Adjutant General, Headquarters, Transport, Medical, Engineering, A1, A2, A3 and A4 sections, plus the Link trainer. All the WACs had been in service for at least 17 months and were all volunteers for overseas duty.

On 1 May, an organisation known as the '8th Air Force Personal Equipment School' moved in on detached service from 'Pinetree'. Its headquarters were on the Technical Site. The instructors at the school were two officers and 10 enlisted men in the Officers' Section, and one officer and one enlisted man in the Enlisted Men's section, there being two schools in operation. Capt Dick Truckman was CO and instructed the Officer's School, assisted by

Top left:
As well as the radio equipment, 1077th men also had to keep their hands in with .50in gun turrets.
B. Downs/113 Association

Centre left:
Lee Roy Sullivan issues a B-24 inner tube from Station Supply.
N. Senter/113 Association

Bottom left:
Luther Walck of the 282nd Medical Dispensary poses beside an ambulance.
L. Walck/113 Association

Above:
Staff of the 282nd Medical Dispensary. Maj Winslow (seated, centre) took his own life with a pistol shortly before he was due to return to America.
L. Walck/113 Association

Right:
Terry O'Lean and Luther Walck of the 282nd Medical Dispensary 'snapped' off-duty in Aylesbury with the local Bobby.
L. Walck/113 Association

Lt Milton Mazer and Lt Robert Bender, who both instructed the enlisted men.

Officers and men attending the schools were from Heavy, or Medium Bomb Groups or Fighter Groups. On completion of the course, the officers became Personal Equipment Officers at their own stations and the enlisted men carried out the maintenance on the equipment. The course varied according to whether the students came from Heavy or Medium Bomb or Fighter Groups. For the Heavy it was of two weeks' duration, Medium five days, and for Fighter Groups one week. Training was in the use of oxygen equipment, maintenance of parachutes, flying clothing, air-sea rescue equipment, flak suits and dinghies of various types.

On 4 June another organisation moved in without aircraft, and was known as the 'Air Crew Evaluation & Research Detachment'. It was composed of six officers and 15 enlisted men, and was inaugurated by Gen H. H. Arnold, Chief of Staff of the USAAF. Its mission was divided into three phases.

● The training and classification test records of personnel assigned to Bomb Groups in the 8th AF were to be collated from basic AF Training Command records, which had been compiled for the detachment. The records were then to be compared with the combat performance of men in key assignments such as lead crew, to determine the value of the records to Squadron and Group Commanders in selecting men.
● To supplement the detachment's existing records by developing and administering to appropriate personnel, certain new tests devised as a result of the survey, and then to validate them against combat performance.
● With the findings from the above work, its task would be to revise and develop tests for the purpose of predicting combat performance, as accurately as possible, at the time aircrew entered operational training units.

The whole idea was that the classification personnel in America would be able to predict, with a high degree of accuracy, which men would make the best lead bombardiers, navigators and pilots. When the evaluation was completed the detachment left Cheddington and presented its findings to Gen Arnold.

In only four months Cheddington had been fully staffed, cleaned, painted and prepared. But what about aircraft? It is true that when the CCRC with its Liberators left, there followed a stream of units with aircraft, but only for short periods. First the Weather Squadron, then the Reconnaissance Wing and then the Courier Squadron, and last but not least, excitement was caused by the arrival of the 788th and 850th Bomb Squadrons, 801st Bomb Group, who were training to supply equipment and agents to resistance groups in Europe on 'Carpetbagger' missions. After initial training, their move out left Composite Command poised for its next task, and the airfield at Cheddington ready for more action. But, with the D-Day landings less than one month away, there were no aircraft to be found on the airfield, let alone a combat unit. But that situation would soon change.

Below:
Capt E. J. Winner, the 9th Station Complement Squadron CO, on duty for the Pay Parade. He is guarded by Sgt Grover Goins and assisted by 1Sgt Vester. Capt Winner was a veteran of the ill-fated Dieppe raid in August 1942. *N. Senter/113 Association*

IV
THE MOUTH OF PSYWAR

Chelveston and Night Leaflet Missions

Psychological warfare — or PsyWar — can claim to be a major force in proving the theory that 'the pen is mightier than the sword', for the clever use of propaganda leaflets, dropped from aircraft, was one of the most effective means of waging psywar during World War 2. This method of delivering messages, information or news was used in every theatre of operations and with considerable success. But Western Europe, with its many large centres of population and concentrations of Allied troops, promised the Allied leaders one of their greatest returns from the leaflets. There were two types of leaflet: 'whites' — true and from

the Allies to friend or foe in enemy occupied areas; or 'black' — claimed to be of enemy origination and for the enemy.

Leaflet or 'Nickeling' missions had been initiated from England by the RAF with a small mission over Kiel on the night of 3 September 1939, and gathered momentum as the war progressed. This type of operation had its opponents however, who thought supplying the enemy with 'toilet paper' to be a waste of resources. Some military commanders refused to accept the idea for a number of years, and a letter from AVM 'Bomber' Harris to AVM N. H. Bottomley dated 25 March 1942, in answer to a request for more leaflet operations, showed he had still not been convinced:

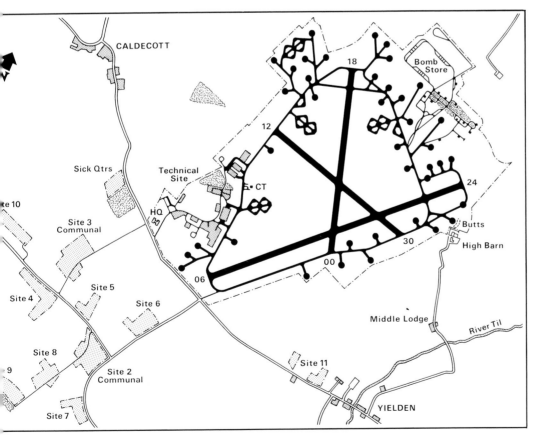

Left:
Chelveston – General arrangement.

39

Right:
RAF groundcrews load leaflet bundles into a Whitley of No 102 Squadron early in the war. *IWM C912*

Below right:
A RAF aircrew member splits open the leaflet bundles prior to putting them down the Whitley's flare shute. *IWM C838*

'Can something please now be done to curb and keep within bounds these uncorrelated and enthusiastic attempts to shower rubbish all over the world at the expense of the bomber effort.

'If it takes 31 tons of nickels to explain to the French why we bombed Renault's, all I can say is that it is a pity we didn't add another 31 tons, drop them in bundles on Renault's, and thereby save the HE which it took to do the damage.

'When it comes to dropping tea, Christmas presents, and Easter eggs, things have really gone too far. Something must now really be done to stop this growing urge of the exiled governments and individual busybodies with idle hands, to play games in wartime when we are more than too busy on serious things.

'I will not drop tea or Easter eggs anywhere unless you guarantee that the packages are lethal.

'The only people likely to be affected by nickles are morons. Notoriously, morons are unable ro read. The only people who are likely to get the Easter eggs are the Gestapo, and why the devil should we feed them Easter eggs? How about quit foolin' and getting on with the war? These jesters are getting completely out of hand and it is high time someone put a heavy foot on them — or behind them. I'm not cross, but I damn soon will be.'

The involvement of the 8th AF with leaflet operations came as a result of just one telegram, number 462, sent on 28 May 1943 by Maj-Gen Ira Eaker to VIII Bomber Command and for action by its three Bombardment Wings. It requested: 'Desire you initiate leaflet-dropping operations as soon as possible.' Thus, for just one piece of paper, an operation was activated that produced and disseminated billions more.

Prior to this telegram, a visit was made by Col Bacon, A-2 of the 8th AF, to the RAF in late August 1942. The visit resulted in Bacon's G-2, Col James Childers, making an exploratory investigation into the RAF leaflet operations. He concluded on return: 'The RAF and PWE have worked out a system for producing leaflets very rapidly. With a simpler organisation, American leaflets should be produced even faster.' He submitted his report in September and requested that immediate arrangements be made to drop propaganda leaflets on bombing missions. The reply from A-3, VIII Bomber Command, was that 'It is wholly impractical to attempt to drop leaflets in loose form from a close formation of aeroplanes, since they would collect in the engine intake and radiators of other aeroplanes, forcing them to land'. This reply, however, put forward a suggestion that a device be developed that would hold the leaflets intact, and only release them when they had dropped below the bomber formations and as they approached the ground. This advice was accepted, and, as a result the A-2 VIII Bomber Command directed the Air Force Engineering Base Air Depot at Burtonwood (BAD 1) to undertake research into such a suitable device.

In a short time BAD 1 had come up with the answer. The leaflets would be tied in bundles by string and as the bundle dropped through the air, the increase in pressure would operate a simple aneroid barometer. This would operate at a desired height by collapsing a set of bellows, whose action would activate a catch releasing a small pin holding the two ends of string, thus allowing the bundle to break open. It was agreed to manufacture 50 test releases that, when attached to the bundles, would be stowed in large plywood boxes. These were to be hung upside down in the bomb bay, with their lids attached by chain to standard bomb shackles. When operated by the bombardier, the lids would swing open, releasing four bundles each containing 16,000 leaflets.

Work started in October, but was held up due to problems with the bellows in the aneroids which had to be redesigned. Research was accelerated again in the first part of March 1943 with flight testing of the complete device held on the 31st. Eight releases of

the containers were made and all were satisfactory, with the bundles clearing the aircraft from both the front and rear bomb racks. The fuses, set for 5,000ft, worked as planned and 25,000 leaflets were released from just one carrier, covering an area of half-a-mile by four miles (in the prevailing 25mph wind). The Development Committee accepted the device and, since the box was light (122lb when full), agreed it could be hung above a regular bomb load without affecting it and therefore no additional aircraft would be required for leaflet missions. It also made a number of other proposals, namely:

● That a Heavy Bombardment Group be designated to conduct further tests from operational altitudes, using a bomb-sight to determine limits of accuracy obtainable, and approximate area of coverage. A crew must be chosen who will take an interest in the development of this equipment.

● If the Office of War Information (OWI) indicates that a large quantity of leaflets will have to be dropped apart from on bombardment missions or on special occasions, it is recommended that development be extended to fighter-type aircraft where containers could be mounted on external bomb racks and less equipment and personnel will thereby be jeopardised.

● That an officer be designated by 8th Air Force to follow through on the development and act as Liaison Officer between the OWI and the operational units.

Maj-Gen Eaker acted on the recommendations and expressed his desire in a letter to the Commanding General of VIII Bomber Command 'to have one Heavy Bombardment Squadron equipped and trained immediately for the purpose of dropping leaflets'.

It may have been Eaker's desire to have a squadron devoted to leaflet dropping, but over the next few months there was no Command decision made as to whether leaflet missions for the OWI was going to be the sole task for a special squadron, or

Below:
USF124: L'Amerique en Guerre
Issue 109 of the French newspaper 'America in the War'. It was disseminated from 9 July to 7 August 1944. There was a total of 114 issues printed, but the first seventeen issues were not disseminated, the first being the 28/29 November 1942 copy.

Below right:
ZH1: Eisenhowers Statement
A joint statement signed by Dwight D. Eisenhower and the Dutch Prime Minister Pieter Gerbrandy. It was dropped over Holland on D-Day by NLS Fortresses, and advised the civilians of the D-Day landings.

whether it would be a mission all Bomber Groups operating over Germany would perform. The answer came in a confidential telegram sent by 8th AF to VIII Bomber Command, dated 28 May 1943, which raised just as many questions as it answered. It did, however, give an outline of the basic objectives of a leaflet programme and an indication of a starting date by stating 'desire you initiate leaflet dropping operations as soon as possible'. It also made clear that there would be two types of operations, both having a strict condition: daylight leaflet dropping in conjunction with heavy bomber raids on targets in Germany. The load desired was for each aeroplane to carry the maximum number of leaflets possible in addition to its existing bomb-load. Night leaflet dropping by B-24s that were at this stage being readied for this type of operation. No leaflets were to be carried by heavy bombers attacking occupied countries.

On paper, for the first time, was the 'way ahead'. It was requested that the 'scale of operations desired is maximum employment of aeroplanes, consistent with ability to maintain availability of operational crews, and a proper standard of maintenance'. Four areas were named for the operations: the Paris area with 7½ tons per week; the industrial north of France including Lille, Cambrai, Roubaix, Douai and Valenciennes; the South of France including the cities of Lyons, Bordeaux, Dijon, Toulouse and Marseilles; and Holland.

To overcome a number of operating problems, including the fact that certain bombs (1,000 and 1,600lb) would not fit in bomb bays with the leaflet boxes, a meeting was held on 4 June, chaired by Col Ordway, A-2 8th AF. Present also were other representatives from A-2, A-3 and A-4 sections. The outcome was successful with a number of problems being solved, including the comment that leaflets should be placed in the last aircraft of each Group to prevent the bundles hitting any other aircraft. Minutes of this meeting were issued, and resulted in a directive from VIII Bomber Command to the Commanding Generals of the Bomb Wings on 10 July, entitled 'Leaflets'. It ratified all the proposals and recommendations that had been made to date and set out the

Message urgent

du Commandement Suprême des Forces Expéditionnaires Alliées

AUX HABITANTS DE CETTE VILLE

Afin que l'ennemi commun soit vaincu, les Armées de l'Air Alliées vont attaquer tous les centres de transports ainsi que toutes les voies et moyens de communications vitaux pour l'ennemi.

Des ordres à cet effet ont été donnés.

Vous qui lisez ce tract, vous vous trouvez dans ou près d'un centre essentiel à l'ennemi pour le mouvement de ses troupes et de son matériel. L'objectif vital près duquel vous vous trouvez va être attaqué incessamment.

Il faut sans délai vous éloigner, avec votre famille, pendant quelques jours, de la zone de danger où vous vous trouvez.

N'encombrez pas les routes. Dispersez-vous dans la campagne, autant que possible.

PARTEZ SUR LE CHAMP ! VOUS N'AVEZ PAS UNE MINUTE A PERDRE !

Z.F.4

S.A 182

ROMILLY-SUR-SEINE

Above:
ZF4: Warning Message
On the eve of D-Day, 6 June 1944, the first Allied aircraft to cross the enemy beachhead were Leaflet Squadron aircraft, which dropped copies of ZF4 over France. This leaflet warned of an impending invasion.

Left:
The 305th Bomb Group's first daylight raid was to Romilly Sur Seine in France on 20 December 1942. A Mosquito of No 540 Squadron RAF photographed the bomb hits after the raid.
Crown Copyright

Top right:
Dan Brennan (third from left) served with the RAF before joining the 8th AF. He is pictured here during training on Whitleys with No 10 OTU at RAF Abingdon.
D. Brennan/113 Association

Above right:
***Foolish Virgin,* 42-30822 the B-17F that Dan Brennan trained on.** *D. Brennan/113 Association*

substituted for those of the 303rd at Molesworth, nearly three times as many leaflets were disseminated. From August to mid-September however, only four leaflet missions were flown and thus the 8th AF commitment of 45,000lb per week was far from being achieved. In an attempt to overcome this failure, a directive from VIII Bomber Command to HQ 1st Air Division on 20 September, directed that the 422nd Bomb Squadron prepare six aircraft 'to carry out extensive leaflet operations at night over Germany and occupied countries as soon after October 1st as practicable'. As a result of this directive, by the end of December 1943, the 8th AF was able to report that leaflet operations had shown a substantial improvement, with 18 missions in the month being tasked and completed. These missions had distributed a total of 21 million leaflets to Germany, pamphlets for Belgium, and copies of *L'Amérique* to France and had ensured that the commitment of 45,000lb per week now had been exceeded!

But why was the 422nd Bomb Squadron selected to drop these leaflets at night, and not bombs by day — the task that it had been trained for? For the planners the decision had been an easy and obvious one.

In September 1943, the 422nd Bomb Squadron, which was one of four squadrons attached to the 305th Bomb Group based at Chelveston, Northants, was ordered to undergo intensive training for night operations. The objective was to use its combat crews as 'Pathfinder' or 'Lead Crews' on night bombing missions by the 8th AF. As the 8th AF had been tasked as a day bomber force, its crews or aircraft had not been trained or equipped for night operations. To rectify this situation and make the 422nd Squadron's aircraft suitable for night-time flying, the 305th Engineering Section was engaged in an arduous programme of design, modification and installation.

In all the squadron's assigned aircraft, the sheet-metal workers installed astrodomes that had been taken from wrecked aircraft, and mounted them on racks constructed from salvage; astro compass installations were also completed in the same way. New and larger navigation tables were installed to accommodate the projections from the ceiling-mounted astrographs. The Instrument Section went to work and rewired the new navigational equipment to the existing equipment, moved instrument panels and rearranged the cabin lighting. It also fitted dead-reckoning compasses and hung special goose-neck lights. New radio antennae, direction-finding and Gee equipment units were installed by the Radio Section. Much of the new equipment required rearrangement of existing compartments for it to fit. Blackout curtains, to separate the navigator's and bombardier's rooms, were found to be necessary and a 1½in black stripe was painted outside the aircraft around the edge of each window. This was to prevent light leakage at the edge of the blackout curtains. All unpainted metal in the interior compartments was painted black to reduce reflection and glare from ground searchlights. Most of the interior surfaces of the waist and tail sections of the fuselage were likewise blackened and had the outside windows painted over so that, in case of any emergency, the dome lights could be turned on without the danger of any light escaping. On six aircraft it was found necessary to replace all the instrument dials whose luminous paint had deteriorated. Red instrument lighting rather than the former blue light, which could be so injurious to night vision, was substituted. New tail lights, interior warning lights, flare pistol sockets and demand oxygen systems were also installed and the bomb bay warning lights on the tail were removed. Flame suppressors, to dampen the light from engine exhaust flames, were fitted on all engines. Also, normal running lights were replaced by English 'resin' lights, which were installed in the same place.

policy to be adhered to, but with a major change contained in proposal 3.

Bomb Wings were to carry leaflets on ALL raids over Germany — therefore operational units would carry on the task; once the initial supply of leaflets had been used the Bomb Groups would have to reorder off their own backs; leaflets were to be carried in the last THREE aircraft of each Bomb Group formation; bombardiers were responsible for seeing that the boxes were hung correctly, and that as the boxes were to be placed on top of bomb racks, they could not be dropped until the normal bomb-load had been released.

This letter not only outlined the policy, but requested that the 1st and 4th Bomb Wings provide the designation of those Bomb Groups which would perform the task. Within 48hr the Groups had been selected and were, for the 1st Bombardment Wing, the 91st, 92nd, 303rd and 305th Bomb Groups; and for the 4th Bombardment Wing, the 95th, 390th and 100th Bomb Groups. However, due to problems in obtaining the required equipment, only five of the Groups were ready for operations by 23 July.

The first leaflet mission to Germany, in conjunction with a daylight bombing raid, took place on 28 July 1943 with aircraft selected from the 1st Bombardment Wing's 91st, 303rd, 305th and 306th Bomb Group, plus aircraft from the 4th Bombardment Wing. These aircraft were loaded with 273,000 leaflets which were dropped successfully. The following day with the addition of aircraft from the 92nd Bomb Group at Bovingdon, which were

The Engineering and Instrument Sections were not the only departments to be given modification work to carry out. The Armoury had to build fire cut-off cams into the gun ports, to prevent the now 'blinded' gunners from firing their guns into the tail or wings of their own aircraft during any defensive action. To suppress the flames created when the guns were fired, 'flash hiders' were likewise placed on all the 0.5in calibre guns. The camera doors were baffled and safety belts for gunners and rear crewmen fitted. All microphone switches, oxygen connections, heating suit junctions and first-aid points were marked faintly with luminous paint. The undersides of the aircraft were painted in a thick coat of gloss black to 'cone-out' searchlights from the ground. Along with the squadron code 'JJ' on the fuselage, the 305th Bomb Group 'triangle G' was painted on the tail. Last, but not least, discreet nose art was liberally applied on many of the B-17s — if selected by the crew and crew chief.

With the modification work completed and the aircraft poised for action, the only thing left to finish was that of crew training for the night missions. Lt Truesdell, the Assistant Operations Officer, must take a lot of credit for this because he designed a night training syllabus for the squadron after liaising with the RAF. It was a great loss when the squadron received news of his untimely death. At 23.30hrs on 31 August, whilst on a training flight over Foulsham in Norfolk, his B-17F, 42-5376 *Eager Eagle* had collided head-on with an RAF Bristol Beaufighter. There were 11 crew on board the Fortress, including a RAF officer, but only two survived. These were the two waist gunners who had baled out.

On completion of the intensive ground and flight training, it was agreed to send the crews to accompany RAF aircraft on a few night bombing missions; the idea was for the American crews to gain actual night combat experience. The first of these joint raids took place on 8 September 1943, when five Fortress aircraft bombed Boulogne. The raid was recorded in the 422nd Squadron records: '23 officers and 30 enlisted men wrote a new chapter in the 8th AF and 422nd Bomb Squadron part in World War 2. Taking-off in 41-24514 *We The People*, Maj Price led his Squadron in the 1st Night Attack on the Enemy, in a Fortress.'

By mid-September the squadron had completed its third 'Secret' night bombing mission over France — the most distant to date — and within five miles of the Italian border. The crews had taken the bit in their teeth with the new task and by October had completed a further three missions. Each mission included a mass take-off from Chelveston, then flying separately the briefed course and timed schedule to the target. Bombing was to be aimed with the help of target indicators that had been dropped previously by RAF Pathfinder aircraft which had been leading the raid.

A total of 35 aircraft were dispatched up to the squadron's eighth raid on 4 October, 32 being effective and two aircraft reported as lost, missing in action. The first, 42-2955 *Centaur*, a B-17F coded JJ-D and flown by Capt Harvey B. Rogers was reported on the 27 as 'coned' over the target area, and going down smoking in a wide spin. The second was on 2 October and was another B-17F, serial 42-3091 JJ-H, and flown by Lt Thomas S. Seay. *Centaur* was the first B-17 lost at night by the 8th AF during World War 2.

Following the results of these first few missions, the 8th AF decided to terminate night bombing operations. The training and effort put in by the 422nd aircrews had not been in vain, however, for the Air Force Planners decided that the squadron was the obvious choice for a new task. With the experience it had gained, it could perfect and use to full advantage the equipment required to fulfill the leaflet distribution requirements of the 8th AF. Thus,

for the 422nd, night bombing missions were slowly replaced by missions whose bomb-loads changed from bomb, to bomb-and-leaflet, then to those of just leaflet. The first solely-leaflet raid was the squadron's ninth night mission, flown on 7 November 1943, and recorded in the unit's diary as follows: 'The mission was a morale builder for the French, using the theory that "The pen is mightier than the sword" — our aircraft carried leaflets instead of bombs.'

When the aircraft left Chelveston for France, an air raid was in progress with a 'Red' showing. When the squadron reached London, which was also on a 'Red', it was fired upon by Allied guns but thankfully without any hits being scored. A natural progression from targets in France was to Germany, and so on the squadron's 24th night mission, which took place on the 30th, eight Fortress aircraft dropped leaflets over German targets.

The year of 1944 saw the airfield at Chelveston become a hive of activity, but for the 422nd which had crews flying bombing missions by day and leaflet missions by night, the continuous pressure of both types of mission began to show. Following a period as Operations Officer, the new CO, **Maj Aber**, who had assumed command on 26 November, recorded in his diary:

'An eventful but hectic day for the squadron. Last night during our initial orientation lecture to the new crews, an alert came through for six Pathfinder aircraft. I had not anticipated this — crews had never flown these aircraft nor met their "Mickey" operators. Even so, with considerable rush, the various sections swung into action. Around 03.00hr, after a short briefing, the six ships took off to their Groups to lead the combat Wings. The target was Berlin. One ship aborted. Stood down the next day so had a chance to meet the crews and test some aircraft. Thirty-three crews in the squadron. Group will have thirty in the other three squadrons combined, which just about makes this the 422nd Group.'

If Maj Aber believed his squadron to be overworked, he was not alone in his thoughts. With his Pathfinder crews proving their worth during the day and his remaining crews flying leaflet missions at night, his commanders were looking at his over-tasked squadron, and seeking a solution. In May they transferred 12 422nd Pathfinder crews from the squadron to Bassingbourn, which left the leaflet crews time to sort themselves out. Maj Aber, who had been busy with the development of leaflet bombs, packing procedures, and operational training, still found time to press for separation of his leaflet and Pathfinder crews. On 4 April he talked with the Deputy Commander General, 8th AF, and found that HQ in Washington would sanction authorisation for a separate squadron to be formed, solely for psychological warfare missions. On the 22nd, whilst at a commanders' meeting, he argued for the separation and gained the authorisation of 305th Bomb Group commander, Col Lawson. Now he had only to obtain Gen Williams' consent for the split to take place — and this he achieved.

Before the squadron separated, the crews flew a number of leaflet missions, one of the most important being on the night of 5 June 1944 — the eve of D-Day. Col Aber, together with 11 other crews, spearheaded Operation 'Overlord' and were the first Allied aircraft to cross the enemy beachhead. Singly and unescorted they dropped leaflets warning the people of 17 villages and cities in France, Belgium and Holland of the dangers of the imminent invasion.

On 9 June 1944, the Chief of Staff AFCC, Col Lee, received news that the 8th AF had decided his command would be assigned to the night leaflet activity, and that the unit was to be relocated at

This page:

On 12 May 1944, 50 officers and men flying in five aircraft took off on a leaflet mission to Denmark. B-17 42-31032 JJ-B, flown by Lt Michael, was attacked by a Junkers Ju 88 which killed its two waist gunners SSgts George Barber and Robert Walker. Both TSgt Louis Hatin the radio operator, and SSgt Nicholas Mastroianni the tail gunner were badly wounded. TSgt Dan Brennan the ball turret gunner also received serious injuries as a result of the attack but succeeded in beating off the Ju 88 before shooting it down. On return to the UK the B-17 landed at RAF Friston where the dead and injured were taken off the aircraft and the flak damage inspected. Note No 2 engine has been feathered.
B. Gunderson/113 Association

45

Above:
Maj Aber shares a joke on the flightline with the 422nd's Squadron Navigator, Capt Travsky. Looking on is Lt Haymon who drove Aber out to the aircraft for the D-Day mission.
E. Webb/113 Association

Right:
Aber gives a last briefing to two of his 'D-Day' gunners. The photograph was taken next to the 422nd's flightline shack.
E. Webb/113 Association

Cheddington. A requirement for dropping approximately 45,000lb of leaflets per week was prescribed, and with effect from 14 June 1944 the responsibility for specialised night leaflet dropping was assigned to AFCC.

Fourteen specially modified B-17 Flying Fortress aircraft, 14 trained combat crews and approximately 45 maintenance and operations personnel were to be transferred from the 1st Bomb Division for assignment to the 858th Bomb Squadron.

Field orders for night leaflet operations were to be issued by HQ 8th AF and the transmission of this information by scrambler telephone to the A-3 Duty Controller was to be the responsibility of HQ AFCC. This was to be transmitted at least 6hr before take-off and was to include information on targets, routes, altitudes and times. The targets themselves were to be selected by the Office of War Information in accordance with the official list of target priorities.

The AFCC's Flying Control was to be responsible for the clearance of all night leaflet aircraft and for all necessary arrangements for night flying aids, such as Pundits, Beacons and Occults. Mission flash reports were to be transmitted by scrambler telephone to the A-3 Duty Controller at HQ 8th AF, upon completion of each operational mission. These reports were also to be confirmed by teletype. The Office of War Information itself was to be responsible for the supply and delivery of leaflet bombs.

At this stage it was planned to eventually replace the B-17s currently in use with B-24 Liberators complete with trained crews.

As a result of this directive, the new squadron was formed by transferring the 858th Bomb Squadron to Cheddington on 21 June 1944, but leaving its combat crews, aircraft and other key operating personnel behind. The following Saturday, the 1st Air Division dispatched from the 422nd Bomb Squadron, Chelveston,

63 officers and 126 enlisted men who were experienced combat crews, plus five officers and 41 enlisted men from the maintenance section. The remainder of the men arrived on the 25th, with Maj Aber flying B-17G 43-37516 *Tondalayo*, the aircraft he would lose his life in eventually. The 422nd Squadron diary recorded: 'The six combat crews who stood-by at this station for last night's mission departed by aeroplane for Station 113. Maj Aber, flying 516, gave much-buzzed site No 6 its most memorable buzz-job by a B-17, as a farewell gesture.'

Once at Cheddington the staff of the newly-formed 858th Bomb Squadron along with its new CO, Maj Hambaugh, unpacked and, with their 13 B-17s, prepared for work. The next day at 21.00hrs the combat crews were called for a mission briefing, but due to bad weather the sortie was scrubbed. But, as crews would soon find out, the weather would have to be extremely bad for this to happen again — much worse than that for a normal bombing mission to be scrubbed!

The squadron's first mission from Cheddington was on 27 June when six aircraft took off at midnight for targets in Occupied France. During the remainder of the month a further 21 missions were flown to targets in France, Belgium and Holland, with the loss of just one aircraft. On 6 July B-17G 42-39811, with Lt Mann as pilot, was posted missing in action. On the 10th, there was a non-combat loss when Fortress '530', with Capt Weil as pilot, took off for a cross-country navigation training flight. Within minutes of take-off a fire broke out in a top turret oxygen pipe. Weil made a hasty landing at nearby RAF Halton, but despite the efforts of

Below:
All that was left of Fortress '530' after it caught fire on take-off from Cheddington. The firemen in the foreground were from Aylesbury.
B. Gunderson/113 Association

the RAF and civil fire service the aircraft was burnt out. There were no serious injuries among the crew, despite Weil being struck by a propeller whilst leaving the wreck. However, the claim to fame as the unit's first true casualty whilst at Cheddington must go to Hulett Collins: he accidentally shot himself in the leg with a .45in pistol whilst on early evening guard duty on 3 August!

The Squadron HQ was located in an old Base Operations building, and the former Chemical Warfare building was used as the Intelligence Library. The aircraft being flown were also not new. In fact the squadron held a unique record, with four B-17s completing 103, 98, 95 and 91 missions; B-17F 42-30791, *Pistol Packin' Mama*, came top with only two aborts, and *Swing Shift* with no aborts and 95 missions to its credit came a close second.

After the Allied invasion of the Continent in June, greater emphasis had been placed on appeals to foreign workers to sabotage Germany's war efforts, and the futility of continued resistance by the German forces was also being played upon in propaganda. Furthermore, there was a change in propaganda policy which resulted in an increase in the total leaflets dropped. In June the 858th dropped 209.6 tons; July on 133 sorties 216.1 tons; and August, a further increase in sorties and of leaflets being dropped. To cope with the increases seven new crews from the 856th Bomb Squadron, 492nd Bomb Group, along with their Liberators, were put on DS at Cheddington. On the 13th, a further five crews were transferred in from the 36th Bomb Squadron and, like the 856th, has also been based at Harrington. The squadron's designation was also changed to that of the 406th Bomb Squadron (Night Leaflet). To complete the changes, Maj Earle J. Aber replaced Col Hambaugh as the new squadron CO, and had a total staff in his care of 80 officers and 387 enlisted men.

Fated Flights

Whilst on a night leaflet mission on 16 August and over the third of its five targets, Fortress 42-30791, flown by Lt Dick Bailey, suffered a fire in its No 1 engine. Dick cut the engine, feathered the propeller and then put the aircraft into a dive, levelling off at 23,000ft. This action extinguished the flames, but as he was still unable to maintain speed, he continued to let down to 15,000ft. At the same time he was engaged by an enemy aircraft, which attacked him from below and which had not been seen until it began to fire its guns. TSgt Charles Williams, the Fort's tail gunner, commenced firing immediately and called Dick to take evasive action to starboard. Dick's top gunner brought his guns to bear upon the enemy aircraft which exploded just as the Fort's gunner was about to open fire. There followed a tremendously bright flash, then pieces of the enemy aircraft could be felt hitting the Fort's fuselage. Charles was credited with one enemy aircraft destroyed and Fortress 791 *Pistol Packin' Mama*, had a swastika painted on her nose to record the 'kill'.

On the 18th, the squadron received news that was not so good and that came as a blow to all. B-24H 42-295238, coded J6-K (J6 having replaced JJ as the new squadron code), flown by Lt Chester Cherrington, was lost whilst on a high altitude cross-country training flight. The intended altitude was 14,000ft but, for some unknown reason, whilst flying at only 100ft the Liberator collided with a chimney at Burghill Mental Hospital (now St Mary's), near Hereford. The Liberator crashed in flames in the grounds of the hospital and was destroyed in the resulting fire. The crew of 10 were killed. At the time of the accident, visibility was two miles and the wind from the southwest, with a cloud-base of 600-800ft. The only indication of the cause of the crash came from the fact that one engine had been feathered prior to impact, indicating possible engine trouble.

Following September, when a total of 105 aircraft were dispatched with 1,050 leaflet bombs to 313 targets, October brought more work. A total of 144 aircraft were dispatched, all but one making it back to Cheddington. On the 12th, Liberator 42-39845 suffered an engine fire and the captain, Lt Shannon, gave the bale-out order. After being abandoned in flight, the aircraft crashed in flames near Rennes in France.

November saw an extra seven crews and their aircraft arrive at Cheddington on Detached Service, to cope with the increase in pressure that was being put upon the NLS for more sorties. The crews were from the 856th Bomb Squadron, and had been on 'carpetbagger' missions (dropping supplies and agents to resistance forces), or 'Gas Runs' (missions with the bomb-bay full of fuel). It was no holiday for them at Cheddington, for after arrival on 6 November, they flew their first leaflet mission on the 8th. **Stan Seger** who was one of the pilots, noted in his diary at the time:

'Take-off: 21.45 hours; landed: 02.30 hours; target: Moulden, Germany. We had rockets fired at us over Chanes at 25,000 feet and flak at intervals over Belgium and Germany. Had trouble with bundles getting out and three were wedged in rear bomb-bay. Front right bomb-bay door was flying loose. Good weather at field, only ice formed was on windshield in traffic pattern, but runway was icy. All went well.'

On 15 November he was tasked for Duisberg in Germany and noted:

'No opposition in or out. Good weather except at Cheddington and was diverted to Oulton. We were weathered there for five days. Left November 20th at 11.00hrs. Lemke's crew took off the 18th and had to return to the field. On his turn on to the final approach, he made a vertical bank and "stalled out" and crashed.'

Murray Peden, who joined the RCAF and then completed a tour of operations with No 214 Squadron RAF, wrote in his book *A Thousand Shall Fall*:

'An American Liberator crew returned one afternoon from operations over Germany and landed at Oulton in the face of generally deteriorating weather. It was like the old times in the mess that night having a scattering of pinks around the bar. The weather kept on deteriorating, so with a full mess and some

warmly responsive guests, the party soared to memorable heights of hilarity. Next morning bright and early, the Americans were in the mess for breakfast, champing at the bit to get back down to the Flights and return to base. They rode up with us in the crew bus, and left us with a volley of friendly insults, in front of Flying Control. In twenty minutes they were all dead! They had taken off under a low ceiling and disappeared briefly into the cloud. Whether the pilot had then decided to make a circuit and try to get back to Oulton, no one will ever know. The Liberator suddenly reappeared, diving out of the cloud in a turn and crashed just beyond one of the maintenance hangars.'

One of the satisfying things about researching events from the past is that, with luck, you discover the background to what really happened. In this case research found that Peden was incorrect, and not all the crew were killed. **Jim Albright**, who was a member of Lt Fred Lemke's crew — the crew who were on the Liberator which Murray Peden saw, recalls:

'For the first time in all our flying as a crew, Les Cazzell, our engineer, and John Koliada, our waist gunner, started up the engines before our pilot and co-pilot climbed in. Immediately after take-off, I looked out the waist window and noticed petrol flowing down the wing near the number three engine, from an open fuel tank cap. I called the pilot who said he was aware of it, and that his main concern was the hot superchargers under the engine, at the trailing edge of the wing. In his last few words to us, he asked if we wanted him to try a landing, or take the aircraft higher for a bale-out. We all agreed on a landing. On the first two passes he was not lined up with the runway and had to try again. On the third attempt, he banked it very sharp and we just seemed to fall out of the sky. I tumbled around like I was in a clothes dryer, and my whole life seemed to pass by in a split second. After things settled down, I got to my knees and noticed an opening above me. I tried to pull myself out, but could not. Someone then "booted" me out, and I tumbled to the ground — I think it was Dan Bradley our

Left:
Herb Trebing with B-24 *Midnite Mistress*. *H. Trebing/113 Association*

Cheddington. His mail had been marked 'Deceased' and was about to be returned to his wife. Also, with the exception of his flying jacket, all his clothing had been either returned to the Supplies Section, or was missing altogether!

The year 1944 came to a very cold, but successful end for the NLS. As it was stood down for two days over the Christmas period, a squadron party was held. Whilst the 'Sad Sacks' band under the musical direction of Rocco Savino played the night away, the men had chance to relax and forget the war for a while.

Whilst at Cheddington, 868 aircraft had been dispatched to 3,067 targets and only four had been lost: one on a training flight, one on take-off, one in flight and one when Lt Abernathy crashed on landing at Woodbridge, Suffolk, whilst returning from the last mission of his tour. The officers and men in the NLS felt happy with their results for 1944, but were soon brought back to reality by the first events in 1945. The New Year started with a loss — a big one at that — when on 3 January B-24H 42-52650, coded J6-E, crashed on take-off with the loss of Lt Ray Hendrix and his crew. An engine had cut and, due to the loss of power at a critical time the aircraft failed to climb and came down in an orchard to the west of the airfield at Buckland.

The next night, the Squadron Operations Section received a telephone call from a Capt Huffner at 'Pinetree', reporting that a Sgt Eaton, a gunner with Lt Bronar's Liberator crew, had baled out of his aircraft along with the rest of the crew. The aircraft had been coned by searchlights over the battle lines in Belgium and had been hit by flak. Sgt Eaton had walked all night until he came to airfield A-89, where he reported in. He thought the rest of the crew, who he had not been in contact with, were all safe.

Following the first tragedy on 3 January, there was nearly another on the 20th when a Liberator on a local training flight was struck by lightning. The aircraft went out of control and one

navigator. I finally stumbled away from the wreck, but was stopped by someone who gave me morphine — well he tried!'.

When the aircraft hit the ground, the left wing struck first and was torn off, throwing the full weight of the aircraft on to the nose and forward fuselage. Lt Bradley, and Sgts Albright and Koliada who were in the waist section, and were the only survivors of the crash, all other crew members being killed instantly.

When the Operations Section at Harrington was informed that one of its aircraft had been involved in a crash, it took no action, for it had no aircraft detailed for missions or training, and was not in contact with those on DS at Cheddington. This presented problems, but they were soon resolved. There was more confusion, however, when Jim left hospital to return to

Below:
Overshadowed by Southend Hill, a Liberator is 'bombed-up' under the watchful eye of a guard. *H. Trebing/113 Association*

of the crew members, Lt Gilman Blake, baled out before the order had been given. He used the ditching exit in the topside of the fuselage, struck the tailplane of the aircraft and was knocked out. Unconscious and unable to use his parachute, he plunged to his death. A short time later his body was recovered from Gade Tower, Hemel Hempstead in Hertfordshire, where it had landed, together with his unopened parachute. As for the Liberator, control was regained and a landing made at nearby RAF Bovingdon.

On the following night, 21 January, an aircraft was lost together with two men. Lt Ferguson was returning from a mission and due west of his last target, when his No 1 engine went off-tune. He was unable to feather it and because it started to vibrate severely, he put the aircraft into a glide to keep up the airspeed. At 12,000ft his No 3 engine started surging and then began to 'run-away'. No 1 started to smoke and, as though it was feeling left out, No 2 began to give trouble. Ferguson had no option but to shut off the fuel to both engines and give the 'bale-out' order. With the exception of Ferguson and Lt Rush his co-pilot, the rest of the crew jumped. As they did, No 3 engine went out. This left just No 4, but that was now whistling. Within seconds the aircraft caught fire and plummeted to earth, exploding on contact with the ground. Both Ferguson and Rush were killed. The radio operator, Russell Onderdonk, broke his leg and before long the rest of the crew joined him in Rheims Hospital with ankle and knee injuries.

Master of Fate

To know where he is, where he is going, and where he has been were three facts a navigator was required to know the answer to at all times. His crew status also required that he worked a longer day, due to the fact that his pre-mission preparation started long before that of his fellow crew members. What was a typical day and sortie like for the 'brains of the crew'? **Howard Bacon** who was a navigator in the Night Leaflet Squadron, recalls:

Above:
Lts Marty Marshall and Art Green from Detachment 113, 18th Weather Squadron.
A. Gulliver/113 Association

Left:
Maj Aber presents the Air Medal to air gunner Jake Sandoval.
J. Sandoval/113 Association

'I don't think you can class any sortie as typical, due to the variability of the targets and the differences in the material we had to deliver, which was diverse in nature. Only our crew remained fairly constant, for which I was eternally grateful. This was because of their vigilance and dedication to all their assigned duties.'

Howard's B-17F, 838, was named *Paper Doll* and coded JJ-O. Some five days after his crew were assigned to it, *Paper Doll* was given some appropriate nose art in the form of a doll, and embellished with the Christian names of his fellow crew members' wives and girlfriends on the engine cowlings. Howard remembers leaflet mission briefings as follows:

'I would get out of my bunk at about 11.00hr, just in time for my lunch at 12.00. Our crew meetings were scheduled for 13.30, at which time the crews going would be selected for the mission. After which, they would be dismissed with the exception of us navigators who were then held for the briefing, and pre-mission preparation.

'Unlike crews in other Bomb Squadrons who flew in mass formations, we in the Night Leaflet Squadron flew alone, and therefore each navigator had his own plans to make up and his own route to plot. So, the responsibility for the accuracy of the mission was squarely in his hands. Instead of making this tougher for us, it actually made it easier in my case, for I felt that I was the "master of my fate" and also of that of my crew, and therefore had to give the best I could. At the briefing I was given flak areas, German fighter airfields, other information that would help me avoid enemy problems, and IFF (Identification Friend or Foe) codes. The entry and re-entry point for the English coast, so that RAF night-fighters would know where and when we would cross the coast (this was to prevent the Germans from sneaking in undetected). Then we were given the most important bit — the targets we were to hit with our leaflet bombs. We were given more than one target per mission, so as to expand the capabilities of reaching more and more people all the time. Last but not least we were given a complete meteorological briefing.'

The 18th Weather Squadron had detachments at every 8th AF base in the British Isles. **Art Gulliver** was assigned to Detachment 113 at Cheddington and, as Leaflet Weather Officer, he recalls:

'We would first give each crew a set of weather maps. These showed the fronts, pressure centres, the precipitation areas along the mission route, and both top and bottom heights of the cloud-base. Also, the expected take-off and landing weather. Attached to the maps was a summary of the conditions, which explained any storms and their direction of movement. A second map was then issued, which showed any high winds and all areas of icing. These areas had their top and bottom heights marked. At all other bomber bases, a horizontal cross-section map was provided for the route. This was not practical at Cheddington however, as each aircraft usually had its own route. Once the maps had been issued, we would brief the crews from a larger map, explaining the expected conditions and stress the hazards, then answer any questions. You could expect the main concern to be the landing conditions when the crews got back — or IF they could expect to get back! We would then explain which airfields were alternatives and the expected conditions there. Crews were also interested in good weather areas over the Continent, as these could be areas where the enemy could sight them from the ground.

'On return from all missions, crews were de-briefed by the same Weather Officer who had briefed them. They would be asked for the conditions that they had experienced on their mission, and which they should have noted on their maps at the time. On completion of the de-brief, we would then return to our office in the control tower, and phone Headquarters 8th AF Bomber Command at High Wycombe. These notes were of the utmost importance to the Weather Officers there, as they would be preparing forecasts for all 8th AF bomber missions which would follow in four to eight hours after the Cheddington aircraft had landed.'

Once the weather briefing was over, it was time to get on with the preparation. **Howard Bacon** continues:

'One of my longest sorties had targets in France at Rennes, Tours, Orleans, and Mulhouse — which was in Eastern France very near to Basle in Switzerland. Armed with all my navaids I plotted the course around any possible trouble areas. On the map it would end up looking great, and I would hope that the flight would go the same way. The exit out of England was Portland Bill which was not a time problem, but as it was also the re-entry point, this did present a problem. It was here that I built in a safety factor, in case of weather changes and in that area there were many. To overcome them, on the way back I would mark a triangle on the map by plotting a heading for a point other than Portland Bill, and then figure out the time at that point for our re-entry time. Then, if we were early we could go further out on the triangle, or if we were late we could cut across the triangle to the turning point to save time, then re-enter at the correct time. The final exactness of the weather report would not be known, however, until our actual flight time.

'When I had finished my planning and plotting at 15.00hrs, I returned to our hut with briefcase in hand, confident I had done the best that I could. Despite the excitement of the moment, I maintained a discipline of not telling my fellow crewmen and brother officers what our target destinations were until they were called to briefing themselves. This was not because I did not trust them to keep their mouths shut, but because I didn't trust myself to keep my own mouth shut. The saying "loose lips sink ships" applied for me at Cheddington, as I had experienced Lord Haw Haw giving the time on our mess hall clock at Chelveston during one of his evening radio broadcasts. The clock was wrong — but he was right! I hate to admit it now, but I would be about to burst trying to keep the target locations to myself.

'Tea was at 17.30hrs, which was followed by odds and ends that I found to do until our full briefing at 20.00hrs, when I would go back briefcase in hand. You could feel the electricity in the air when the time came for target assignments, and when it really sunk in where the crews were going, you could feel their excitement. After the briefing we put on our Mae Wests and picked up our parachutes, then off we went to the aircraft. The 406th Squadron dispersal was over on the northeast side of the field, away from that of the 36th.

'Once in the aircraft my equipment had to be checked out, my first concern being the "G" Box radar unit, which provided me with information I couldn't do without. This was an accurate indication of the wind direction and its speed, but I could only get this after we were in flight. The box had such accuracy in England that I could find my location and with it, our limitations for altitude all round the Base, should there be any fog. We could therefore land without crashing into any of the hills. It required special hyperbolic-type maps with lines defined in three colours. These indicated three different radar sources, and were identifiable as different blips on the screen. I would have to get at least two different blips, and where the lines crossed, that was where we were at that instant in time. If I took a series of these "fixes" I had enough to establish the flight line, and from that result could extract the effect of the wind during the flight, and thus the wind direction and speed. For me the big problem was the shortness of the accuracy range, for once across the Channel the accuracy diminished in relation to the distance away from England. From then on it was "dead reckoning" or DR, and hoping that the winds remained constant throughout the mission.

'After all my checks had been completed, the only thing then left for me to do was wait it out and see if we would go. The mission could be scrubbed at any time, and we would then have to stand down. The worst thing about a mission was to be ready, then have the red flare signal fired by Flying Control indicating to the pilot that his mission was off.

'Once our engines were turning over, I made a last-minute check to make sure the blackout curtain between me and the bombardier was safely in place. This was so that no light could leak out. I would also check my oxygen, then after a green light, brakes were released and we were off. The time was 02.00hrs and for me this was the time I felt like a "one-armed paperhanger". It was the critical period when I had to get the winds while we were climbing to reach our mission altitude, with the pilot following the course I had set for him at each turn. I took for granted he would follow this course as accurately as possible, and I know he tried to maintain it. Things looked good for us as the winds given in briefing were coming from the right direction, and we departed Portland Bill on time, and en route for France. Checks were now made from time to time to verify the wind speed and direction. Even though it was night, the rivers and towns were used to identify our track over the ground, and so could give us an accurate computation of the wind speed and direction.

'On this particular mission, we had just crossed the Channel and were over the bay of St Malo. We had all settled down into our basic routines, with the bombardier anticipating the first drop, when I realised something was wrong! We were too early for the crossing and had arrived there much too fast. A sinking feeling then started to creep in, and I wondered what had gone wrong with my computations. Checking with the bombardier, who agreed with me on identification of St Malo, I quickly refigured our wind speed and direction, and came up with a weird answer for our speed over the ground. The wind pushing us in flight — or the wind mass we were flying in — had reached the unheard-of velocity of 125kt and were cruising at 155-160kt. This meant that we were flying through France at a ground speed of some 280kt. This is all very well, but take the flip side of the coin and it meant we would be crawling back home out of France at only 30-35kt!

'Knowing the problem but not the answer, with the assistance of our bombardier I concentrated on checking landmarks to verify our position, and soon was able to reconfirm our way-points with their new arrival time. We raced into France dropping our leaflet bombs on our assigned targets, with the last drop at Mulhouse way ahead of my original eta. Once we had completed the bomb-run, I informed the rest of the crew about the problem so they would understand the situation, and the reason for the long slow haul home. I then kept constant watch on our ground speed and refigured our time to the re-entry point. The old "Radius of Action" triangle technique worked, and we made our re-entry point right on the nose and were soon back home.

'We landed at 05.50hrs in between day take-offs, and reported in for de-briefing and our usual shot of whisky (if you wanted it). We then all sat down at a table for interrogation and then each individual had his own de-brief. I thought the weather man would

turn inside out when I reported the winds we had encountered. I told him the direction was accurate but the speed far exceeded anything I had ever run up against. It was soon 06.30hrs and time for breakfast — real (not powdered) eggs, toast, and cocoa, then into the sack at 07.00hrs for a good day's sleep, or until our next briefing.'

Those winds Howard encountered are now fully understood, and are known as jetstreams — high altitude almost horizontal winds exceeding 80kt found at the boundary of warm and cold air currents. For Howard it was just another mission, another to help make his final total of 45. Despite being witness to take-off crashes, despite seeing one aircraft shot up so badly that it had to be scrapped, and despite seeing one return with three dead and six wounded on board, what kept him going? He claims to have had a good crew, a first class pilot, a tremendous crew chief who, with his men, always worked above and beyond the call of duty. And that whilst he sat on his 'flak flap', Lady Luck sat on his shoulder.

The Bomb

When leaflet missions first started in 1943, the method of dissemination in bundles with barometric releases was acceptable. That is until their failure was brought to light by a Col Wallace from VIII Bomber Command, who stated:

'We are not getting satisfactory results from the aneroids we are using on our leaflet bundles. The slipstream causes the bundles to

Below and below right:
One of many booklets that gave the man in the street instructions on how to delay or destroy the German war machine. WG2F had 32 pages in both French and German. It was disseminated from 5 September to 28 October 1944.

open up directly below the aircraft, which means that leaflets destined for Paris end up in North Africa or Turkey. Either this or the leaflets go all the way down in a bundle. Will you see what you can do on this?'

His statement was no exaggeration of the situation, for week after week errors became the norm. On one of the first leaflet missions, aircraft of the 422nd Squadron had to drop leaflets destined for the Paris area over Brussels! This was just to combat the prevailing 60mph winds that were present at 30,000ft. As for the problem of the leaflets falling intact as a bundle, *The Manchester Guardian* reported that 'one fell solidly on to a small German barge, went through the bottom, and sunk it. Another bundle crashed through the roof of Notre Dame Cathedral...'!

A new problem was highlighted when VIII Bomber Command changed the strategy of its bombardment campaign from explosive, to the devastating effect of incendiary bombs on German urban areas. Little did anyone think it would change leaflet operations or policy, but it became increasingly evident that, due to the number of internal aircraft fires being started by the pre-ignition of bomb fuses, the mixture of incendiary bombs being transported along with leaflets added a new hazard to bombing missions. Leaflets could be loaded in bomb-bays with 500 and 2,000lb bombs, but would not mix with clusters of incendiaries. Crews were also faced with, and complained of, the additional drag that was being caused by the extra weight of up to

---

Gibt es wirklich keine Brücken mehr....

zwischen dem deutschen Volk und der freien Welt?

Die Antwort auf diese Frage bestimmt in diesen Stunden das Handeln oder Nichthandeln aller deutschen Menschen. Von dieser Antwort hängt DEINE Zukunft ab!

Goebbels sagt: „Das deutsche Volk hat alle Brücken hinter sich abgebrochen...."

Für Goebbels, Hitler, Himmler und Co. ist das kein Problem. Für die besessenen Fanatiker und zum Untergang verurteilten Führer der deutschen Tragödie gibt es in der Tat keine Brücke. Weder eine Brücke zur europäischen Zivilisation — noch zu einer besseren deutschen Zukunft.

Für die Partei und SS-Fanatiker gibt es nur den UNTERGANG.

UN APPEL AUX TRAVAILLEURS FRANCAIS ET BELGES EN ALLEMAGNE

L'Allemagne a perdu la guerre !
La fin de la plus grande guerre de l'histoire approche — mais....

VOUS ETES EN DANGER !

A mesure que la guerre tire à sa fin le régime nazi deviendra de plus en plus impitoyable. Chacun de vous dorénavant est sous le coup d'UN DOUBLE DANGER. Le DANGER émanant des terroristes nazis qui, pour obtenir le maximum de rendement de votre part, useront contre vous de tous les moyens. Et le DANGER — chaque jour plus grand — des ATTAQUES AERIENNES.

Vous serez contraints à vivre et à travailler dans les régions qui renferment les plus dangereux des objectifs choisis par les Forces Aériennes Alliées — tandis que les adolescents allemands de seize ans et les vieillards de soixante ans et de plus seront dirigés vers le front pour servir de dernières réserves de chair à canon dans les batailles de Hitler acculé. Ne dites pas: Nous savons ce que sont les bombardements.

VOUS N'AVEZ ENCORE RIEN VU.

Vous serez versés de force dans l'armée allemande pour combler les rangs ravagés de la Wehrmacht vaincue.

800lb of leaflets. This made it difficult for the captain in each of the three B-17s in the tail-end position to keep up, and as a result they lost the protection of the large box formations of bombers.

At the same time as the crews were having misgivings on mixing bomb-loads, engineering officers at American bomber bases were beginning to think that the additional weight of the leaflets (now being transported in heavy canvas bags) might cause the aircraft to buckle during violent, evasive action from fighters or flak. The bags had replaced the wooden boxes and were strapped to the main longerons of the aircraft. When the last bomb was released, it jerked open the neck of the bag which had been kept closed by wire, thus allowing the leaflets to fall out.

A solution to the airframe distortion possibility was submitted by Lt Bloomer, a junior engineering officer in VIII Bomber Command. He suggested loading bundles of leaflets into many large wooden boxes rather than just one, but using only ONE aircraft. This aircraft could then carry 3,500lb of leaflets in each of the large slatted boxes. Thus, each aircraft alone could carry more than the 24,000lb that were being carried by three aircraft using the bags, but still keep the aircraft light for manoeuvring. This method was accepted and put into practice.

Despite the changes and improvements in the equipment, and the increase in volume of leaflets now being disseminated, the British PWE reported that an average of only 4% of leaflets dropped were finding their way into the hands of the enemy. What was needed was a device that would allow accurate dissemination over the required target area. The idea of using a readily available device that was present on the airfield at Chelveston came first to the 305th Bomb Group Operations Officer, Capt James Monroe. He investigated some old laminated paper containers that had housed M-17 incendiary bombs. They were 48in long, had a diameter of 16½in, and were light but strong with the ends enclosed by cardboard caps. Furthermore, they were NOT needed. Capt Monroe, with foresight, saw they had potential. With the addition of just a pair of standard

General Eisenhower taler til de besatte Lande i Europa

VESTEUROPAS FOLK!

Troppestyrker fra de Allieredes Ekspeditionshær er gaaet i Land paa den franske Kyst. Denne Landgaa et Led i de forenede Nationers fælles Plan, som er lagt sammen med vor store, russiske Allierede, og som Sigte paa at befri Europa.

Jeg bringer Dem alle dette Budskab. Selv om det indledende Angreb maaske ikke er blevet foretaget i I eget Land, er Befrielsens Time dog nær.

Alle Patrioter, Mænd og Kvinder, Unge og Gamle, har en Indsats at gøre, naar den endelige Sejr skal vi Til Medlemmerne af Modstandsbevægelserne, hvadenten de faar deres Ordrer hjemmefra eller udefra, siger " Følg de Instruktioner, De har faaet." Til Patrioter, som ikke tilhører organiserede Modstandsgrupper, jeg : " Udsæt ikke Deres Liv for unødig Fare, men fortsæt Deres passive Modstand, indtil jeg giver Dem Sig til Rejsning og til Angreb paa Fjenden. Den Dag vil komme, hvor jeg faar Brug for Deres samlede Styr Indtil den Dag paalægger jeg Dem den haarde Opgave at udvise Disciplin og Tilbageholdenhed.

FRANKRIGS BORGERE!

Jeg er stolt over atter at have Frankrigs tapre Styrker under min Kommando. I Kampen ved deres Allie Side vil de spille en fortjenstfuld Rolle under deres Fædrelands Befrielse.

Fordi den første Landgang har fundet Sted paa Deres Lands Jord, gentager jeg over for Dem med en større Eftertryk mit Budskab til Befolkningerne i de andre besatte Lande i Vesteuropa. Følg Deres Led Instruktioner. En forhastet Rejsning af alle Franskmænd kan komme til at forhindre Dem i at yde Deres I den størst mulige Hjælp i det kritiske Øjeblik. Vær taalmodige og hold Dem beredt !

Som Øverstkommanderende for de Allieredes Ekspeditionshær er det min Pligt og mit Ansvar at træffe nødvendige Forholdsregler i Forbindelse med Krigsførelsen. Det er af største Betydning, at de Ordrer, jeg udste bliver efterkommet hurtigt og villigt.

En effektiv fransk Civiladministration maa foretages af Franskmænd. Enhver maa fortsætte sit nuvær Arbejde, medmindre han modtager andre Ordrer. De, som har gjort fælles Sag med Fjenden og saaledes forr deres Land, vil blive fjernet. Naar Frankrig er blevet befriet for Undertrykkerne, maa det franske Folk selv v sine Repræsentanter og den Regering, det ønsker at leve under.

Under dette Felttog, hvis Maal er Fjendens endelige Nederlag, vil De maaske lide yderligere Tab eller Sk Hvor tragisk dette end er, er det en Del af den Pris, der maa betales for Sejren. Jeg forsikrer Dem om, at je gøre alt, hvad der staar i min Magt, for at lette Deres Prøvelser. Jeg ved, at jeg nu i lige saa høj Grad som tidli kan regne med Deres faste Holdning. Den tapre Indsats, der er blevet gjort af de Franskmænd, som baade i Frankrig og overalt i det franske Imperium har fortsat Kampen mod Nazisterne og deres Lejesvende i Vichy, været et Eksempel og en Inspiration for os alle.

Denne Landgang er blot den indledende Fase af Felttoget i Vesteuropa. Der ligger store Slag foran os. opfordrer alle frihedselskende Mennesker til at slutte sig til os. Vær tillidsfulde og standhaftige ; — vore St kræfter er resolutte ; — sammen vil vi vinde Sejr.

Dwight D Eisenhower

DWIGHT D. EISENHOWER.
Øverstkommanderende for de
Allieredes Ekspeditionshær

AVIS DU COMMANDEMENT SUPREME ALLIE AUX HABITANTS DES ZONES DE COMBAT

RAIDS AERIENS—VOTRE VILLE PEUT ETRE UN OBJECTIF !

Même s'il n'y a pas actuellement de troupes allemandes dans votre région, il peut se trouver dans votre ville des ponts, des viaducs, des installations ferroviaires, des réservoirs de carburant, des usines, des ateliers de réparations, etc.... qui pourront être à un moment donné d'importance vitale pour l'ennemi, au cours de sa retraite de France.

L'attaque de ces installations par les forces aériennes alliées peut faire partie des opérations de la libération. *Il ne sera pas toujours possible de vous avertir à l'avance de ces attaques.* En conséquence...

1. Dites-vous toujours que l'apparition de bombardiers alliés peut signifier que des troupes allemandes ou des installations vitales de votre ville sont sur le point d'être attaquées.

2. Si vous en avez le moyen, quittez la ville. Si vous devez rester là, ne traînez pas dans les rues ou sur les ponts : réfugiez-vous dans les abris, dans des caves profondes, ou au rez-de-chaussée de votre maison, sous l'escalier ; couchez-vous par terre, écartez-vous des verres.

AVANT QUE LA BATAILLE APPROCHE

Soyez prêts à quitter la ville au premier avertissement. Les armées de la libération se déplacent rapidement.

1. Préservez vos biens de l'ennemi, y compris les vêtements civils.

2. Ayez toujours prête une réserve de nourriture et d'eau, suffisante pour plusieurs jours, et dissimulez-la à l'ennemi.

3. Construisez une tranchée ou un abri dans la campagne, aussi près que possible de chez vous, mais assez loin des routes, des chemins de fer, des ponts, et autres objectifs militaires.

4. Que votre tranchée ou votre abri soit assez large pour recevoir votre famille et assez profonde pour vous per mettre de vous coucher par terre. Couvrez-la avec de branches et du gazon.

ZWEI WORTE die 1 600 000 Leben retteten

„EI SÖRRENDER" sagten allein im Westen 1 600 000 Deiner Kameraden, weil sie einsahen, dass ihre Lage hoffnungslos war.

„EI SÖRRENDER" bedeutete für 1 600 000 Deiner Kameraden, dass sie aus der Hölle der Materialschlacht in Sicherheit gelangten.

„EI SÖRRENDER" bedeutete für 1 600 000 Deiner Kameraden, dass sie die Heimat nach Kriegsende gesund und wohlbehalten wiedersehen.

Auch für Dich öffnen ZWEI WORTE den Weg in die Heimat. ZWEI WORTE: „EI SÖRRENDER"

Above:
ZF10 People of Combat Zones
Disseminated over France from 14 August up to and including 19 November 1944. It advised all local civilians to keep clear of roads, bridges and railways.

Right:
ZG126: I Surrender
One of a number of leaflets that were directed at German troops. It pointed out some facts on who had surrendered, and advised them to do the same. It was disseminated on the nights of 13 to 17 April 1944.

A D-Day follow-up information leaflet, signed by Dwight D. Eisenhower. It was dropped over Denmark on the night of 10 June 1944.

'U-bolts', they could be attached to the normal issue bomb shackles. The containers, when full of leaflets, could then be hung in the bomb-bays of B-17 Flying Fortress aircraft. All he now needed was to find out if they would be stable in flight and if they could be made to open at a desired height for the contents to empty and cover the nominated target area.

Working in one of the 305th's hangars, he conducted research into the fitting of standard M-111 bomb time-fuses into the end of the containers. Then after drilling down both sides, he fed primer cord through the ½in diameter holes that were spaced at 6in intervals. The cord was terminated next to the explosive fuse, which was sunk into a length of pipe so as to increase the explosive effect of the detonation. When assembled, Monroe took the completed bomb outside the hangar, then, after detonation of the nose fuse, saw that the container had been blown apart! All that was now required was some drawings of the device so that additional 'Monroe T-1 Bombs' could be made and then test-flown. The first test was held on 21 January 1944, when a T-1 was loaded into a B-17 flown by Capt Hitchcock. Also on board as an observer was Gen Robert McClure, Chief of the PWD section of the Supreme Headquarters Allied Expeditionary Forces (SHAEF), with which Monroe had just been placed on Detached Service. Monroe was on board an observation plane flown by Maj Aber and Capt August Weil (Weil had just replaced Monroe as the new Operations Officer). Aber's crew also included Jake Sandoval the tail gunner, who recalls the test and claims, 'I saw nothing'.

The intended height of the test was to have been 5,000ft, with split-second timing. To achieve this, radio contact was to have been established on the frequency used as the 305th Command Frequency, but at the time of the test it was being used for a mission! The two aircraft were thus unable to communicate, and in manoeuvring to the test area over the North Sea, missed each other. All Aber could do now was to put on a second test when there was a lull in missions, and if the weather permitted. The chance came on 4 February, when the Fortress dropped the test bomb from 10,000ft. A total weight of 300lb of paper had been packed in the bomb, most in the fuse end to make it stable in fall, and Jake's observation aircraft with Monroe and camera on board flew at 6,000ft. Also on board were Allan Challas who was head of the Office of War Information (OWI), Sam Boal, of the London OWI, Maj Robert Garey, Liaison Officer at HQ 8th AF, and Sqn Ldr Peter Branch RAF, SHAEF. A free radio frequency had been obtained and allowed contact to be maintained between the two aircraft. As a result, at 15.00hrs and on a Gee signal, the bomb fell free from the bomb-bay, rolled twice, then — when at 1,000ft below the Fortress — detonated. The paper contents showed good dispersal and began to separate into single sheets with the bomb disintegrating into harmless bits. As a result of the test, a report was submitted three days later by Maj Aber and Capt Monroe to the 305th Headquarters, detailing the events and reporting the fact that leaflet bombs could now be brought down to explode from 30,000ft to 2,000ft, and target an area as small as a half to one mile, or as large as required.

The first operational use of the Monroe bomb was on 18 April 1944, when the 422nd added a new location for squadron operations — Norway. The intention was for five B-17s to drop 2,560,000 copies of leaflet N4 entitled 'Come it Will' over the Stavanger, Oslo, Bergen and Trondheim area. With Aber's crew

Below:
Leaflets were packed into Monroe Bombs by Ammunition Company staff, intially at Sharnbrook Depot in Bedfordshire. *IWM OWIL29624*

DAS ENDE EINER DIVISION

Überlebende der 716. I.D. (Kreml-Division) sind jetzt in Sicherheit in England. Ihre Berichte sind EINE WARNUNG FÜR ALLE TRUPPEN AM ATLANTIKWALL — DIE AUF ENTSATZ WARTEN

Hier ist einer der Berichte :

„Am Dienstag war der erste Angriff auf unseren Abschnitt zwischen Arromanches und Ouistreham. Da kriegten wir gleich den Befehl : Aushalten — Verstärkung im Anmarsch !

Am Donnerstag waren wir praktisch schon überrannt und eingekesselt. Rückwärts war der Feind mit kanadischen Fallschirmjägern. Vorne lag der Feind mit Schlachtschiffen und zerharkte uns die Stellung. Und über uns da hing der Feind mit einer dicken Fliegerdecke und jagte uns mit Flächen-würfen die letzten Minenfelder hoch.

Kein deutscher Jäger zu sehen. Keine Verbindung mehr mit rechts und links — alles was wir wussten war : der Amerikaner landet dauernd Truppen und schweres Material auf beiden Seiten.

Und von Verstärkung keine Rede. Nur wieder der Befehl vom Kommandeur kam durch : Aushalten bis zum letzten Schuss !

Da lagen wir so gut wie nackt in unseren ausgeschlitzten Bunkern und sollten mit unseren Maschinenpistolen und MGs und Pak-Geschützen die Stellung halten bis zum letzten Schuss — und kamen garnicht zum Schuss. Ab und zu hat einer nach den Fliegern geschossen, das war alles.

Am Donnerstag abend hiess es wieder : Es kommt Ver-stärkung. Wir werden 'rausgehauen. Von Caen sind Panzer unterwegs.

Die Panzer haben wir nie zu sehen gekriegt. Das war nur eine schöne Geste, — mehr nicht. Eine Abteilung von der 21. P.D. mit Panzer IV — mit sowas kamen sie an am dritten

ZG 11

Above left:
ZG61: Safe Conduct
The very successful 'safe conduct pass'. Disseminated from 10 September 1944 to 8 March 1945. Over 70% of prisoners of war had these with them when they surrendered.

Above:
ZG11: A Division Written Off
Another tactical leaflet aimed at the German soldier, informing him of the loss of a unit. It was disseminated from 15 June to 14 August 1944. There were a total of 95 tactical leaflets produced in the 'ZG' series.

Left:
ZG82K: What Is To Be Done?
Disseminated from 13 November 1944 to 8 March 1945.

in the lead aircraft, the 10hr mission — with 'Tokyo Tanks' to carry the extra fuel — went as planned, but as a leaflet drop at night it was unsuccessful. Norwegian reports which arrived in London afterwards said that whilst leaflets had been spotted and picked up in fairly large quantities at a small town southeast of Oslo, only three of the other target areas had seen them, and near Bergen and Trondheim the leaflets had burst over a fjord. Also, many leaflets had landed in too high a concentration and could therefore be easily and quickly picked up by German troops. Monroe's explanation in a report to SHAEF was that the M-111 fuses had been set for too low an altitude and had exploded at only 20 to 25ft. The wind therefore was unable to disseminate them. He stated it would not happen again, as issue of the M-111 fuse had dried up and the British Type 860 barometric fuse would be utilised on all future missions. This fuse was set to detonate at 2,000ft, was available in large numbers, and had proved to be more reliable when fitted to parachute flares.

Left:
F73: Le Courrier De L'Air
**The 5 July 1944 issue of *Courier,*
disseminated from 10 July to
7 August 1944. It was a four-page
French newspaper which
preceded *L'Amerique en Guerre.*
Very pictorial and with the latest
war news for the French people.**

LE COURRIER DE L'AIR

APPORTE PAR AVION — *LONDRES, LE 5 JUILLET 1944.*

Dans Cherbourg libérée

QUATRE PAGES DE PHOTOGRAPHIES

Le 27 juin 1944, les forces américaines commandées par le major-général Collins, faisaient leur entrée dans Cherbourg.

A l'exception de quelques forts, les Allemands, commandés par le lieutenant-général Carl von Schlieben, mettaient bas les armes.

Ainsi s'est terminée la deuxième phase du débarquement allié sur le sol normand; la libération de Cherbourg, première grande ville française à être affranchie du joug allemand, offre aux Alliés une base dont toute l'importance se fera sentir dès que les travaux de réaménagement du port seront terminés.

L'expérience acquise en Afrique du Nord permet de croire qu'ils seront rapidement achevés.

La libération de Cherbourg constitue le point final d'une brillante manœuvre des troupes américaines.

Brièvement, la bataille s'est déroulée comme suit :

Les Américains ont d'abord coupé, sur un front étroit, la base du Cotentin entre Carentan et Barneville.

Contrairement aux prévisions du Haut Commandement allié, les Allemands ne réussirent pas à contre-attaquer utilement l'enclave américaine, ni au nord ni au sud.

Au nord, une seule contre-attaque fut lancée mais elle fut brisée par l'artillerie.

Au sud où, sur la carte la situation était éminemment favorable à une manœuvre décisive de la part de Rommel, rien de tel ne fut tenté.

Pour comprendre cette carence de Rommel, il faut examiner quelle était, au moment où les Américains ont lancé l'assaut de Cherbourg, la situation dans le secteur britannique entre Caumont et Caen.

Les puissantes formations de blindés mises en action par le général Montgomery au sud-est de la tête de pont alliée y avaient fixé quatre divisions blindées allemandes dans une bataille statique et défensive.

Rommel, durement pressé, sachant qu'une rupture de son front dans ce secteur aurait des conséquences incalculables, fut contraint de choisir de deux maux le moindre.

Assignant à la majeure partie de ses blindés disponibles un rôle d'arrêt entre Caen et Caumont, il n'a pu gêner sérieusement le déploiement américain dans le Cotentin.

M. Stimson, Ministre américain de la Guerre, rendant hommage aux troupes britanniques, a déclaré que la victoire américaine dans le Cotentin était due en grande partie aux opérations menées par les Britanniques et les Canadiens dans le secteur Caumont-Caen.

Le drapeau blanc remplace la croix gammée. Le général von Schlieben sort de son P.C. souterrain

Von Schlieben arrive au Quartier Général du major-général Collins

As for bomb manufacture, the men at Chelveston constructed the first few Monroe bombs, but as the requirement for more arose, a detachment of an Army Ammunition Company at nearby Sharnbrook in Bedfordshire took over the production. In a short time, and due to a report claiming that the Sharnbrook personnel handled the explosive components in a dangerous way, production was changed to the 8th AF Ordnance Depot at Melchbourne Park. The first Monroe bombs manufactured there came off the production line on 16 May 1944, and by D-Day there were some 4,000 bombs ready. By the end of 1944, a total of 75,277 had been produced — some with assistance of a civilian contractor — and from this total 6,000 were for shipment overseas. Both the T-1 and latter versions of the bomb that had fins and a Type 860 fuse, known as the 'T-2', turned haphazard leaflet bombing missions into an accurate and essential operation.

To keep pace with the Monroe bomb that could not only disseminate leaflets better, but hold more, the production of leaflets had to be quickened. The Luton-based printers Home Counties Newspapers, who owned and published the *Luton News* and many other local newspapers, can take much of the credit — if not all — and were engaged on important war-related leaflet printing work from the onset of war in 1939. Their original leaflet commission, from the Political Intelligence Department (PID) of the Foreign Office, was for half-tone and line blocks of print. To complete this order long hours of work were required which included daily collection of the print blocks by car from nearby Woburn Abbey, from where many famous journalists had been conscripted to write the copy. The success of the operation so impressed the PID that, in 1940, it requested a new weekly production — *Courier de L'Air*. The *Courier* which was a 'White' propaganda newspaper in French, was produced by gravure at other printers, but the typesetting contract was given to the *Luton News* and resulted in the work being completed during the evenings. The text was set at four times its finished size then the proofs reduced photographically. Before long, staff were setting papers in five languages and working two evening shifts to comply with the mandate.

In 1944 the staff of the *Luton News* produced what became one of the finest achievements for the provincial press. Early in March a contract was issued to produce the first daily newspaper for German troops, *Nachrichten für die Truppe*. The idea was to give enemy troops the real truth about the military and general situation on both war and home fronts. In April the PID provided a test issue of two pages measuring 13in × 9in in size, for the *Luton News* to print. Arrangements were made to cut the paper at the associate firm of Leagrave Press, which was also based in Luton. On 25 April the first issue was printed, and after being tied up in convenient bales on the publishing bench, was transported the 2½ miles to the Leagrave Press, 'knocked up' by female labour then put through two guillotines, the first of which cut off the fold, the second dividing the two copies. They were then loaded into leaflet bombs and transported by men of the NLS to the airfield to be flown out that night.

Production of *Nachrichten* continued up to 6 June 1944, 'The Big Day', when process staff came in at 03.30hrs. By 10.00hrs they were running the greatest war story ever to roll off local or national presses, official, and with full details. The staff who until then had been locked in the factory, had been unable to say a word to anyone outside their building!

From the initial edition of 200,000 single-sheet copies, production rose to 1,000,000 on D-Day. The print run was then set at 800,000 copies of a four-page newspaper, seven days a week. As the Allied advance approached the River Rhine in early 1945, the daily order was increased to 1,000,000 again and carried on at this figure until the German surrender in May.

To put on record the thanks of the Political Intelligence Department, its Chief, **Harold Keeble**, sent the following letter to John Gibbs of the *Luton News* on 8 April 1945:

'Now that your Presses have turned out the last issue of *Nachrichten*, I should like you to know how much I personally appreciate the great work which you and your staff have put in on this paper.

'I hope it is some satisfaction to you all to have launched the world's first airborne daily newspaper. I hope, too, that the splendid enthusiasm which you have shown in the production of the *Nachrichten* will be echoed in our new enterprise which starts on Tuesday.

'This new paper — which is to be called *SHAEF*, with the subtitle *The Official Organ of the Supreme Allied Command*, also breaks new ground in publishing history. It is the first time a Supreme Commander has been able to sponsor a venture of this kind and Gen Eisenhower believes that its development will have an important part to play during the period of chaos and collapse.

'Again, my warmest thanks to you all'.

One way of assessing the effect leaflets had on the enemy was by interrogation of prisoners of war. *'Leaflet Reactions'*, — a notice issued by SHAEF at regular periods, reported the results of these interrogations and also gave the latest news on PsyWar Operations. The following examples display its style and content.

'Out of a sample group of 200 prisoners captured in and around Aachen in the middle of October, approximately 50% had leaflets on their person at the time of their capture.'
'An interesting commentary on the value attached to our Safe Conduct Leaflet ZG61 by the German soldier comes in a report from the Third Army. They have received information from prisoners that Allied 'Safe Conduct Leaflets' have a high trading value for cigarettes and other items in special demand within the German lines.'

'A report from the 21st Army Group says that almost all prisoners taken along their sector of the front prove to have had some contact with our leaflets. One was particularly impressed by a leaflet describing the conditions in prisoner-of-war camps.'

'The Peoples Court of Innsbruck has passed a sentence of death on Joseph Axinger for "the offence of picking up and distributing dropped leaflets".

'Out of a sample group of 69 prisoners taken at Lorient, 29 stated that Allied leaflets had influenced their decision to give themselves up. 70% of the group reported that they had seen Allied leaflets; of these 50% were familiar with the Safe Conduct Pass. 40% recalled one or more of the following: *Nachrichten* (T series), *You Are Surrounded* (ZG38), *How Your Comrades Fared* (ZG54), *Polish Language Leaflet* (ZG10) and the special *Lorient* leaflet (ZG47).'

The back of the *Counter Attack* leaflet (ZG77) carries a 'five Minute Blitz Course for German G.I.s' consisting of German-English translations for a number of key phrases. 1st Army reports the course seems to be getting results. Many have come over, leaflet in hand, shouting the words 'I surrender'.

'A Prusso-Phobe Bavarian read the PWB leaflet containing the text of the Aachen ultimatum. He decided to desert, took a Viennese comrade along, and persuaded eleven others to join. They marched to the US lines waving the leaflets and white flags.'

'The Commanding Officer of the 2nd Battalion, 1215 Grenadiers, 462 German Infantry, has given his troops a strong warning to those who find Allied leaflets to turn them in UNREAD.'
'A group of fighters were used for the first time in this theatre to carry the psychological warfare campaign to the enemy. Instead of bombs, Thunderbolts dropped leaflet ZG34 (*German Generals Proclaim Peace Government*) near Chartres and between St Quentin and Compiegne. 31 July.'

' "Clumping" by leaflets in bundles will now be avoided by the use of leaflets bombs. Dissemination of *Arc en Ciel* over Belgium for July (XB18, XB19, XB20, XB21) amounted to 1,544,000 copies.'

'You will be interested to hear that when the final count came in for Le Havre it showed 11,302 prisoners out of a garrison of 12,000. Analysis show that over 75% had leaflets on them.'
'Korvetten Kapitän Fritz Otto, now a prisoner, informed us that with leaflets falling all around his troops he found himself leading a "bunch of neurotics" and gave the whole thing up — coming over to us ... Thanks again for the great assistance, and please pass on my thanks to the gang who are actually doing the dropping. They are doing a great job and it is really being appreciated.'

Life in the Squadron

Life for an officer or enlisted man in the NLS was far from dull. If there were no missions to be flown, there was training, and if there was no training, there were always the rules and squadron policies to be adhered to. Col Aber implemented these rules not to confuse, heckle, or depress his staff, but to let them know exactly what he required of each and every one of them so they could all

Right:
The bomb designer, Lt James Monroe, sets the barometric fuse on a T1 bomb. *IWM OWIL29625*

Below:
To prevent vehicles crossing an active runway, staff from the 9th Station Complement Squadron mounted guard.
N. Senter/113 Association

Below centre:
Gloss black paint was used to deflect searchlights from NLS Liberators.
N. Senter/113 Association

Bottom:
Liberators of the 406th taxi out for an evening take-off in 1944.
N. Senter/113 Association

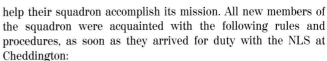

help their squadron accomplish its mission. All new members of the squadron were acquainted with the following rules and procedures, as soon as they arrived for duty with the NLS at Cheddington:

Formations

New crews had to have formation meetings every day at 09.00 and 13.30hrs, that were held on the Instructional Site. Once combat training had been completed and the crew operational, only one formation meeting had to be attended each day. This was held at 13.30hrs in the Briefing Room. All crews, both officers and enlisted men, had to be present and attendance lists were taken to ensure this was complied with.

Passes

The men were expected to 'work like hell' while on duty at the Base, but when off duty their time was their own to do with what they liked, provided of course it was within 'Theatre Regulations'. New crews could expect their first pass to be issued after being on Base for two weeks and after having their security lecture. After that a crew could expect to go off the Base 'on Pass' every two to three weeks. Passes were granted by operations in co-ordination with the Orderly Room. They began at 12.00hrs, and terminated 48hr later. The Pass Roster was kept in Operations so the First Pilot could ascertain when his crew would be off the Base. The 13.30hrs Formation Meeting held the day the Pass started could be missed, but it had to be attended on the day of return to the Base. All officers had to sign-out in the register that was kept in Operations, when leaving the Base and likewise on return to the Base. It had to be signed personally, and in addition, one of the 'Duty' Operations Officers had to be informed. There were only two cases when this was not necessary: for absence of less than two hours from the Base, or when going on the 'Liberty Run'. These runs consisted of several buses that left the Base gym every night at 19.00hrs for the American Red Cross Club in Luton, and returned to the Base at 23.00hrs. For enlisted men, green Class 'B' passes were available for off-duty hours and were good within a 25-mile radius of the Base. They expired at 01.00hrs and had to be returned after being used.

Bulletin Boards

Any official squadron or command notice was displayed on two notice boards. One located in Site 3 and the other in the Operations Building. Each officer had to read and initial them daily, for Aber claimed 'an officer who reads the notice board knows what's going on in his squadron'.

Uniforms

The only item of flying equipment that could be worn off the flying line was the now-famous 'A-2' leather jacket. It could be worn around the Base, but never in the Mess or Officers' Club. For the evening meal either the blouse or battle jacket was acceptable but, if flying a mission that night or having flown that afternoon and the crew member did not have time to go to his quarters and change, he could wear his Class 'B' uniform. For all formal occasions including the squadron dances that were held each month, the blouse had to be worn. When off the Base either the blouse or battle jacket was acceptable, as well as the well known 'crusher' hat. Whilst cycling it was not necessary to wear either the jacket or blouse, but one had to carry one or the other and wear one's cap. Officers were allowed to wear GI shoes, but not the rough-finished type. They had, however, to be kept very well polished. White socks were forbidden, only tan being worn. There were inspections to ensure these conditions were being met and 'dog tags' being worn and, if pullovers were used, that they could not be seen. The only true personal choice was the wearing of 'pinks' — beige trousers with green shirt, or vice versa.

Below:
A number of the airmen made good friends whilst in England and were often taken in and treated as one of the family.
J. Reeve/113 Association

Below right:
Sixty-plus even got married, including the 406th Gunnery Officer Lt Gugenhein. *B. Gunderson/113 Association*

Promotion

Just because an individual was an aircrew member, it was not necessarily a guarantee of promotion. The following standards were considered, however, when selecting officers for promotion to 1st Lieutenants, or Flight Officers to 2nd Lieutenants:

Pilot

He had to complete a sufficient number of operational hours to demonstrate unquestionable proficiency as pilot on the type of aircraft he flew. He had also to demonstrate, both in the air and on the ground, the qualities of a well disciplined officer, and in particular the way he handled his crew and how he discharged his ground duties. When a pilot satisfactorily demonstrated that he possessed the right qualities he was then recommended for 1st Lieutenant. Subsequently, out of the entire group of pilots, the three most outstanding in proficiency, initiative, aggressiveness and 'officer-like' qualities were chosen as Flight Commanders. This position carried the rank of captain, provided the officer continued to measure up to the high standards. He also had to remain with the squadron after his tour of combat had been completed for a period of about one to two months, in order to help with the flight training of replacement crews.

Co-Pilot

He had to complete a minimum of 100 operational hours before assessment as first pilot in the type of aircraft he was assigned to. To enable him to do this his pilot was allowed to give him transition flight training until he considered him to be proficient. The co-pilot would then be given a check ride by the Flight Commander who would look for good aircraft control during take-off, approaches and on landings. He would also expect a good circuit to be flown and see a good mastery of all emergency procedures. If found acceptable, the co-pilot would then be given another check ride, this time by Col Aber, or either his Air Executive or Operations Officer. He would also have to be an efficient officer, both in the air and on the ground.

Navigators

Likewise, he had to be efficient, fly a minimum 100hr on operations and demonstrate a high degree of skill in all types of

Left:
A NLS B-24 that left runway 26 too early! *N. Senter/113 Association*

navigation, in particular DR (dead-reckoning) and the use of the G-Box.

Bombardiers

In the NLS he occupied a peculiar position due to the fact that there was no opportunity for him to demonstrate his proficiency as a Precision Bombardier. Other standards were therefore devised to determine his eligibility for promotion. The Navigation Department conducted a school in DR and G-Box for all bombardiers, which enabled supervisory personnel to make observations on the individual's ability to navigate, his eagerness, initiative, attitude and attention to duty. In addition, the conduct of each bombardier, both on the ground and in the air, was carefully noted. All these observations taken together formed the basis on which bombardiers were recommended for promotion.

Enlisted Men

They had to prove themselves deserving of promotion by being good crew members, and good NCO material. All would be sergeants before flying operationally and subsequently the radio operator and engineer would become a staff sergeant, and the latter a tech sergeant. All gunners became staff sergeants.

Inspections

Enlisted men's barracks were inspected each day by the Flight Commander at 14.15hrs. On Saturdays, at 13.00hrs, the Squadron Commander also inspected them. In addition, he inspected the officers' quarters at the same time.

Tour of Combat and Awards

In accordance with the policy set by HQ 8th AF, the tour of combat for heavy bombardment crews in the latter stages of the war was

Above:
Lt Heusser and his crew along with *Paper Doll*. Standing left to right: Lt Heusser, pilot; Bill Taylor, waist gunner; Rusty Emerick, radio op; Ted Lewis, co-pilot; Herb Bobinger, ball turret. Kneeling: Dean McConn, navigator; Walt Rogells, tail gunner; Ray Sefrna, bombardier; Ed Stearns, flight engineer; Joe Roden, waist gunner.
B. Gunderson/113 Association

Right:
Against the backdrop of a wintry landscape in March 1945, the crew of B-24 *Dark Eyes* pose for the camera. Standing: Eugene Chambers, pilot; Walt Longanecker, co-pilot; Don Van Heest, navigator; James Kennedy, bombardier. Kneeling: Gunners Chas Higgs, Howard Rackett, Richard Dunham, Don Slumpff, James Hoestman, James Pocsatko.
W. Longanecker/113 Association

set as 'unlimited', The tour of combat for the NLS, however, was set at 250hr of combat time. Flying awards were made as follows:

Air Medal	40hr of combat
1st Oak Leaf Cluster	80hr of combat
2nd Oak Leaf Cluster	120hr of combat
3rd Oak Leaf Cluster	160hr of combat
4th Oak Leaf Cluster	200hr of combat
5th Oak Leaf Cluster	240hr of combat

Distinguished Flying Cross

This was not an automatic award as some members of the squadron thought, but given only for acts of extraordinary achievement whilst on air operations.

PX Ration Cards

Post Exchange ration cards were available for periods of eight weeks at a time. They were issued by name and number to each individual on the squadron. To have more than one PX card was a court martial offence!

Fuel

Wood, coal and coke for the 'pot-bellied' stove that was in each man's quarters was available on each site — in theory. But, it was treated as gold for it was hard to obtain. In fact many night 'ground operations' were carried out by members of the squadron when they set out under cover of darkness to raid the coal/coke store. Don Childress' crew even used Very Pistol flares in their fire one cold evening! Col Aber was not amused, however, when he saw the base illuminated as the flares came out of the crew's chimney!

Bicycles

Government-issue bicycles were a boon. They were not available to combat crews, so were often bought from civilians. When finished with, they were traded in for other goods or sold to the highest bidder. All bicycles had to be fitted with a white front light and red rear light, and could not be ridden on grass or the walkways. Many however ended their days 'MIA', after failing to complete the return leg of the mission home from the pub and along the nearby canal towpath.

Orderlies

These were available to officers for 10/- or £1.00 per week, depending on the quarters occupied. The fee had to be paid promptly to Lt Hlava the Supply Officer, each month.

Gas Masks

These had to be worn, adjusted to the face, from 10.00 to 18.30hrs on the last Wednesday of each month.

Equipment

Each aircraft was fitted with the following communications equipment:

- 10 Headsets
- 10 Throat Microphones

Above:
The tail of '726' *Shady Lady* deflects the late evening sun at Cheddington from *Tondalayo*. *N. Senter/113 Association*

Right:
The prize — a bottle of whisky. This bottle was sold to an airman by a local publican. On the way home, and the worse for drink, the airman dropped the bottle. It was found by the publican the next morning and resold that night. *H. Trebing/113 Association*

- One B-458 Transmitter for contacting the control tower on 5770Kcs.
- Four crystals for the VHF SCR-522 set
- Flash-lights
- 10 Oxygen Mask Microphones
- One Liaison set for contacting MF/DF Stations and Operational Control. Also to monitor 4795Kcs in the event of a recall message being sent, weather changes or airfield diversions. One Command set for contacting all control towers in the UK.
- One VHF set for navigational aid, air-sea rescue and communication with Cheddington
- One Inter-phone for contact with all crew members. As well as inter-crew communication, its use was essential when oxygen was being used. Each crew position was contacted regularly by the co-pilot to ensure that there were no problems being caused by frozen masks. The crew member concerned would not be aware of this problem until he passed out. This was the case with Sgt Ed Szymczak, who suffered oxygen loss whilst on a mission on 11 March 1945; as a result he died
- One Gee set as a navigation aid
- One Boozer set. This was a device consisting of three coloured lights that were monitored whilst on missions over both enemy and Allied continental territory, where night-fighters could lurk; and also where the Wurtzberg chain of flak and ground control stations were located, a dim red light indicated the enemy was tracking them. A bright red=flak; a yellow light=enemy fighters in the area
- One IFF set to show if an aircraft was 'Friend or Foe'. As this device could be monitored itself by the enemy, its use was restricted to emergency situations only
- One Radio Compass for homing in on low-frequency beacons, but this was not used on missions. Two sets used, however, were Loran and the SCS-51. Loran was a long-range Gee set, capable of some 1,000 miles range at night, but slightly inferior to the usual Gee set. The SCS-51 was a blind-landing system that aided night landings in unfavourable weather conditions. Its disadvantage was that, unlike Cheddington, very few airfields were equipped with the ground station for its use
- Ten heated flying suits. Originally all heated suits were pooled and a crew member could be issued with as many as seven suits for as many missions. As the months went by the supply department obtained enough to make a personal issue of one set to each man. The only item pooled then was the A-3 chest-pack parachute. This pooling was not due to shortage, but to enable 10-day inspections and 30-day repacks to be accomplished.

For each mission, a Communications Section Officer or NCO would brief all crews and ensure each radio operator was issued with:

- The HF/DF station to contact and the call-sign
- All Control Tower coded call-signs — Cheddington being 'Hillside'
- Resin Light colours for that time period
- The arbitrary QFF for decoding weather reports
- The Operational W/T call-sign for the mission, and the collective call-sign of those aircraft involved
- The R/T call-sign for all aircraft
- The beacons being used
- The Gee coding and other data required to use the Gee system
- All Occults and Pundits
- All recognition signals for the period of the flight
- Flak Helmets: each aircraft in the 8th AF was authorised three flak helmets, but NLS aircraft were issued with six!
- Pistols: all crews should have been issued pistols for their own use before arriving at Cheddington. If anyone had not, they were issued one on arrival.

As well as the rules for the use of equipment, there were also rules for the Equipment Section:

- Officers and EM were not allowed beyond the service counter in the Equipment Room, without permission from any authorised personnel of the department
- Each individual was given a number which was his bin and hanger number. Equipment was called for by that number
- Heated suits or parachute packs could not be left in the bins they had to be put in their respective places in the drying room
- Heated gloves and shoe-inserts had to be attached to the heated suit when left to dry after each mission
- Oxygen masks had to be washed on completion of a mission and also left to dry on hooks over each respective bin
- Faulty or lost equipment has to be replaced at a time other than that of take-off time

Supply Section

Like the Equipment Section, the Supply Section also functioned with a set of rules. Laundry for enlisted men had to be turned in to the Supply Room every Tuesday and was returned 10 days later. Each man was allowed nine pieces a week with a pair of socks being counted as one item, and three handkerchiefs the same! Mattress covers and fatigues could be turned in on the same day and were not deducted from the allowance. Only one pair of fatigues, however, could be turned in each week, no matter how much oil or grime they had accumulated from the constant work on the Fortress or Liberators. Fatigues and dry cleaning had to be marked with the letters 'TT', together with the last four numbers from the individual's service number. TT was also the identification mark for shoe repair tickets, as the 406th Squadron designation was never allowed to be marked on any item of clothing or equipment, in case the user came into contact with the enemy. Dry cleaning had to be turned in each Sunday and was also returned after 10 days. Regulations forbade the use of 100 octane gas (aircraft fuel) as a cleaning agent for uniforms, and violators were punished severely if caught.

Training

It was agreed by most on the airfield that the proverbial 'band of providence' a mere strong effort of will, or the lucky rabbit's foot

in the back pocket, were not enough to assure the successful completion of a tour of combat. Training, even though it brought restless sighs of boredom, was the only way to be prepared for nightfighters, flak and searchlights. It also kept at bay the authors of that War Department telegram 'We regret to inform you that your son . . . '. Training therefore in the NLS had to be completed in the following three subjects before combat flights could be undertaken:

- At least 7½hr instruction in night vision, with gunners and radio operators in their respective positions
- A minimum of 2hr of lectures on security and prisoner-of war procedure
- 1hr of hygiene instruction

Night Vision

As most, if not all the NLS combat flying was completed at night, the squadron put a heavy emphasis on night vision training. A school was opened to ensure that the crews would be just as prepared as the enemy for night flying vision; to see them, if not before, at least in time to get in the first shot. The school's purpose was to make the combat students 'blind as bats'. Nature has seen to it that the eyes best suited to night work are those in nocturnal creatures, for example the bat and the owl. These creatures are born with 'night eyes' which have evolved differently to the 'day eyes' of most other creatures. All humans have 'bat elements' in the outer portions of their eyes that are little used in daytime, and by training, the school taught how to use these parts to see better at night.

It was discovered that the ability to see on a flight in daylight was accomplished because human eyes are naturally adapted for day vision which is binocular and central, or 'foveal'. To see an object in daylight we use the optical centres of the eyes, giving colour and detail. Below moonlight, this central portion is blind and off-centre, and so peripheral vision must be employed, resulting in perception of motion, contrast and size, but not detail or colour.

Therefore seeing at night is a much different and more difficult matter than in daylight, and necessitates special training to develop and use the peripheral or parafoveal 'night portions' of the retina which are normally neglected by civilised man.

After crews had been trained in daylight for their specific jobs, they were quickly adapted for night work by the school. This was with the exception of a small handful who turned out to be 'night-blind', and who were weeded out by the standard SAM, Heehct-Sabler, RAF Hexagon or Heyford night tests. Training was carried out in a completely blacked-out building, which has shutter-controlled lighting to simulate any degree or angle of night illumination, such as high, low, right or left moonlight, half moonlight or starlight. When used with relief maps this controlled, but variable, illumination made the teaching of night aerial observation of terrain possible. The same lighting system was used in an apparatus for several off-centre eye exercises. Also in the same building were a night-simulating epidiascope (an instrument use to teach estimation of range and recognition of aircraft and ground targets) and a cine projector.

Lectures were given to between six and 12 crew members at a time and consisted of basic anatomy, physiology, and physics of night sight. They were told what dark adaptation was and how to preserve it while in searchlight cones. They were taught the tactical value of low light contrast and scanning, what the basic principles of ground and aerial night observation were, and what part constitutional factors, such as oxygen, played in eyesight. How to seek and how to avoid a foe over water, land, above or below cloud, in clear or hazy conditions of moonlight, and at what range enemy aircraft could be spotted. Constant use was also made of a RAF night gunnery (Lamplough) trainer. It presented an erratically moving (in a horizontal plane) night aerial target which, due to the low illumination, students had to follow using their parafoveal vision. The American Done trainer was preferred, but was unobtainable.

The final step in the training was when the students were blindfolded and had to familiarise themselves with every surrounding of their particular stations in the aircraft. Then, after being given the 10 Commandments of Night Sight, they had to memorise and follow them until they were prepared, and forewarned, for what to expect in combat.

Above:
Don Childress, his ground and aircrew with *Channel Fever Baby*. Don was elected to confront Maj Aber about the feelings of the squadron on promotion — or the lack of it. Many felt Don's departure from the ETO on completion of his tour was held up by this confrontation with Aber.
D. Childress/113 Association

Gunnery Training

Each day, whilst the crews were on combat training at Cheddington, they were expected to climb out of their comfortable beds and attend lectures on aircraft recognition, radio, tactics, ammunition loadings and maintenance. They also kept their hand in on the Skeet range which involved a moving target fired upon by .5in guns mounted in a turret. Guns were cleaned each day, and every 24hr they were inspected; ammunition was inspected once a week. There was also great detail given to where to look for the enemy by each gunner as follows:

● **Tail Turret:** watch from eight to four o'clock, concentrating on high areas
● **Left Waist Turret:** cover all areas as high and as low as possible, between eight and three-thirty
● **Right Waist Turret:** also as high and as low as possible, plus between four and two-thirty
● **Chin Turret:** area between ten-thirty and two-thirty on the aircraft's bow, concentrating and varying the search between high and low areas
● **Top Turret:** 360°cover with particular attention being height, and above the tail between three o'clock and nine o'clock
● **Ball Turret:** keep turret depressed below horizontal position

so that while searching low, the ball turret gunner can see no part of the underside of his aircraft. The search was made from four o'clock to eight o'clock, varying the angle of depression occasionally to 80°. A final reminder was given to all gunners not to search the other crew members' positions, as a few minutes' loss of cover could cause the enemy to attack without being seen — and could result in death!

Nightfighter Attacks

In case of attack by nightfighters whilst on leaflet raids, gunners were trained to be ready to open fire instantly and at the same time call over the intercom what evasive action the pilot should take. For dead astern attacks between five-thirty and six-thirty it would be either a right or left-hand corkscrew, according to the angle of attack. For attacks between six-thirty and nine o'clock the gunner would fire then call 'dive left!', remembering always to turn into the attack in order to give the attacking pilot a maximum deflection shot.

Lights Over Enemy Territory

Should a light be seen by a gunner who could not be certain if it was a star, a motionless light on the ground or a moving light in the sky, he was taught to position the light in his ring sight and then check for any apparent motion. He was told not to alarm his pilot by calling out numerous reports that could be unconfirmed, unless he was sure. If a nightfighter was spotted, the gunner, if possible, would check to see if it was showing any lights. The reason for this was that most twin-engined German fighters used either red, green or white lights to signal another fighter to join in the attack. If the fighter was at — say — nine o'clock and showing a red, the gunner would check at three o'clock for the other fighter.

Advice was also given on two other forms of enemy lighting: flares that gave a huge orange light and that seemed to hang motionless, were dropped above Allied aircraft from higher flying German machines and would illuminate them once underneath, thus showing the enemy a good silhouette of the Allied aircraft. The second form of lighting was the searchlight. If 'coned' by an enemy searchlight the crews were told not to dive straight down whilst attempting evasive action, but to fly at full speed straight ahead in a gradual dive. If caught in one or two lights, either sideslip, dive or stall — according to what action seemed correct to the captain at that time. Crews were also reminded that a blue light was the master beam for the cone.

Enemy nightfighters did not have it all their own way against the NLS, as there were a number of claims by the Fortress and Liberator crews. There were, however, two other unfortunate 'own goal' claims made, the first being an Allied P-61 Black Widow that was shot down, and on the last day of December 1944; a Beaufighter with an American crew was also shot down by an NLS crew. A copy of the American services newspaper *Stars and Stripes* reported the shooting-down in full, which did little to keep the incident quiet!

Operation 'Infatuate'

In September 1944, with the aid of the Belgian Resistance Forces, the Armoured Division of Gen Dempsey's 2nd Army secured the city of Antwerp. The use of its port as a supply base, however, was denied to the Allied troops since the Germans had dug in well and controlled the 40-mile river approaches that led into Antwerp. The port's facilities could handle up to 40,000 tons of supplies each day. For the Allies to send cargo vessels down this route would have been suicide.

Cherbourg was the only ship-fed supply base available to the Allied forces, but it lay several hundred miles to the rear of the advancing troops, and could only send supplies to them by truck. It was therefore of the utmost importance that a major forward supply base should come into use. Field Marshal Montgomery had accepted this and stated that the Allies' need for Antwerp 'makes the capture of the Walcherens a matter of the utmost urgency'. Hitler, once he had lost Antwerp, had given his 15th Army orders to hold Walcheren Island and use it as a fortress. This order resulted in the island and its dykes, along with the Breskens Pocket — both of which straddled the river mouth — becoming an ideal holding point. More than 86,000 men, artillery pieces, and 6,000 vehicles were moved in, building up a strong resistance against any attack by Allied troops. The engagement of these enemy forces by units who had been involved in the fight for Antwerp had been delayed for two reasons. First, Montgomery had decided to gather all his available forces and attempt a Rhine crossing before winter came. Second, an order to tie up large numbers of men, or expend large amounts of ammunition in breaching the strongly defended islands, could wait, for there were other plans to be used first — Operation 'Infatuate' held the key. A daylight bombing raid by the RAF, followed by a ground attack by British Commando forces. The time had now come for its implementation.

Walcheren was saucer-shaped and rimmed by high sand dunes, with a flat lowland interior, most of which was below sea level. There were gaps in these dunes that were filled by dykes, the largest located near Westkapelle at the western end of the island. The RAF was given the task of bombing the dykes, as it was these that held back the heavy tide of the North Sea. It was expected that, as a result of breaching them, most of the interior — including the German garrison city of Middelburg — would be flooded under 3 to 6ft of sea water. The raid, due to be launched on the afternoon of 3 October by 252 Lancasters and seven Mosquitoes of RAF Bomber Command, would include a second attack to strafe the enemy coastal batteries. After a period of waiting by the Allied forces, it was hoped that by this stage the Germans would be slogging around in the cold waters of the North Sea, and would either surrender or withdraw. If not, a commando raid would follow. For the Allied commanders

Above:
Lt Dale Wilkes (back, right) and crew with Liberator *This is it Men*, photographed on 25 February 1945. *D. Wilkes/113 Association*

Left:
The route that Col Aber and Maj Weil took on Operation 'Infatuate'. *113 Association*

planning 'Infatuate', there was just one last problem — 8,000 Dutch civilians! Gen Eisenhower was very concerned for them, and so ordered that all civilians who were in the projected danger zone should receive warning, in similar fashion to the Pre-D-Day leaflet raid in June by aircraft of the NLS.

By special order of Gen Eisenhower, the NLS was tasked to fly two daylight sorties. This was to ensure the accuracy of a widespread leaflet drop that would cover the main populated areas of the island. Leaflet ZH-3 was produced, warning that the Scheldt Estuary would be subjected to a long and heavy bombardment. All civilians were also told to move away from roads or military objectives and to keep off the lowlands.

Maj Aber felt that he could not miss this raid, so after selecting two crews — Maj Harry Gaddy and Capt August Weil — he announced he would fly as pilot in the No 1 aircraft with Maj Gaddy. After briefing at 14.00hrs, both crews took-off — Maj Aber in '516' at 15.48hrs, and Capt Weil in '167' at 15.55hrs. The two aircraft climbed out from Cheddington and, after meeting their escort of eight P-51 Mustang fighters, set course on Mission No 275. For the NLS it was its second anniversary on leaflet operations, and Maj Aber, his 30th mission of his second tour of combat duty.

Aber's aircraft was first to release its T-1 leaflet bombs when, at 17.05hrs, he dropped the first on Flushing, followed by Middelburg, Kapelle, Goes and Kortene. Capt Weil covered Domburg, Biggekerke, Arnemuiden and Westkraalert. Maj Aber caught some flak that was accurate, and heavy, over Flushing and Middelburg, but when his flightpath crossed that of Weil's the enemy guns followed Weil. German fighters also joined in the attack on both Fortress aircraft, but soon backed off when they saw the Mustang escort.

On the return journey both pilots saw a fleet of ships in a bay far below, and considered that it must be the Germans preparing to evacuate. Both crews landed safe at Cheddington, Aber at 18.41hrs and Weil at 18.37hrs.

The RAF followed next with 1,262 tons of high explosives, and as a special gift for the coastal batteries, 6.7 tons of incendiaries! The seas poured in and the Dutch took to what high ground they could find, most of it in attics or on house roofs. As for the Germans, as many of their defence positions were on the high dunes, they were unharmed. To observe the effect of the raid, Spitfire PR XIXs from No 541 Squadron, RAF Benson, were dispatched on reconnaissance missions to photograph the area. Flg Off Arnold, who took off at 14.30hrs in PL850, reported back at 16.55hrs that: 'flooding had extended approx half-a-mile inland as far as Tol and Lichitore, and water was rushing through the break in the dyke at Westkappel at a considerable rate'. The PR missions flown from Benson continued each day, and on the 4th, Flt Lt Garvey in Spitfire PR XIX RM643, flying at 1,000ft, reported the flooding had extended inland for 1¼ miles. Two days later whilst flying RM637, he reported flooding had extended inland for 3 miles but was now at sea level. He also claimed what must have been a 'first' for an unarmed reconnaissance aircraft — one enemy aircraft destroyed! This claim came about when on the mission he saw two German FW190s. One gave chase and, to avoid its guns, Garvey dived his Spitfire towards a wood. When at zero level, he pulled the stick back and made a tight roll away from death! The Luftwaffe pilot, close on his tail, failed to pull up and his aircraft exploded as it hit the trees 8 miles to the east of Bruck.

A commando attack by the 'Green Berets', of the 4th Special Services Brigade, followed on 1 November, and after several days of hard, wet fighting they 'Flushed out Flushing'. By the 4th, the Island was liberated and as soon as all the mines in the harbour had been removed, the estuary was opened to Allied shipping.

The raid was a success for the Allied troops, but for the Dutch it was a disaster. Crops were ruined and due to the lack of fodder, cattle had to be killed. Most houses were uninhabitable and if not, sanitary conditions were deplorable. Great attention was given by the Press to the raid, and to try and offset the unfortunate side effects, the part played by the 'Special Leaflet Squadron' was revealed in USAAF Press releases. These were printed in the National newspapers of both England and the USA. Set against the damage caused by the water, they showed that the leaflet warnings more than made up for it, as there were very few — if any Dutch injured in the Allied attack. As for missions over Holland, Maj Aber would be back, but it would cost him his life.

Aber's Last Mission

The night missions continued and so did the losses, but they culminated on the night of 4 March 1945 in a blow that was felt by every member of the squadron. For Mission No 864, 12 aircraft were tasked to drop leaflets on targets in Germany and Holland. One of those aircraft dispatched to Holland was *Tondalayo*, with Col Aber as captain. He was tasked to drop leaflet 'XH-95', the 4 March edition of *The Flying Dutchman* newspaper over Amsterdam, Rotterdam and Utrecht. His bombardier, **Connie Morton**, recalls that flight:

'My normal pilot was Ed Leahy, but I was out of action for a time because an armour plate fell on my finger whilst working on a jammed machine gun. Ed and the rest of our crew completed their tour of combat, and returned to the States. I then flew as an

Right:
XH95: De Vliegende Hollander
The 110th Issue of *The Flying Dutchman*. It was this four-page issue of the Dutch newspaper that Maj Aber had dropped over Holland on the night he was killed by Allied flak.

Below:
Tests were conducted at Cheddington on a container to air-drop food. The device worked and it was used over Holland.
N. Senter/113 Association

unassigned crew member with other crews, to make up my missions, so as to complete my tour.

'My 42nd sortie was on the night of March 4th, when we went to the Netherlands. The flight went well with only some distant flak. As we headed home, I spotted flak a number of miles away in the general area of the English coast, at the point where we were to make landfall. I was sure it was anti-aircraft flak, and we discussed that it might be English shore or naval batteries practising. The Colonel directed me and the other crew members to keep a close watch. We were then at 20,000ft and about to cross into England at Clacton-on-Sea. At 10,000ft, just as we crossed, I spotted a German bomber coming head on towards us. I yelled "Bandit at 12 o'clock", but we didn't get a shot because the rate of closure was so fast. We almost collided and just as the German plane passed under us, we were hit by a burst from the English batteries. The hit blew in part of my bombardier's plexi-glass compartment and I was hit in the right leg, and hip, in five places. I also had small splinters in my forehead and cheeks and one small steel splinter embedded in my right eye-ball. The first blast put our right inboard engine on fire and also part of the wing area. The plane was hit again, this time in the waist area.

'The B-17 has a compartment for the bombardier in the nose, and the navigator behind him. On this flight, we had three in that compartment: Paul Stonerock our navigator, who had flown many missions; a young navigator, Billing, who was flying his first combat operation, and me.

'When I was hit, I fell slightly backwards into the navigator's area. Paul Stonerock told Billing to stay on the intercom while he assisted me. Billing said "The colonel wants a heading to Woodbridge". Woodbridge was a base equipped especially for emergencies. It had advanced communications, the runway was wider and had special lighting. Stonerock made calculations and gave the heading and the approximate time that it would take us to reach there. Just as he did this, Billing excitedly said "Colonel said bale out". With that, Billing unhooked his intercom, and started towards the escape hatch. Stonerock said to me "Are you going to be alright?" When I replied "Yes", he said "I'm gone".

'I had decided that since I was hurt and partially blinded, I would ride the plane down if we had a chance of making Woodbridge. However, as I got to the escape hatch I decided to bale out because we were burning so badly. I said a short prayer and dropped out into the night. I had on a chest-type parachute, and at first yanked the handle instead of the rip-cord. Then I realised what was happening and pulled the rip-cord. Because of my error, I had a fairly long free-fall drop before my parachute opened.

'I could not see where I was landing, and landed abruptly and with considerable force. My parachute came down over my head and body. I had landed in shallow water and in unbelievably mucky mud. I was afraid at first I had landed in some quicksand — I couldn't stand up and could hardly see, so I sat there for a minute and tried to get my bearings. Off to the right I could see the fire from the aircraft, which had crashed and exploded. At this time I had no idea how many of our crew had got out in time. I could tell from the flames that there was water between me and the plane, and I was able to determine that the water was flowing from my back, so I figured it was headed towards a bigger body of water. Off to my left I could see what appeared to be hills, so I decided to try to crawl in that direction. As I crawled my arms would go into the mud up to — or almost to — my shoulders, and I became afraid of the quicksand. I would crawl awhile then rest. The blackout was on, of course, so my thoughts were to get to land and rest.

'It never occurred to me that the anti-aircraft crews and others had seen the aircraft go down in flames. I then saw what I thought was a small light on shore, moving towards me. I yelled, but there was no answer. I began to think it was a mirage, then it seemed to come closer so I yelled again. A man's voice said, "who are you?". I replied, "I'm a Yank". The voice replied, "talk awhile". He said if he came out he would get stuck, so directed me towards him and the bank. After a time, he did come out in boots, and got me to the bank. When on the bank he, along with two other men and a woman, removed the mud from my face, and escorted me to an area where I was placed on a stretcher and put in a truck. I was then taken into Harwich. Later, the rest of the crew, who had also baled out and who had also been assisted by local villagers, came to see me. They told me Col Aber and Maurice Harper, our co-pilot, had gone in with the aircraft at 21.20hrs, and that divers had been sent down to the wreckage to recover both bodies, but had very little luck. Only a hand that belonged to Aber was found, and that was only identified by his class ring.'

A full military funeral was held at Cambridge American Cemetery within a few days, when the coffin containing the hand, escorted by members of the squadron along with many other high-ranking officers, was buried. Col Aber had been with the squadron since it entered into leaflet operations; Lt Harper had flown Spitfires in the RCAF prior to joining the US 8th AF.

Connie Morton never saw his crew again for, by the time he was ready to leave hospital, they had all returned to America. Who he did see again was Maj Harold Gaddy, Aber's replacement as the new Squadron Commander.

It had been the summer of 1944 when **Harold Gaddy** first joined the 406th, having flown across the Atlantic to Valley in North Wales, thence by train to Cheddington. The news that confronted him on arrival, though, came as a shock. He recalls:

'I was greeted by Col Aber who informed me that his squadron flew B-17s. I told him that I had been B-24 trained, had even flown one over to England, but had never been in a B-17! He told me this presented no problem and to prove it, took me out flying the next day for about 45min in a B-17. The following night I flew as a co-pilot on an operational mission in another, and from then on was the aircraft commander for all my future missions. For the Colonel this was acceptable, as I had four years' training under my belt and some 2,000hr flying time and, at 24, was a Major. I soon came to prefer the Fort to the Lib, as it was infinitely more pleasing to the eye. It was a joy to fly and could take tremendous punishment. There was also a "feel" to flying it which was simply lacking in the B-24. I can recall that we also said the B-24 was the crate the B-17 came in — but this comment provoked some severe responses!

'In March 1945, I had finished my "Tour of Combat" and was waiting around the base for the squadron to return from a mission. Aber, who by then was a Lt-Col, had gone on the mission, as he would occasionally do, when word came through that his aircraft had been shot down and had crashed on the tide-banks near the mouth of the River Stour. Throughout the rest of the night reports filtered in from surviving crew members who had baled out, but none from Aber or Lt Harper, his co-pilot. The next morning I took a B-17 and flew to a field as near as possible to the site of the crash then went to a small detachment of the Royal Navy. They took me in a launch as close as they could — probably 100yd from the site — but, due to the low tide and shallow water, I could go no further. My co-pilot, Lt Leftwich, who was with me, and I were given some rubberised coveralls. We put them on then went over the side of the launch into the water, and slogged our way to the scene. The depth varied from waist deep at first, gradually shallowing to about 8 to 10in. Upon arrival we made the sad determination that Col Aber had been killed in the crash.

'On return to Cheddington I went immediately to Col Goodrich, the Base Commander, and reported our findings. Ironically, the previous day I had received orders transferring me to Wing Headquarters, and was supposed to report there the following day. Col Goodrich asked me if I would stay and assume command of the 406th, provided he could attain the revocation of my orders. "Of course", I said, "Yes" — what Major says no to a Colonel? Besides, I was the ranking officer in the squadron, and it was clearly my duty. Thus, it was the tragic loss of Col Aber that thrust me into command of the 406th Night Leaflet Squadron. Col Aber had been a superb organiser and moreover loved his job, hence I inherited a smoothly running squadron.'

The squadron continued flying regular missions for the next few weeks until orders were received by Gaddy to transfer the squadron to Harrington in Northamptonshire. As a squadron

```
;
4SSSS .STAN  BY   STAND   BY  USLIST PA -PC   AL:  ALC   103
   CDD       EVERYBODY  STAND   BY

USLIST PA - PC V BMP NR 7 -OP OP-

FROM: BMP 070929O MAY 45
TO : 1. USLIST PA
     2. USLIST PC
BT
MULTIPLE ADDRESS
---------------SECRET - SEND IN CLEAR.

iAD M-335-G

FOLLOWING MESG RECEIVED FROM 8TH AF. " QIOTE
PARA CNE PD A REPRESENTATIVE OF THE GERMAN HIGH COMMAND SIGNED
THE UNCONDITIONAL PAREN FROM SHAEF FORWARD SIGNED EISENHOWER CITE
SHGCT UNPAREN SURRENDER OF ALL GERMAN LAND CMA SEA CMA AND
AIR FORCES IN EUROPE TO THE ALLIED EXPEDITIONARY FORCE
AND SIMULTANEOUSLY TO THE SOVIET HIGH COMMAND AT ZERO ONE FOUR
ONE HOURS CENTRAL EUROPEAN TIME CMA SEVEN MAY UNDER WHICH ALL
FORCES WILL CEASE ACTIVE OPERATIONS AT ZERO ZERO ZERO ONE BAKER
MINE MAY PD PARA TWO PD EFFECTIVE IMMEDIATELY ALL OFFENSIVE
OPERATIONS BY ALLIED EXPEDITIONARY FORCE WILL CEASE AND TROOPS
WILL REMAIN IN PRESENT POSITIONS PD MOVES INVOLVED IN OCCUPATIONAL
DUTIES WILL CONTINUE PD DUE TO DIFFICULTIES OF COMMUNICATION THERE
MAY BE SOME DELAY IN SIMILAR ORDERS REACHING ENEMY TROOPS
SO FULL DEFENSIVE PRECAUTIONS WILL BE TAKEN PD PARA THREE
PD ALL INFORMED DOWN TO AND INCLUDING DIVISIONS CMA
TACTICAL AIR COMMANDS AND GROUPS CMA BASE SECTIONS CMA AND
EQUIVALENT PD
NO REPEAT NO RELEASE WILL BE MADE TO THE PRESS
PENDING AN ANNOUNCEMENT BY THE HEADS OF THE THREE GOVERNMENTS PD
UNQUOTE

FOR INFO AND COMPLIANCE

              TURNER COMAIRDIV ONE

DT 070929B MAR 45
AS
LS   AR K
AS FOR R
CDD R ............070953B   SSW   AR
T  ........ .... ......
```

move is not as easy as one would think, Gaddy sent Capt Weil on ahead several days in advance to aid in the preparations for the squadron's arrival, and reported that Weil did an excellent job.

Harrington

By 'peep and jeep, luck and truck' was how the move to Harrington was recorded when the men and their equipment moved by road and air on 13 March 1945. For one crew, that of **Lt Ed Canner** who flew *The Leading Lady*, it was without luck and became a tragic flight. Ed remembers:

'We loaded our personal belongings into the aircraft and I attempted to start the engines. I got three going, but the fourth one would just not start. I had been assigned two other flying officers to transport to Harrington, but as I had tried three or four times to start the engine with no luck, they left my plane and went with another crew. After about 30min, I finally got the last engine running and we were on our way. Shortly after take-off, at about 1,000ft, one of the engines failed. I cannot recall if it was the one that had been giving trouble on the ground or not. It appeared at that time that something else happened, because normally with three engines running, a B-24 could actually climb. But, even though both my co-pilot and I were on the right rudder, with the loss of that one engine we could just not maintain altitude and it was quite obvious we were going to crash. My navigator went to his station, which was below the flightdeck, and directed us towards Harrington. When I sighted the field, I called down and ordered him to come back on deck; he said he was going to shut off the equipment. I ordered him again to come back up immediately, but once more he said he was going to shut off his equipment!

Above:
Teleprint Message.
On 7 May 1945, Cheddington's teleprint room received a teleprint message. Its content was the news all were waiting for — the war in Europe was over.

Right:
Echoes of the motion picture *The Way to the Stars*: men from the NLS throw a Christmas party for local children — December 1944. *113 Association*

Left:
**B-17 *Tondalayo* and her happy
crew — the Fortress in which
Col Aber would eventually lose
his life.** *113 Association*

Below:
**Paul Stonerock expresses doubt
at his captain . . . well, it was a
posed picture.** *IWM OWIL29628*

Right:
A group of Liberators taxi into the mist at Cheddington for an evening take-off.
A. Gulliver/113 Association

Below:
Harrington — General arrangement.

Far right and following pages:
Pencil sketches of scenes depicting day-to-day life at Harrington in 1945 by Richard Sizemore, a radar mechanic attached to the 801/492nd Bomb Group.

'I could not turn the plane and was therefore intending to land on the grass portion of the Base. We were coming in on a normal approach, when I saw what I believe was an out-house in the path of the plane. I remember seeing someone come out of the out-house running as fast as he could, trying to get out of our way. At the time it looked very funny.

'When it appeared that we would not make the airfield, I called for the wheels to come down. The engineer put the wheel lever down and as they came into the slipstream they slowed the plane just enough so that we landed probably two seconds sooner than I had expected. Both wheels were down, but one wheel was not locked. When we hit the ground the aircraft was flying at about 125mph and the unlocked wheel just folded up. The whole thing just rolled — I remember going end over end for what appeared to be quite a long way. The wing fell off and caught fire, but

fortunately it was about 20yd away from the cockpit. The cockpit section I was in was probably no more than about 12ft long and had five people in it.

'Dutch, my navigator, had waited too long to come out of his navigation quarters and was killed instantly when we hit the ground. When the plane stopped rolling the cockpit section was upside down. The instrument panel was still there, but nothing was in front of it. I had my seat belt on and when I released it, I fell to the ground and simply walked out of the side of the aircraft. There was no more aluminium on the side of the plane, it had all been worn away by the tumbling.

'When I got out of the aircraft I noticed that when I bent over my back hurt, but when I stood up straight, I had no pain. I ran to the aft section of the aircraft that held at least three of my men. It was very close to the fire and when I got to it, the 0.50 calibre

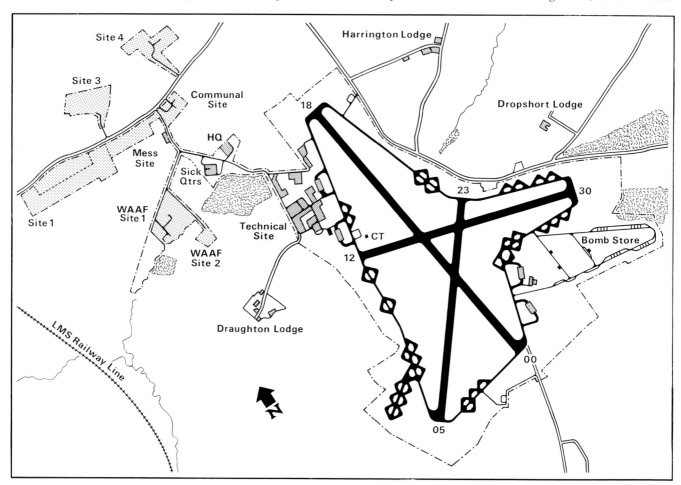

epairing a 'Lib'.

The Chow Line at the Mess Hall.

machine guns on board started to explode and I took-off. Probably within two minutes of the crash, a fire engine was on site along with an ambulance. They put me on a stretcher and carried me to hospital.'

Ed was given X-rays and found to have had a compression fracture of the first and second lumbar vertebrae. After being fitted with a plaster cast, he was flown back to America and home.

When both the air and ground sections of the 406th arrived at Harrington, the squadron set up camp — and camp it was, for both the officers and enlisted men had to sleep in tents that were erected in 'Mud City'. It was so wet and damp around the site that the men had to build small moats to carry the rainwater away. One officer even grew mushrooms under his bedding!

March had been a busy as well as tragic month, with missions on 24 out of the 31 nights. Of the six non-operational nights, two were stand-downs whilst the squadrons moved from Cheddington to Harrington, and the other four scrubs were due to poor weather. The missions flown were to France, Holland, Germany, Luxembourg and Belgium.

For the next few months, the 406th — which was no longer an independent squadron, but attached to the 492nd Bomb Group — continued its leaflet task night after night, as and when required. There had also been some extra tasks for the crews, one was that of dropping carrier pigeons! Some were dead and had false messages attached to their legs, the idea being to mislead the enemy when he found the birds. The live ones — that is those who not only survived the flight but also the descent — were used for Resistance groups to send messages back to London (that is if they could ever fly again). Pilot Dale Wilkes recalled how he plucked souvenir feathers from the frightened birds — without

Above:
Lt-Col Harry Gaddy promotes Al Weil to the rank of Major.
B. Gunderson/113 Association

Below:
Ed Canner's crew of *The Leading Lady*. Standing, left to right: Lts 'Dutch' Cohoorn, Ed Canner, Marcina Parker-Butts and Mike Markovitch. Kneeling, left to right: Gunners Jim Mancuso, Walter Mark, Reuben Hill, Jim Keaton, Ralph Featherstone and Chas Bunnell. 'Dutch' Cohoorn was the only member killed in the crash at Harrington when the squadron moved from Cheddington.
E. Canner/113 Association

Base Radar Shack.

View from my hut, Barrack Site No 3.

telling other crew members. So did his navigator, and the bombardier and the tail gunner... The first 'Pigeon Raid' was on the night of 11 April. Aircraft flown by Lts Callaghan, Pard and Pardue, in addition to their normal bomb-load of leaflets, carried 10 'live' pigeons each. These were parachuted out over three German towns in the hope that, when retrieved, they would fly back to their homing cotes in Times Square, Piccadilly Circus, London. During the remainder of April, 340 additional pigeons in groups of 10 were all dropped over strategic and tactical targets in Germany.

In addition to leaflets and pigeons, there were a number of other 'special deliveries' by the NLS, including forged German ration cards. These were dropped to inflict severe strain on the German economy. This came about when large numbers of the public, unaware of the deception, descended on their local butcher or grocer and bought up all the available supplies with the forged cards. Another item delivered by the efficient services of the now well known 'News Boys', were 'Braddocks'. These were celluloid 3in square time-fused incendiary devices that, when dropped behind German lines, could be planted in homes or factories by civilians who were against the Nazi regime.

The original concept was Winston Churchill's, but was dropped when RAF Bomber Command, under AM Arthur 'Bomber' Harris, refused permission for RAF aircraft to carry the bombs. Those in command of PsyWar jumped at the chance however, and formulated plans for the Braddocks to be dropped with instructions for use in various languages. Also enclosed were suggestions for targets that were easily accessible by the foreign workers, and who were on the Allies' side. The use of the Braddocks had another sinister purpose. Once the enemy knew about their existence, it was possible for large fires or explosions to be blamed on the incendiary devices when they were not the actual cause. This created suspicion between German workers and their police. One of the requirements for the Braddock was that they should not be dropped within a radius of 25 miles of any POW camp. This became impossible by April 1945, and so their use was discontinued.

With an end to the hostilities, 'Tactical PsyWar Runs' came to a close, but were soon replaced by 'SHAEF Runs'. These were leaflet sorties to drop news sheets printed in English, French, Russian or Polish, to keep the many displaced people and foreign nationals up to date with current news and any important

Red Cross Club.

Right:
Walt Longanecker Jr (second left) and his crew pose for the camera at Charleston AFB, South Carolina, in September 1944 prior to posting and assignment to the 406th Bomb Squadron at Cheddington. *W. Longanecker*

Above and right:
B-24J of the 36th Bomb Squadron, photographed from Jack Wrenn's aircraft.
M. Wrenn/113 Association

military instructions being released. The squadron's last leaflet mission took place on the night of 6/7 May, when 10 Liberators were dispatched to France, Holland and the Channel Islands. Once this task had been completed the war-weary crews could still not put up their feet, for there was another task to be undertaken. One that not all the men agreed with or indeed understood the reason for.

The Base Commander at Harrington, who had been a graduate of the US Military Academy at West Point, took immediate action to see that his troops did not get into mischief because of idleness. His first step was to announce that there would be a Saturday inspection of all squadrons, quarters, grounds, equipment and personnel. Harold Gaddy, who had been a flying cadet at Randolph Field and who had observed these 'West Pointers' in action, knew the matter of inspections was very important to them. So, along with his Executive Officer David Usser, whom he classed as competent and highly conscientious, he set about following the inspection requirements. By the following Saturday, everything was in first-class condition in the 406th, including the quarters, grounds and equipment. They even had their men in fresh, clean uniforms. The Base Commander was extremely pleased, which made Gaddy very proud indeed of his squadron.

The next few weeks were busy times indeed for his men, accomplishing much-needed maintenance, attending classes and lectures and generally retracing their way back to a 'spit and polish' military organisation. When the orders came for the squadron to return to America, all was in fine order. The orders, dated 28 June, directed that the squadron depart via Valley in North Wales on the best available route to Bradley Field, then on to Camp Miles Standish, Boston, which was the Port of Embarkation (P of E). This was for rest and recuperation prior to any further assignment. Thus the 20 aircrews left Harrington and flew home, with Gaddy in the lead aircraft but only this time he crossed the Atlantic from east to west and in a Fortress! The remainder of the groundcrews who could not find space on the aircraft followed later by sea.

As 'the Mouth' of PsyWar during World War 2, the Night Leaflet Squadron had used a weapon that many did not know existed, but which was so successful and efficient that its use continues to this day.

Above:
'Germany Quits' – the long and hard-fought struggle to crush Nazism is over.

Right:
Reaping the whirlwind – scenes of devastation in Germany photographed at the war's end on one of the many 'Cook's Tours' for groundcrews and non-flying personnel.

V
THE EARS

No 100 Group RAF

From the outbreak of war, RAF Bomber Command sent its aircraft far into the enemy homeland without the protection of countermeasures against any form of enemy radar, the reason being that at that time the Allies had no proof of its existence. Evidence, however, started to come to light from December 1939, when an aerial that had been removed from the scuttled German pocket battleship *Graf Spee* at Montevideo was examined by a British radar expert. A second clue came with the repeated use of the word *Freyer* in intelligence reports that were received during the middle period of 1940. *Freyer* was finally uncovered as a radar, in February 1941, when its frequency was located and identified. This allowed the plotting of *Freyer* sites by British radio operators searching the frequency bands, and by October a total of 27 sites had been located. In less than a month, another site at Bruneval had been located by aerial photography. This caused much excitement because the site contained a new type of radar. As the site was located close to the French coast it allowed for the now-famous Operation 'Biting' to take place, when 119 men were parachuted in from Whitley aircraft. This raid resulted in 17 British casualties, but also the capture of three German operators who, along with their radar receiver, amplifier, modulator, transmitter and aerial, were brought to England for interrogation and examination. The Germans, who expected a second raid to take place, increased the security of all the other sites and surrounded them with barbed wire. This move however, made the sites more conspicuous from the air, thus aiding the photographic reconnaissance Spitfires and Mosquitoes from RAF Benson and allowing more intelligence to be gathered by the Allied forces. As a result, by July 1942 a good picture had been built up of enemy radar operations.

If there was any doubt as to the German ability to jam British radar, it was removed on 11 July 1942 when the German cruisers *Scharnhorst* and *Gneisenau* sailed up the English Channel. This provocative act was accomplished in broad daylight whilst jamming the British radar systems to avoid attack. It resulted in the start of British offensive radar countermeasures (RCM), and a race to produce equipment, test it, then form squadrons to put it to use. RAF Fighter Command was the first off the blocks, with aircraft equipped with 'Moonshine' jammers. These, developed by the Telecommunications Research Establishment (TRE), pro-

duced spurious returns on the enemy's *Freyer* early warning radar system. It worked by re-transmitting the *Freyer* signal, and therefore increasing the strength of the 'spoof' echo. Bomber Command took over the lead in the race with the formation of No 100 Group on 8 November 1943, and used the previously formed No 80 Wing as a foundation. This Wing, based at Radlett in Hertfordshire and under the command of AVM Addison, had commenced testing of prototype equipment. The Group's brief was to operate airborne and ground RCM equipment to deceive or jam enemy radar systems, wireless signals, and radio navigation equipment. It was also to examine all intelligence on enemy radar systems and radio navigation equipment, to enable tactics or modifications to be made to Allied aircraft or operations.

The Group's first operational unit was No 141 Squadron, formed on 3 December 1943 at West Raynham, and equipped with Beaufighter VIf and Mosquito Mk II aircraft. By mid-January 1944, No 100 Group consisted of the following squadrons and flights:

- No 141 (SD) Squadron — Beaufighter, Mosquito
- No 169 (SD) Squadron — Mosquito
- No 192 (SD) Squadron — Wellington, Halifax, Mosquito
- No 239 (SD) Squadron — Mosquito
- No 515 (SD) Squadron — Beaufighter, Defiant
- No 1473 (SD) Flight — Anson
- No 1692 (SD) Flight — Beaufighter, Defiant.

Sculthorpe

The first 'Heavy' squadron to join the Group was No 214 at Sculthorpe, Norfolk, on 17 January 1944. This squadron had been equipped with four-engined Short Stirling aircraft, but was converting to the American B-17 Flying Fortress. To convert crews on to the Fortress, No 1699 Flight was formed. Its staff put the ex-Stirling crews through seven days of ground training, followed by 25hr flying time. This time included air firing, fighter affiliation and cross-country flights. Following a 'Bullseye' sortie, pilots went on a 'second dickey' operation as second pilot with an experienced crew, before returning to their own crew for their first operation together.

The use of the B-17 came about because of its performance and suitability, plus its availability. The decision to use the type was made at HQ RAF Bomber Command, High Wycombe, when several requirements were drawn up.

- RAF Bomber Command requested the supply of 14 B-17 aircraft from the US 8th AF, plus replacements. These aircraft were to be replaced in American service by an equal number of B-17G aircraft, off-set from future British Lend-Lease contracts.
- In terms of electronic equipment, each aircraft would carry H2S, Gee or Loran, API and AMU, a DR compass, 'Monica' IIA, MF and HF communications, HF and VHF R/T, 'Jostle IV' and four 'Airborne Grocers'. The installation of 'Jostle' and 'Airborne Grocer' would be acceptable.
- Each aircraft would carry a rear, mid-upper and ball turret gunner.

With regard to aircraft performance, the following estimates were arrived at: aircraft complete with all electronic equipment and armament having an overall weight of 60,500lb (27,442kg) — a range of 1,150 miles (1,851km) at 135mph (217km/hr) at an operational height of 30,000ft (9,144m). A range of 1,400 miles (2,253km) at 215mph (346km/hr) at an operational height of 25,000ft (7,620m). For an aircraft without H2S or vertical turret, and having an overall weight of 59,000lb (26,762kg) — a range of 1,220 miles (1,963km) at 230mph (370km/hr) at an operational height of 30,000ft (9,144m). A range of 1,500 miles (2,414km) at 212mph (341km/hr) at an operational height of 25,000ft (7,620m).

Above:
Sgts Jim Fettig, Bob Lathrop and Johnny Redd on 'station' transport.
B. Downs/113 Association

Left:
One of the first RAF Fortress aircraft to be fitted with ECM equipment by Scottish Aviation at Prestwick. The aerials flanking the twin tail guns are 'Airborne Grocer', and 'Monica' below the guns.
IWM ATP13090D

Below left:
Fortress 'BU-S' No 214 Squadron RAF shows proud its H2S radome beneath its nose. In the background is 'BU-U'. *RAF Museum PO17128*

The crew would comprise a pilot, navigator, flight engineer, wireless-operator, special operator, bombardier (to act as second navigator/air gunner), and two air gunners.

The first B-17, 41-24577, arrived on 20 January 1944, and was used for conversion training and then fitted with jamming equipment. To train the English air and groundcrews of No 214 Squadron on the American aircraft, a small detachment of men from the 8th AF was moved into Sculthorpe. On 28 March, General Order No 5 was issued from AFCC at Cheddington, directing that the detachment would become the 803rd (Provisional) Bomb Squadron (H). Under the command of Capt Paris, the squadron was then deemed to be the 8th AF RCM detachment. At first the squadron was involved purely with the training of English crews, but within a short time efforts were taken to integrate them with those of the RAF, and for the RAF to provide its initial equipment. On 10 February, six crews arrived with their B-17s from the 96th Bomb Group, 8th AF, who had all completed their 25-mission tour of combat. They had been selected from a number of other crews at Snetterton Heath who were due to return home to America. These six crews, therefore, were all new to each other and unused to each other's way of work. This formation caused morale to fall like a stone!

By 1 April, the following equipment had been fitted into the B-17s:

one aircraft — three 'Carpet' sets, one 'Mandrel' set;
two aircraft — four 'Mandrel' sets;
two aircraft — six 'Mandrel' sets;
one aircraft — one 'Blinker', one S27, one SCA587.

Above:
A 'Boozer II' indicator unit fitted on to the instrument panel of a B-24. A red light indicated the presence of enemy *Würzburg* radar transmissions and a yellow lamp, that of FuG 202/212 transmissions. *Royal Signals & Radar Establishment, Malvern (RSRE)*

Left:
A selection of 'Mandrel' antennas from the T1408 A to the T1408 F. Each antenna was cut to the required length for the frequency range being jammed, and mounted under the aircraft's wing. 'Mandrel' was essentially a standard IFF set, altered so that it could receive and transmit continuously. When an enemy signal was received, the set was switched to transmit thus jamming the incoming signal. *RSRE*

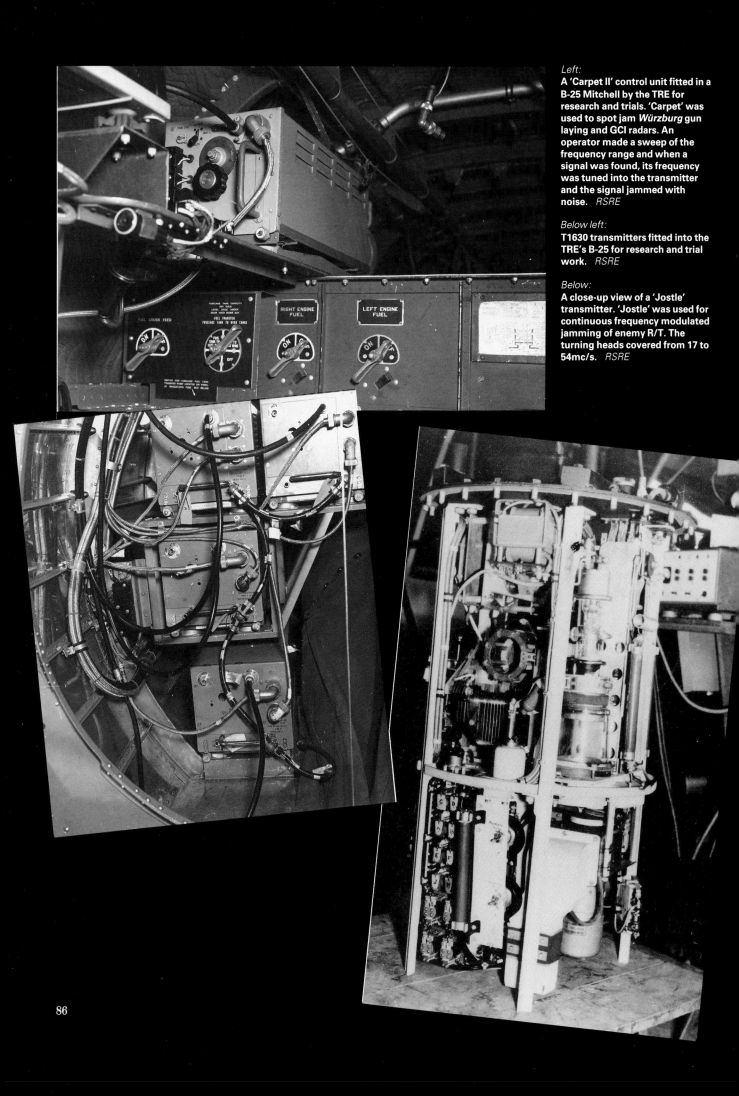

Left:
A 'Carpet II' control unit fitted in a
B-25 Mitchell by the TRE for
research and trials. 'Carpet' was
used to spot jam *Würzburg* gun
laying and GCI radars. An
operator made a sweep of the
frequency range and when a
signal was found, its frequency
was tuned into the transmitter
and the signal jammed with
noise. *RSRE*

Below left:
T1630 transmitters fitted into the
TRE's B-25 for research and trial
work. *RSRE*

Below:
A close-up view of a 'Jostle'
transmitter. 'Jostle' was used for
continuous frequency modulated
jamming of enemy R/T. The
turning heads covered from 17 to
54mc/s. *RSRE*

Above:
A RAF officer and a NCO stand beside their American bomb truck, modified to carry the 'Jostle' transmitter in a vertical position to the aircraft dispersal point. *RSRE*

Left:
When at the dispersal it was lowered into a specially dug pit. The aircraft was then brought over the pit and the jammer winched up into the bomb bay. *RSRE*

87

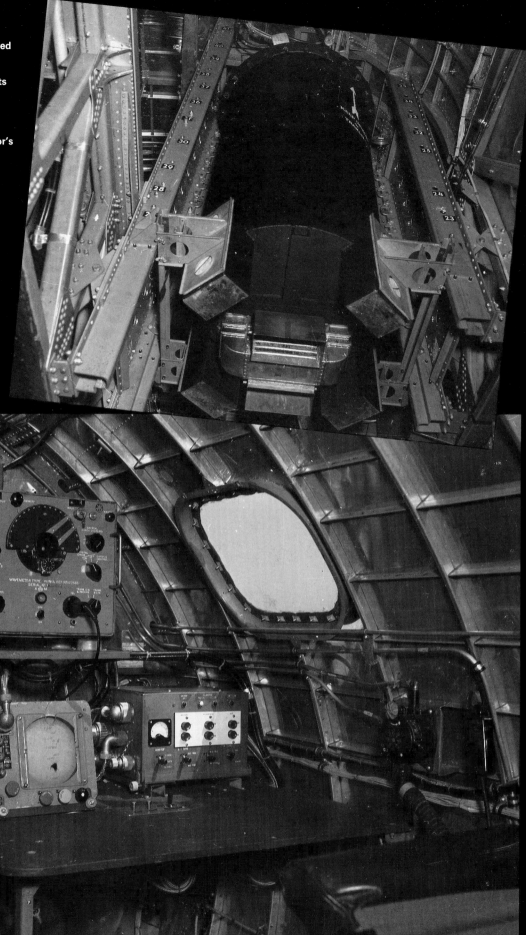

Right:
A 'Jostle' T1524 transmitter fitted into a B-17 bomb bay. It measured 51in high, 24.5in in diameter, weighed 600lb, and its case was maintained at a pressure of 35lb/sq in.   *RSRE*

Below:
The B-17 Special Radio Operator's section showing a T11991A wavemeter, a Type 2000 visual display unit, and alongside, a 'Jostle' control panel. Fortress and Liberator aircraft were the only types that could carry 'Jostle'.   *RSRE*

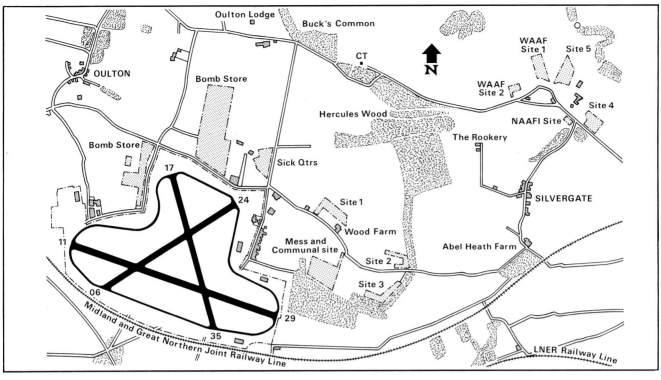

Oulton

On 25 April, Capt Paris became the Operations Officer and handed command of the squadron over to Maj Scott. A further change occurred on 16 May when RAF Sculthorpe was closed, and both Nos 214 and 803 Squadrons moved to RAF Oulton, some 20 miles away. At the time of this move considerable thought had been given to the use of the 803rd on operations, and so its aircraft were equipped with 'Carpet' and 'Mandrel' jammers, and its crews trained to operate them.

The squadron's first operation came on the night of 5/6 June 1944, when along with other aircraft of No 100 Group, a 'Mandrel' screen was put up by four 803rd B-17s to mask the progress of the Allied invasion fleet, heading towards the French coast. The aircraft took off at 22.00hrs and started to jam at 22.35hrs. They continued until 04.50hrs, then returned safely to Oulton. Operations continued into June with the 803rd sending 27 aircraft out on five nights to provide a screen for RAF bombers. Of the 31 sorties, 28 were effective as there was one abort on the 22nd and two on the night of the 27th. The screens were flown at 15,000ft until the night of the 27th, when tactics were changed and the height increased to 19,000ft. This height was maintained during July, when 58 sorties were flown on 14 nights. On 12 July the 803rd sent its first B-24 Liberator out on a mission. The Liberator was destined to replace the squadron's Fortresses for it was now accepted to be a more suitable aircraft for RCM operations. The changeover to an all-Liberator fleet was completed by 28 July.

Above:
Oulton — General arrangement.

Right:
96th Bomb Group groundcrew take a rest from working on their 'Fort'. *R. Stutzman/113 Association*

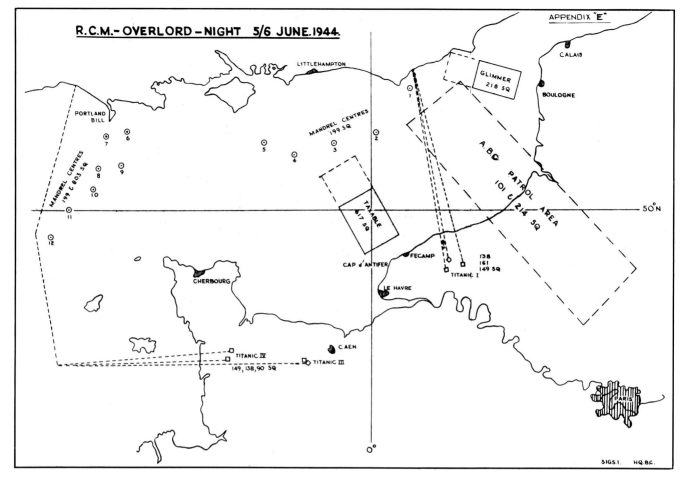

RCM - OVERLORD - NIGHT 5/6 JUNE 1944.

APPENDIX 'E'

36th Bomb Squadron (RCM)

August saw more changes, including a new Commanding Officer, Maj Hambaugh, who had been the squadron's Liaison Officer with No 100 Group RAF, also a new type of mission, with 'spoof' sorties being flown. The main change was on the 13th, when the 803rd merged with the 856th Bomb Squadron, changed its designation to the 36th Bomb Squadron (H) (RCM), and moved to Cheddington alongside the NLS, sharing its Operations Room. The Operations Room was not the only item that the 36th shared with another unit. Whilst its Liberators made lone patrols, adorned with the new squadron code 'R4' painted on their fuselages, other aircraft lurked in the night. Was it accidental or intentional on the part of the 8th AF that those letters were the same ones used by the Luftwaffe nightfighter unit *Nachjagdgeschwader 2* (NJG 2). This unit had been formed in September 1940, with its *Gruppen* (Squadrons) and *Stab* (Headquarters Flight) using Dornier Do17Z-10, Do215B-5, Do217J-1 and Junkers variants, including the G6b.

The remainder of August saw 'Mandrel' operations continue including four ELINT (Electrical Intelligence) gathering sorties, where radio bands and frequencies were searched to locate those in use by the enemy. The 'Mandrel' screens were in support of RAF raids to Germany (six), France (five), and one 'spoof' raid. The same format continued into September with 87 aircraft being dispatched on 'Mandrel' duties. The 'Mandrel' screen was now a 'creeping' screen on all missions, unlike the original sorties that remained stationary and did not move towards the enemy coast. Work also continued on navigation training and the staffing of a 'Special RADAR School' that had been opened at Cheddington to train radio operators from other Bomb Groups in the operation of 'Mandrel', 'Monica' and 'Jostle' jammers.

Above:
RCM cover for Operation 'Overlord' — 5/6 June 1944.

RCM cover for Operation 'Overlord' — the Allied invasion of France — consisted of five separate operations:

1. 'Taxable'
2. 'Glimmer'
3. 'ABC'
4. 'Titanic'
5. 'Mandrel'

'TAXABLE'
A combined naval and air diversion against Cap d'Antifer with 16 aircraft from No 617 Squadron RAF.

'GLIMMER'
As with 'Taxable', 'Glimmer' was also a joint naval/air operation but against Boulogne. No 218 Squadron RAF provided six aircraft.

'ABC'
Operations consisted of 24 aircraft from No 101 Squadron RAF along with five aircraft from No 214 Squadron providing VHF jamming support for Operation 'Taxable' and 'Glimmer'.

'TITANIC'
'Titanic' consisted of 34 aircraft from Nos 90, 138, 149 and 161 Squadrons RAF, which provided three feint airborne attacks towards Caen.

'MANDREL'
The 'Mandrel' screen was provided by 16 aircraft from No 199 Squadron RAF, and four aircraft from the 803rd Bomb Squadron USAF, consisting of two screens with 12 centres.

October saw the first 'Mandrel' screen in support of the 8th AF when, on the 10th, seven aircraft were tasked to provide a daylight screen to mask B-17 and B-24s returning from a leaflet raid. This mission set the pattern for all future sorties. The screens continued into November, providing protection for departing RAF and returning 8th AF bombers, but from the 25th, cover was extended for the 8th AF and retracted for the RAF. This was due to the gradual phasing out of involvement with No 100 Group operations. From 25 November, the 8th AF screen was also flown in daylight and used to mask radio chatter coming from the B-17 and B-24 bombers assembling prior to setting out on their bomb raids. Sorties were then flown each day until the 30th. Up to 25 November, 78 aircraft were dispatched to support RAF operations and following that date, one 'Mandrel' patrol each night. The Group Intelligence Officer summarised the missions in a short poem that said it all:

Above right:
Capt Stutzman, Lt-Col Scott and Capt Robinson of the 36th Bomb Squadron. *R. Stutzman/113 Association*

Right:
Maj Robert F. Hambaugh from Birmingham, Al, who took over the command of the 36th Bomb Squadron from Col Scott, pictured in the pilot's seat of an Airspeed Oxford. *F. Wilkins/113 Association*

Below:
Form 5 — Individual Flight Log.
Each month Form 5 was completed by the squadron's Operations Officer. Vane Glendening recorded his 52 missions with the 36th Bomb Squadron (RCM). His total operational hours of 301 worked out at 5.7hr per mission.

THE NIGHT OF 23/24TH NOVEMBER 1944

Bomber Command had laid on a raid,
To be carried out with 100 Group's aid.
But Bomber considered the weather was poor,
So Group took a hand at alerting the Ruhr.
They put up a suitably placed Mandrel Screen,
Through which, so they hoped, not a thing could be seen.
They sang to the Hun a Serrate serenade,
Round the beacons they danced a Perfectos Parade.
They intruded up high, they intruded down low,
(Just to be beastly they'd put on this show).
The Window force windowed 100 per cent,
And came through the screen with offensive intent.
The Hun plotted hundreds of Heavies around,
But hadn't a hope of control from the ground.
He put up some fighters and led them astray,
In a huge mass of blips that faded away.
Our immediate analysis shows in the main,
That the poor bloody Hun had been fooled once again.

In November, the first 36th Squadron crew was killed when, on the night of the 9/10th, B-24 42-51226 coded R4-L, crashed. The aircraft, flown by Lt Joseph Hornsby, was returning from a mission when fire broke out in one of the four engines. Joe gave the bale-out order but for some unknown reason three crew members failed to jump. Lt Fred Grey the navigator, Sgts Ray Mears and Frank Bartho, who were both gunners, died in the abandoned aircraft when it crashed in flames near Boucly in

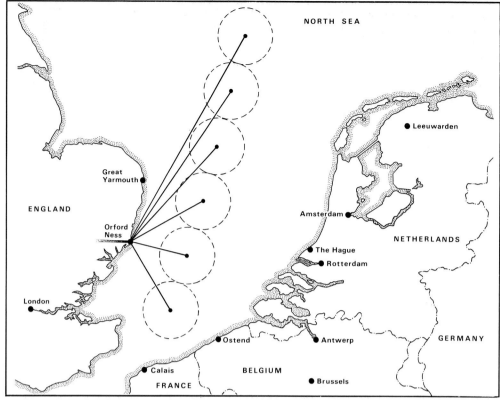

Northern France. A second crash occurred at 23.48hrs on the night of the 15th, whilst B-24 42-51219 coded R4-I, was taking-off for a 'Mandrel' screen mission. Norman Landberg, the captain, made a normal take-off from Cheddington's runway 08 and climbed out following the 2,000ft lane of red warning lamps which extended from either side of the runway. The aircraft cleared the railway line, but came down again about 3,000ft east of the tracks and just left of the runway centreline. The tail gunner, **George Eberwine**, recalled the crash:

'One minute we were up — the next we were down. I had my back to the bulkhead and that saved me as the Lib just folded up. After we came to a halt I just ran to get clear of what I thought would be an explosion. I then realised there were only two of us so went back to do what I could for the others whilst my buddy went for help.'

Lying dead in the shattered wreckage were the navigator, Walter Lamson, and one of the gunners, Leo Smith. The cause of the crash, following an investigation, was put down to instrument failure and pilot error.

December brought more deaths for the squadron. On the 19th, whilst returning from a mission, B-24 42-51232 coded R4-J was diverted to RAF Manston in Kent as Cheddington was 'closed in' due to fog. The crew remained there until the 22nd, when they set off for home at Cheddington. Again due to the weather, Cheddington was closed, so Bill Lehner, the B-24's navigator, gave a course for RAF Valley to his captain, Harold Boehm. The Lib with its crew of 10 set off for the Welsh airfield, but the extra flying time proved to exceed the aircraft's fuel reserves, and the crew were forced to bale out three miles southwest of Valley. Only Harold Boehm and his co-pilot Don Birch survived. The other eight crew members, whose bodies were never recovered from the Irish Sea, were reported as 'Missing In Action', presumed drowned. As for missions in December, support for the 8th AF raids continued with screens provided to mask the radio chatter

Above:
Irl Fife, the crew chief of *Ramp Rooster*, pictured at Cheddington. The lightning strike marks beneath the cockpit indicate jamming missions. *I. Fife/113 Association*

Right:
***Ramp Rooster* before her nose art was completed.** *113 Association*

Below right:
B-24J 42-51230 *LiL Pudge* and her unknown co-pilot of the time. *N. Senter/113 Association*

on 23 days, and a further nine screens provided to mask the RAF's operations.

The squadron recorded a 'first' on the 28th, when a 'Jackal' mission was flown. Liberators R4-E *Li'l Pudge*, R4-H *The Beast of Bourbon*, and R4-K *Lady in the Dark*, set course for the enemy front-line in Belgium. When the three aircraft were in position, they orbited the area for 4hr, jamming enemy army vehicle and tank radios that were participating in the 'Battle of the Bulge'. To test how effective the jamming was, Liberator R4-N *This is it Men*, was used with an S27 search receiver which monitored the enemy frequencies. As jamming also affected Allied aircraft bombing equipment, it was stopped when Allied aircraft approached.

The year 1944 came to a very successful end for the 803rd/36th staff, who had achieved a lot in a very short time. Mission tactics had been perfected and equipment tested, approved, and installed. Commendations had been received from both 8th AF and RAF for the effectiveness of the squadron's jamming. Their aircraft were the most powerful jamming machines in Europe. But the war was not yet won and there was still a lot of work to do, both in training and equipment installations. The missions could be broken down into three types:

Right:
The Beast of Bourbon taxies past the station Control Tower. *The Beast* was lost in a take-off accident on 19 February 1945.
N. Senter/113 Association

Below right:
Rum Dum was the personal mount of Sam 'VAT '69' Ziff.
N. Senter/113 Association

Below:
Mandrel Jamming Patterns:
Racecourse (right). A racecourse screen comprised two aircraft which flew a 10min diagonal circuit, consisting of two long and two short legs. These legs, flown up and down Gee lines, required accurate timing by the pilot and navigator in order to maintain the position of the screen.
Shifting Racecourse (left). Starting on 17 July 1944, the screen became a 'creeping mandrel', its centre slowly moving towards the enemy coast. This was achieved by making the downwind leg longer that the following upwind leg.

Mandrel:

A screen provided to mask the radio traffic caused whilst Bomb Groups were assembling, thus preventing enemy ears from having advanced indication of the numbers of Allied bombers involved.

Spoof

Three aircraft would try to deceive the enemy into thinking that a second bomber formation was assembling, by operators reading typical Bomb Group formation messages from a script.

Mandrel R/T

Jamming aircraft would travel with the Bomb Group formations towards the target to screen R/T messages.

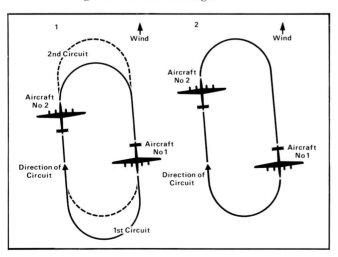

As for the jamming equipment installed in the aircraft, the situation was much more complicated and must have been very confusing for the ground crews and staff from the 476 Sub-Depot, who had been moved into Cheddington on Detached Service to fit, remove and then re-fit the equipment. The following aircraft had jamming equipment installed by the end of 1944:

Jackal	Carpet I	Jostle	Dina	Mandrel	ELINT
50665	250665	251311	250665	250385	250622
50476	250476	251315	251230	250665	250671
51230	251230		251685	250750	
51685	151685		295221	250844	
95221	401609		250385	251546	
01609	251331		251239	295221	
	251315		251308		
	251315		251576		
			250671		

In addition to the fitting of jammers, a number of other modifications were made to the aircraft. These included the installation of a floor in the right rear bomb-bay to carry the extra equipment; the fitting of overhead lighting, oxygen and flight-suit heating points for the Special Radio Operators; the fitting of the required number of aerials either under the wings or on the tail section. The ball turret was removed to be replaced by 'Jostle' jammers. The 'Jostle' itself was transported by a converted bomb-truck, then lowered into a pit that had been dug in one of the aircraft disposals. The aircraft would then be manoeuvred into position over the pit and the jammer raised into the Liberator's ball turret position.

The cold Christmas of 1944 gave way to January 1945, but there was no let-up in the missions. Out of a total of 24 missions, two 'Mandrel' screens were provided for the RAF, with the rest being the now regular VHF screening for the 8th AF. **Odis Waggoner**, a gunner in the 36th, recorded the month and his missions in his diary:

1st: We started off the New Year by flying another morning mission in 188 — Uneventful; 6hr 45min.

2nd: We had a practice mission this afternoon, testing a new antenna.

3rd: Nothing to do today. Went to the aero club with Sid and Way tonight.

4th: Nothing to do today. Went to the show on the Base tonight.

5th: Flew another mission this morning. Got back after our two-day pass had started. Went into London with Way tonight: 6hr 30min.

6th: Way and I ran around together today. Then Way, Catt, and I saw *30 Seconds over Tokio* this afternoon.

7th: Returned to our Base this afternoon. Caught the 11.35 train from Euston. Walked from the crossroads outside Tring to base.

8th: Flew another mission this morning in 188. Had to abort after we had been in position about an hour. Got credit for the time: 3hr 30min.

9th: Flew another morning mission in 'L'. Were recalled early and I was glad −46°C at 21,000'. Had two teeth filled: 3hr 30min.

10th   Nothing to do today. Lt Young's crew finished up.

11th   Nothing to do today.

12th   We were woken for a mission this morning but they scrubbed it before we got dressed for chow. Nothing else today.

13th   Nothing to do today. Put pictures in my new album tonight.

14th   Nothing to do today. Woke up late to go to church.

15th   Flew another mission this morning in 'T'. Kept smelling gasoline all through flight otherwise uneventful: 6hr 15min.

16th   Nothing to do today.

17th   Flew another mission this morning in 'P'. Uneventful: 5hr.

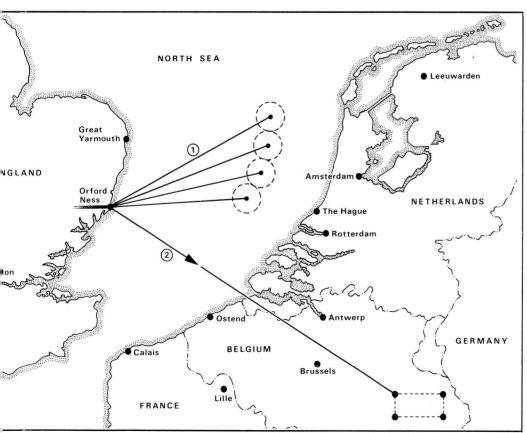

Top:
Two of the 36th Bomb Squadron's B-24s taxi back after a mission.
N. Senter/113 Association

Left:
Mission plan for 2 January 1945:
1. Four aircraft Mandrel screen.
2. Three aircraft Jackal screen.

18th Nothing to do today.

19th Slow timed '188' this morning. Had a tooth filled this afternoon.

20th Flew another mission this morning in '188'. −48°C at 22,000'. Uneventful. I went into London on my class 'B' pass tonight to see *Castle Arford*: 5hr 30min.

21st Went to church this morning. Nothing to do today.

22nd Nothing to do today.

23rd Nothing to do today. Went to the show on the Base tonight, saw *Summer Storm*.

24th Flew another mission in 'F'. We were diverted to Woodbridge and then went by truck to Martlesham Heath to sleep: 5hr 15min.

25th Mission was scrubbed.

26th Flew another mission this morning in 'F'. We were diverted to Linton. No 1 engine lost oil pressure on the final approach. Need new engine: 5hr 45min.

27th We started on a mission in 'M' this morning but they scrubbed it after we got to the end of the runway. I slid off the wing whilst I was checking the gas. I broke a bone in my left hand. They took me to York and put a cast on it. I removed the cast around midnight — severe pain.

28th The pain eased this morning. Then I went back to Cheddington this evening by plane. Stayed in the hospital overnight: 1hr 45min.

That was the end of combat for Odis. He was given credit for the mission, making a total of 50 missions. His operational flying time was some 296hr 15min, and total flying time 554hr 15min.

Jamming

January may well have seen the end of operations for Odis, but for **Lee Hendrickson** it was only the start. Lee remembers:

'After sixty-eight days' training which included one hundred and one hours' transition training as co-pilot on B-24J aircraft, my crew and I departed November 1st 1944 for processing and a two-week overseas ocean voyage to Liverpool, England. Of the fifty-two crews on our shipment, half went without bombardiers, ours amongst them.

'Upon arrival in Liverpool, we were assigned and transported to the HQ 70th Replacement Depot at Army Air Force Station 594,

Below and below right:
When You Are Overseas.
A leaflet given to all American airmen prior to service in England with the 8th AF. It gave information on writing home, military mail and civil V-mail, cables, careless talk and capture!

War Department Pamphlet No. 21–1   29 July 1943

WHEN YOU ARE OVERSEAS

THESE FACTS ARE VITAL

Writing home

THINK! Where does the enemy get his information—information that can put you, and has put your comrades, adrift on an open sea; information that has lost battles and can lose more, unless you personally, vigilantly, perform your duty in SAFEGUARDING MILITARY INFORMATION? CENSORSHIP RULES ARE SIMPLE, SENSIBLE.—They are merely concise statements drawn from actual experience briefly outlining the types of material which have proved to be disastrous when available to the enemy. A soldier should not hesitate to impose his own additional rules when he is considering writing of a subject not covered by present regulations. He also should guard against repeating rumors or misstatements. It is sometimes stated that censorship delays mail for long periods of time. Actually, mail is required to be completely through censorship within 48 hours.

There are ten prohibited subjects

1. Don't write military information of Army units—their location, strength, matériel, or equipment.
2. Don't write of military installations.
3. Don't write of transportation facilities.
4. Don't write of convoys, their routes, ports (including ports of embarkation and disembarkation), time en route, naval protection, or war incidents occurring en route.
5. Don't disclose movements of ships, naval or merchant, troops, or aircraft.
6. Don't mention plans and forecasts or orders for future operations, whether known or just your guess.
7. Don't write about the effects of enemy operations.
8. Don't tell of any casualty until released by proper authority (The Adjutant General) and then only by using the full name of the casualty.
9. Don't attempt to formulate or use a code system, cipher, or shorthand, or any other means to conceal the true meaning of your letter. Violations of this regulation will result in severe punishment.
10. Don't give your location in any way except as authorized by proper authority. Be sure nothing you write about discloses a more specific location than the one authorized.

INCLOSURES IN LETTERS:—Do not inclose anything in a letter that would violate any of the foregoing rules.

PHOTOGRAPHS, FILMS.—Special rules apply to the transmission of photographs and films. Do not send them until you have ascertained what regulations are in effect in your area.

540677°—43

2

POST CARDS.—The use of post cards may or may not be authorized. Find out first, and then be sure that the picture or printed part of the card does not violate censorship regulations.

Letter addresses

ADDRESS.—Always leave room for a forwarding address to be written in. *On mail to civilians.*—Use normal address and form. *On mail to military personnel.*—Give name, grade (rank), Army serial number (if known), unit and organization, and location if in United States. If addressee is also overseas use his APO number c/o Postmaster ——. If in the same general locality as the sender see Army Postal Service for authorized address. *On mail to prisoners of war held by enemy.*—Obtain full information from local Army Postal Service.

RETURN ADDRESS.—Every letter or post card must have a return address. Place it in the upper left-hand corner, leaving a margin of ½ inch for resealing in case of censorship beyond the unit censor. The ½-inch margin rule applies equally to mail from officers and from enlisted men. Both are subject to examination by base censorship detachments.

    Sgt. John Smith, 6749318,   Free
    Co. C, 299 Inf., A. P. O. 1005,
    c/o Postmaster, New York City, N. Y.

                  Mrs. John Smith,
                  123 First Avenue,
                  New York City, N. Y.

The return address must include (1) full name, including grade (rank), (2) Army serial number, (3) unit (company, battery, etc.), (4) organization (regiment, etc.), (5) APO number, (6) c/o Postmaster (city assigned). Return addresses on mail written to prisoners of war are subject to specific regulations. Obtain information locally.

No geographical location of sender may be shown on an envelope or other outside cover.

Official military mail

Special regulations are provided for official military mail. They are not covered herein.

Mailing your letter

Reread your letter to be sure you have complied with all regulations. This will protect you and assure the most expeditious delivery of your letter. Five minutes now will save later delay and prevent possible suppression of the letter. It will protect you from punishment for unintentional violations.

ENLISTED MEN.—Place your letter unsealed in your organization mail box, never in any civil post office box. *You are required to use the Army Postal Service, and the Army Postal Service only.*

Left:
'V Mail'.

Once letters had been written, they had to be approved by the censor. Then, to make way for more valuable goods to be shipped, they were photographed on to microfilm and shrunk. V-Mail proved a very good way to save space — but hard on the readers' eyes.

Stone, Stafford. There we were briefed on customs and courtesies of the British people, language and behavioural differences and the avoidance of such words as 'bloody' in mixed company. We were relieved from assignment to that station on November 30th, and ordered to proceed on December 1st to Cheddington. On arrival we were assigned to a hut, furnished to our satisfaction with steel beds. These had straw-filled, three-piece "biscuit" mattresses and a pot-bellied stove for which we were rationed three and a half pounds of coke per man per day. We heated the hut from 16.30hrs to 22.00hrs each day, and felt privileged to have had the only hut on our site with adjoining toilet!

'Happy at last, after six months of continuous moves, we settled down to training. This consisted of ten flights during the month to familiarise our crew with England, foggy weather landings, navigation using Gee systems and searchlight locating of bases, and, at long last, actual practice in the use of the radio and radar-jamming equipment. After some sixteen hours of English flying weather we flew our first mission on January 6th 1945.

3

OFFICERS.—Seal the envelope, sign your name without comment in the lower left-hand corner to indicate your compliance with censorship regulations (your letter is subject to further censorship examination by base censorship detachments), and deposit in the organization mail box. *Use only the Army Postal Service.*

V-mail

This is an expeditious mail program which provides for quick mail service to and from soldiers overseas. A special form is used which permits the letter to be photographed on microfilm, the small film transported, and then reproduced and delivered. Use of V-MAIL is urged because it greatly furthers the war effort by saving shipping and airplane space.

Censorship rules apply to V-mail with such adjustments as are necessary due to the form used and special processing features.

Blue envelopes

Enlisted men who wish to write of private or family matters and who feel that censorship of a specific letter by their unit censor would cause embarrassment may be authorized to use a blue envelope which will allow censorship action to be taken by the base censor rather than the unit censor. Blue envelopes should be obtained from your organization and must be addressed to the final intended recipient. Only one letter may be placed in each envelope and the envelope should be sealed prior to mailing.

Censorship regulations apply to blue envelopes as well as to all other communications.

Warning

Written communications may be sent only through the facilities of the Army Postal Service. Any attempt to avoid this restriction by mailing letters in civil postal systems or by having travelers transport communications will result in severe disciplinary action against both the sender and the intermediary.

Cables; radiograms

Every cable message goes through the hands of at least 12 people. Radiogram messages are available to all who wish to "tune in," including the enemy!

Constant effort is being made to provide you with approved, rapid, cheap electrical communication.

Under no circumstances can cables be sent over commercial or foreign outlets until their use is authorized by proper military authority. "Safe Arrival" messages, identifiable as such, are prohibited at any time. There are two types of electrical messages generally available: Senders' Composition Messages (SCM's), which are like the cablegrams and radiograms you know at home, and Expeditionary Force Messages (EFM's) which are fixed text messages sent at a very low rate, much like Christmas and birthday telegraph messages in use in the United States, but with set messages composed to meet your normal requirement.

As soon as safety allows you will be assigned an APO cable address. Until it is assigned only serious, emergency messages may be sent, and then only if first approved in writing by the theater or area commander or his authorized representative. The Red Cross can handle certain extremely urgent personal matters by cable.

Ask your unit censor how to send messages, either SCM's or EFM's. Under no circumstances may you mention your unit or organization, or any military establishment; nor may you mention in the text any APO number other than your own.

4

Cable addresses

Outbound.—First give *your* cable address; next, the full name, street address, city, and State of the person for whom the message is intended; then the message, and finally sign your full name. Example:

AMTRAG (typical APO cable address)
Mrs. John Smith, 1616 Main St.,
Zenith, Ohio.
XXXXXX Message XXXXXX
XXXXXXXXXXXXXXXXXXXX
John T. Smith.

Note that addresses and signatures do not include Army serial numbers, unit or organization designation, or APO numbers, nor do they show your location in any manner whatsoever.

Inbound.—Cables and radiograms should be addressed to you, giving your full name, Army serial number, and *cable* address, but not your unit nor organization.

Talk

SILENCE MEANS SECURITY.—If violation of protective measures is serious within written communications it is disastrous in conversations. Protect your conversation as you do your letters, and be even more careful. A harmful letter can be nullified by censorship; loose talk is direct delivery to the enemy.

If you come home during war your lips must remain sealed and your writing hand must be guided by self-imposed censorship. This takes guts. Have you got them or do you want your buddies and your country to pay the price for your showing off? You've faced the battle front; it's little enough to ask you to face this "home front."

Capture

Most enemy intelligence comes from prisoners. If captured, you are required to give only three facts: YOUR NAME, YOUR GRADE, YOUR ARMY SERIAL NUMBER. Don't talk, don't try to fake stories, and use every effort to destroy all papers. When you are going into an area where capture is possible carry only essential papers and plan to destroy them prior to capture if possible. Do not carry personal letters on your person; they tell much about you, and the envelope has on it your unit and organization.

Be sensible; use your head

Published for the information and guidance of all concerned.
By order of the Secretary of War:

G. C. MARSHALL,
Chief of Staff.

Official:
J. A. ULIO,
Major General,
The Adjutant General.

U. S. GOVERNMENT PRINTING OFFICE: 1943

CAPTAIN HUBERT N. STURDIVANT AND COMMUNICATIONS SECTION - 2
8ᵗʰ AIR FORCE

ALCONBURY, ENGLAND - - MAY 23, 1945

Above:
Capt Hubert Sturdivant and his men from the Communications Section at Alconbury, 1945. *J. Steininger/113 Association*

'Preparation for missions consisted of arising at 02.00hrs, breakfast of real eggs, ham, coffee and that thick crusted English bread. Mission briefing gave us the weather and assigned our Gee position over the English Channel which was relative to the other squadron aircraft. Also, the timing of our jammers, both on and off. Take-off was usually between 04.00 and 05.00hrs, in order to be in position ahead of the bomber formations that we would be screening, and which at that time would be forming over England. Visibility for most missions was so bad that aircraft awaiting take-off ahead of you were just about seen, and resulted in a number of accidents. One resulted in me becoming the possessor of an A-2 leather flying jacket, formerly owned by Glenwood

Poindexter, who was in a crew which reported at Cheddington with us.

'Usually four to eight aircraft would take-off thirty minutes before the bombers, to position singly about 10 miles apart, in an arc 50 miles east of the bomber assembly area. We would then fly a counter-clockwise racetrack orbit and jamming transmissions made for two to three hours as altitude was increased. Our screen would gradually advance towards the enemy territory or was shifted towards the North Sea. Whilst flying the racetrack, we occasionally observed the bright arc of a V-2 rocket vapour trail, lit by the rising sun as it ascended from the still dark horizon. These we could report, in the hope that action would and could be taken.

'As daylight appeared and we observed the bomber formations approaching from the west, we shut down our jamming equipment and dodged our way back to Cheddington, through the high, low and medium altitude squadrons, coasting out on their bombing missions.'

Loss of the Beast

February saw 24 VHF screening missions in support of the 8th AF and for the first time no aircraft provided a 'Mandrel' screen for the RAF. A total of 156 aircraft had been dispatched with the loss of just two. The first was on the 5th of the month when Liberator 42-51239 coded R4-C *Uninvited*, with a crew of 10, failed to return from its mission. All crew members were reported MIA — presumed shot down over the North Sea and drowned, as this was the area for their RCM patrol. On the 19th, *The Beast of*

Left:
I Walk Alone said it all for a 36th Bomb Squadron aircraft.
L. McCarthy/113 Association

Stanley J. Dombrosky, a gunner with Lt Corder's crew, uses his .50in calibre gunbelt as a scarf. *V. Glendening/113 Association*

Bourbon. painted with very colourful nose art in the form of a monster, crashed on take-off for a mission. This Liberator, 42-50385 R4-H, with a crew of 10, included two members of another crew. They were being taken on a 'check-out ride' to assess their capabilities for combat after completion of their squadron training. **Henry Parke**, who was a radio operator/gunner on Bert Young's crew, remembers that day:

'I flew most of my missions on Bert's crew, but then had a spell in hospital. When I came out my crew had completed their tour but I was left with 10 or so missions to do. Carl Boehm had lost his crew except for his co-pilot over the Irish Sea, because they were not wearing life jackets, so I talked him into taking a few of us "left-overs" as crew, to complete our tour. He agreed and we were known as "Boehm's Bums"! We were scheduled to fly on the 19th but were told another crew had one more mission to fly, so we let them have our ship to fly the mission. If we had not . . .'

The weather at Cheddington was poor, with visibility only 100yd in fog. With a wind speed of only 2mph from the south-southeast, there was little chance of an early clearing. In fact, by the time of take-off at 09.15hrs, the fog had closed visibility to 30yd! The

Above left:
Gunner Dean McComb on the day his crew (Flt Off Bert Young) passed out for combat at Cheddington.
D. McComb/113 Association

Above:
Louis McCarthy and crew.
L. McCarthy/113 Association

Left:
Gunner Vane Glendening (standing, right) with his crew. From left to right: Lts Dan Jenkins, Don Albinson, Bill Corder (captain) and Joe Thome. Kneeling, left to right: Gunners Jim Marchello, Ralph Ramos, Stan Dombrosky and Wesley Crowther.
V. Glendening/113 Association

Liberator, with brakes released, rumbled out to the marshalling point next to runway 26. The captain, Louis McCarthy and Vic Pregeant, who was with him being checked out, made a pre-take-off check which showed everything to be in order. One last engine run-up was made, perhaps because the aircraft had been in dock for engine work the day before, but all was well. Brakes were released and, when the ground speed reached 105mph, rotation. The *Beast* took to the air and reached 110mph by the time the runway had been cleared. Due to the poor visibility, flying was immediately on instruments with the aircraft being held in a flying attitude to build up air speed to 135mph. All engines were operating at full throttle and sounding normal, with gauges indicating 43in of vacuum and 2,500rpm. Within half-a-mile of the runway, and just to the right, the *Beast* came down. The mark of its path indicated that it was in a proper attitude at the time of contact, and the altimeter showed 45ft — as it had not reduced. After hitting hedges and trees, Louis cut the throttles and Vic Pregeant cut the ignition switches, which possibly delayed the fire and explosion that took place within minutes of the crash. A local farmhand, seeing the tragic event, rushed over to help. Despite being burned, he removed three trapped members from the burning hulk. Three gunners, Pts Fred Becker and Howard Haley, and SSgt Carl Lindquist, were all killed.

Below:
Alconbury — General arrangement.

Alconbury

February came to a black and very sad end for the squadron. It was not just the crashes that were responsible, tragic as they were, for on the 27th the whole squadron left Cheddington for a new base — the airfield at Alconbury in Cambridgeshire. This move was the beginning of the rundown for operations at Cheddington and, had the 36th remained, the airfield would have witnessed the activities that continued at Alconbury. These consisted of the continuation of 8th AF VHF screens and, from the 16th, actual jamming of enemy radar during the Bomb Group assembly period. In addition to these Liberator missions, there was the start of operations by three P-38J 'Droop Snoot' Lightning aircraft. These were flown by 7th Photographic Group pilots from Mount Farm, Oxfordshire, but used 36th Bomb Squadron observers — Lts Zeider, Holt and Stallcup — on the six ELINT missions which were flown. These were to monitor enemy radar in Holland and along the German front line. Of the three P-38s, one was reported MIA, and 43-28479 crashed on take-off. A take-off crash also caused the loss of Liberator 42-50844 on 20 March 1945 whilst being flown by Lt Sweeney, but this was thankfully the squadron's last Liberator accident and was non-fatal.

May 1945 gave way to new — but short-lived — missions in June, with the transportation of squadron members on 'sightseeing' trips over Germany. Ten passengers were carried at a time, with a minimum of crew to man the aircraft. Forty-four of

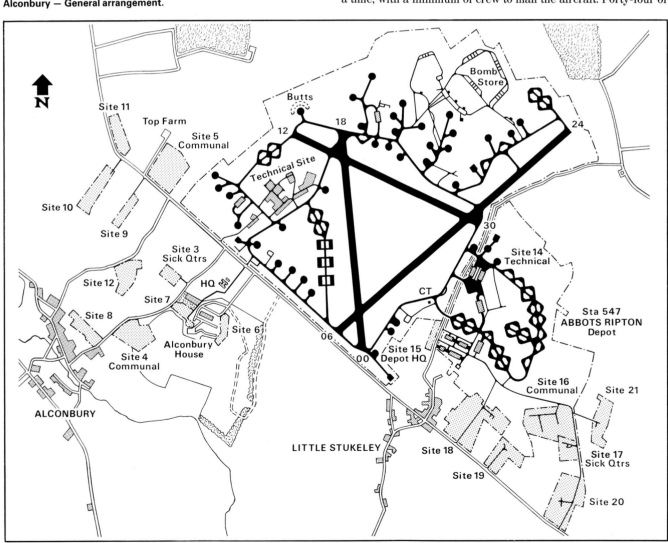

these flights were flown during the month, plus 134 other 'passengers' to Paris for their 48hr pass. The only other flights made were celestial navigation night flights, for the benefit of the 20 squadron navigators preparing for the long flight back home to America. The order for these return flights came from 1st Air Division on 5 July 1945, and directed that the squadron's 20 Liberators, with Capt Jack Wrenn leading in 42-95221 *Ready N' Able*, depart via RAF Valley by the best available air route to Bradley Field, Windsor Locks, Connecticut, then on to Camp Miles Standish, Boston, for 'rest and recuperation'.

And so the electronic war against the Nazi regime was over, and with it the protection that crews in both the Mighty Eighth and Royal Air Force had been given by the 36th. This protection from the prying eyes and sharp ears of the enemy prevented, or hindered, them from bringing their guns to bear on the Allied bomber formations and fighter escorts. And that, without doubt, resulted in the saving of many, many Allied lives.

102

652ᴺᴰ BOMB SQUADRON (H)
ALCONBURY, ENGLAND — AUGUST 1945

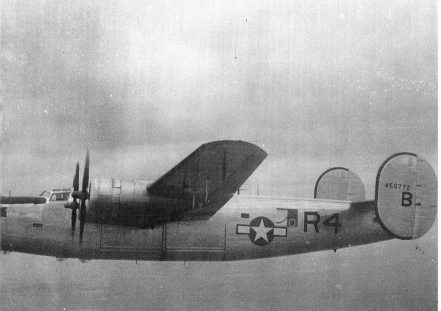

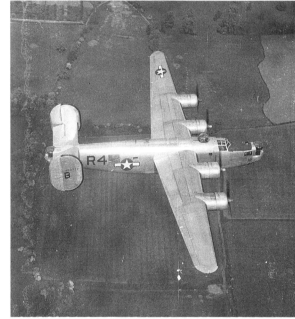

Above:
R4-B with its underwing 'Mandrell' and 'Dina' antennae. On top of the fuselage is a 'Jostle' antenna.
M. Wrenn/113 Association

Above right:
A fine air-to-air shot of late-built B-24 45-0772 R4-B, taken from Jack's aircraft.
M. Wrenn/113 Association

Right:
Jack relaxes from the rigours of operational flying with a round of golf. *M. Wrenn/113 Association*

Right:
A view of Jack's B-24 cockpit showing the tail of B-24J 44-10609 R4-S.
M. Wrenn/113 Association

Far right:
Jack Wrenn with *Ready n' Able*.
M. Wrenn/113 Association

Below right:
The men of the 1077th Signal Company go 'State-side' on the *Queen Elizabeth*.
B. Downs/113 Association

Bottom:
The most photographed B-24 at Cheddington, *The Beast of Bourbon*, with Lt Jack Wrenn and his crew — 5 January 1945.
113 Association

VI
THE REUNION

The sky was blue with just an odd fluff of white cloud. A small group of men and women gathered in silence. Lost for words, their thoughts known only to themselves, they gazed skywards as a formation of aircraft approached. That group, which included a navigator, pilots and gunners from both Night Leaflet and RCM squadrons, aircraft mechanics, a communication expert and the captain of the Women's Army Corps along with some of her girls, could see 'Star and Bar' markings on the aircraft. There was no battle damage to be seen, or flares being fired to indicate injured or dead on board. As the formation made its third pass, a lone Piper Cub broke away, circled, then made a final run towards the group. When overhead, its pilot released a bundle of leaflets that fluttered to the ground. Not propaganda leaflets or news of the Allied armies' advance, but each one bearing the name of every man killed whilst based at Cheddington during World War 2. What the group had seen through their tears was not a formation of bombers overflying Cheddington during the war years, but a formation of nine light aircraft overflying Cheddington in the 1980s. This event marked the second reunion of the Cheddington

(STN 113) Association. The first was when a memorial was dedicated to the 8th AF on the site of Cheddington's old main gate.

Why had there been a reunion? Back in 1980 I tried to find out about the old airfield. Its buildings were empty, the runways gone. I searched books and official records — all to no avail. I decided that my only option open would be to form an Association with the aim of tracing as many as possible of those who had been based at Cheddington and obtain first-hand their experiences of those events and missions. Missions that until now had escaped attention, and had not been given the credit they deserved. Missions that were held in conditions of such secrecy that even some members of the aircraft crews did not know why, or where they were going! Those missions, and the assistance they received from the various support units, enabled many Allied lives to be saved, and tactics proven to such a degree that operations with the same structure are tasked to this day.

To all those who either supported or served with those 'Secret Squadrons', I say thank you.

AIR FORCE INTELLIGENCE SERVICE
UNITED STATES AIR FORCE

CERTIFICATE OF APPRECIATION
TO
The Cheddington (STN 113) ASSOCIATION

for the honor of participating
in the dedication of the
CHEDDINGTON MEMORIAL
as a representative of
THE UNITED STATES AIR FORCE

20 OCTOBER 1982

WALTER B. LONGANECKER, JR.
Major General, USAFR
Mobilization Assistant to the
Assistant Chief of Staff, Intelligence

Left:
Certificate of Appreciation.
In 1980 the Cheddington (STN 113) Association was formed with the following aims:
1. **To research past events at AAF Station 113, Cheddington**
2. **To locate those who served there with the US 8th AF**
3. **To erect a memorial to all those killed.**

Some 700 men and women have now been located. At the Association's first reunion in 1982 when a memorial was dedicated, Maj-Gen Walter Longanecker, USAFR, presented the Association with a Certificate of Appreciation from the Air Force Intelligence Service, USAF.

APPENDICES

Research Sources

United Kingdom

Imperial War Museum, London
Public Record Office, Kew
RAF Museum, London
Science Museum, London

United States of America

US Air Force Historical Research Center, Maxwell AFB, Alabama
Battle Monuments Commission, Washington DC, Defence Audio
    Visual Agency, Washington DC
US Air Force Inspection & Safety Center, Norton AFB, California

----

Selective Bibliography

8th Air Force Yearbook, J. Woolnough, (8AF News, Texas, 1981)
Air Force Spoken Here, J. Parton, (Adler, Maryland, 1986)
A Thousand Shall Fall, M. Peden, (Canada's Wings, Stittsville,
    1981)
Carpetbaggers, B. Parnell, (Eakin Press, Texas, 1987)
Confound and Destroy, M. Streetly, (Macdonald & Jane's,
    London, 1978)
Fortress of the Big Triangle First, C. Bishop, (East Anglia, 1986)
Iron Eagle, T. Coffey, (Crown, New York, 1986)
Luftwaffe Handbook, A. Price, (Ian Allan, London, 1977)
Mighty Eighth, R. Freeman, (Macdonald & Jane's, London, 1970)
Mighty Eighth War Diary, R. Freeman, (Jane's, London, 1981)
Mighty Eighth War Manual, R. Freeman (Jane's, London, 1984)
Mission With LeMay, Gen C. LeMay, (Doubleday, New York,
    1965)
US Strategic Bomber, R. Freeman, (Macdonald & Janes, London,
    1975)

Unpublished Primary Source Material

Maxwell AFB, Alabama

B0797/8	2nd CCRC Group
A092	9th Station Complement Squadron
B0548/9	36th Service Group, USAAF
B0811	38th Service Group, USAAF
A0606/7	406th Bomb Squadron, USAAF
A0609	422nd Bomb Squadron, USAAF
A0667	858th Bomb Squadron, USAAF
A0464	1077th Signal Company, USAAF
B5118	Composite Command Records
A0470	Station 113 Records

Public Record Office, Kew

AIR	14/737	RCM Equipment
AIR	14/1427	Operation 'Infatuate'
AIR	14/6005	Leaflet Policy
AIR	20/1492	RCM 1939-45
AIR	25/777	No 100 Group Operations
AIR	28/104	RAF Bovingdon Operations Record Book (ORB)
AIR	28/143	RAF Cheddington ORB
AIR	29/669	RAF Wing ORB

Aircraft Used by 406th Bomb Squadron (NL)

SERIAL	TYPE	CODE	NAME/COMMENTS
42-38167	B-17G	JJ-L	—
42-6174	B-17F	JJ-K	Home-Sick Angel/Stripped for Action
43-37516	B-17G	JJ-T	Tondalayo. Shot down Clacton 4/3/45
530	B-17		W/O 10/7/44
43-37530	B-17G	JJ-A	W/O 4/1/45
42-30656	B-17F	JJ-D	Miss Mickey Finn, also JJ-W
42-37717	B-17G	JJ-B	Channel Fever Baby
42-37726	B-17G	JJ-N	Shady Lady
42-37771	B-17G	JJ-Q	—
42-30775	B-17G	JJ-P	—
42-39790	B-17G	JJ-F	—
42-30791	B-17F	JJ-J	Pistol Packin' Mama
42-59811	B-17G	JJ-E	MIA 6/7/44
42-30838	B-17F	JJ-0	Paper Doll
42-39843	B-17G	JJ-G	Daley's Male
42-51210	B-24H	J6-0	—
42-51217	B-24H	J6-R	—
42-37522	B-24H	J6-	Miss Stardust
42-95238	B-24H	J6-K	W/O 18/8/44
42-52251	B-24J	J6-L	—
42-50479	B-24J	J6-L	—
42-50483	B-24J	J6-I	Midnite Mistress
42-50484	B-24J	J6-	W/O 21/1/45
42-51492	B-24J	J6-B	—
42-52510	B-24H	J6-U	—
41-29522	B-24H		856BS on DS. W/O 11/12/44
42-50555	B-24J	J6-G	—
42-51555	B-24J	J6-Q	—
41-29602	B-24H		856BS on DS
42-51574	B-24J	J6-P	—
41-29598	B-24H		—
41-29599	B-24H	J6-	—
41-29601	B-24H	J6-M	—
41-29602	B-24H	J6-Q	856BS on DS. Black Zombie
44-10619	B-24J	J6-T	—
42-52637	B-24H		—
42-52650	B-24H	J6-E	W/O 3/1/45
42-50651	B-24J	J6-F	—
42-50652	B-24J	J6-W	Dark Eyes
42-94756	B-24H	J6-C	—
42-94775	B-24H	J6-	W/O 18/11/44
42-94824	B-24H	J6-S	—
42-39845	B-24H	J6-	W/O 12/10/44
42-94851	B-24H	J6-E	—
42-94865	B-24H	J6-H	—
869	B-24H	J6-	—
41-28871	B-24H	J6-	The Leading Lady. Crashed 14/3/45
42-94873	B-24H	J6-Y	—
41-28880	B-24H	J6-Y	—
44-50929	B-24M	J6-	—
42-50844	B-24J	J6-	—
41-6205	P-47C		—

Named aircraft that are unknown

—	—	—	Swing Shift
—	—	—	Foxy Lady
—	—	—	She Wolf
—	B-24H	J6-	The Night Night
—	—	—	Betty

(W/O = Written Off; DS = Detached Service; MIA = Missing in Action)

422/858/406th Bomb Squadron
Mission Summary

CHELVESTON: October 1943-June 1944
Missions:	128
Sorties:	662
Leaflets:	536,220,000 (6,703 bundles)

CHEDDINGTON: 27 June 1944-13 March 1945
Missions:	160
Sorties:	1,292
Leaflets:	1,121,600,000
L/Bombs:	14,020

HARRINGTON: 14 March 1945-25 April 1945
Missions:	27
Sorties:	378
Leaflets:	285,580,000
L/Bombs:	3,571

TOTAL: October 1943-25 April 1945
Missions:	315
Sorties:	2,332
Leaflets:	1,943,500,000
L/Bombs:	24,294
Targets:	6,816
Pigeons:	200

6 June 1944 — D-Day
Missions:	1
Sorties:	6
Leaflets:	3,000,000
L/Bombs:	60

Tons of leaflets dropped by all 8th Air Force Units
October 1943-May 1945

MONTH	UNITS ON BOMBING MISSIONS	422/406th BOMB SQN	492nd BOMB GRP	MONTHLY TOTALS
1943				
Oct	—	24.4	—	24.4
Nov	—	100.8	—	100.8
Dec	3.3	112.1	—	115.4
1944				
Jan	27.6	118.6	3.8	150.0
Feb	37.4	131.6	6.9	175.9
Mar	99.1	146.3	12.9	258.3
Apr	74.8	134.9	27.9	237.6
May	123.5	102.4	35.3	261.2
Jun	73.1	209.6	43.1	325.8
Jul	53.6	216.1	42.3	312.0
Aug	87.8	203.1	37.6	328.5
Sep	152.8	180.4	1.1	334.3
Oct	165.8	240.5	—	406.3
Nov	151.1	315.3	—	466.4
Dec	138.1	261.6	—	399.7
1945				
Jan	165.8	182.0	—	347.8
Feb	196.6	276.3	—	472.9
Mar	247.0	407.9	—	654.9
Apr	186.8	370.5	—	557.3
May	102.4	—	—	102.4
	2,086.6	3,734.4	210.9	6,031.9

In May 1945, the 406th Bomb Squadron flew four missions of 30 sorties over 56 targets. 354 leaflet bombs were dropped containing 28,320,000 leaflets. After VE-Day, 18 non-combat missions of 141 sorties over 96 targets were flown. 1,549 bombs were used.

Aircraft Used by 36th Bomb Squadron (RCM)

SERIAL	TYPE	CODE	NAME/COMMENTS
42-3438	B-17F	—	—
42-3518	B-17G	—	—
42-6080	B-17F	—	—
42-30039	B-17F	—	*Liberty Belle*
42-30066	B-17F	—	—
42-30114	B-17F	—	—
42-30177	B-17F	—	—
42-30178	B-17F	—	—
42-30353	B-17F	—	—
42-30363	B-17F	—	—
42-37743	B-17G	—	—
41-29144	B-24	R4-B	—
42-51188	B-24H	R4-O	*Lady Jane.* First 'Dina'-equipped aircraft
42-51219	B-24H	R4-I	W/O 15/11/44
42-95221	B-24H	R4-A	*Margie/Ready N'Able*
42-51226	B-24J	R4-L	W/O 10/11/44
42-51230	B-24J	R4-E	*Li'l Pudge/Rum Dum*
42-51232	B-24J	R4-J	W/O 22/12/44
42-51239	B-24J	R4-C	*Uninvited.* MIA North Sea 5/2/45
42-51304	B-24J	R4-B	—
42-51307	B-24J	R4-Q	—
42-51308	B-24J	R4-M	*Modest Maid*
42-51311	B-24J	R4-T	—
42-51315	B-24J	R4-U	—
42-50385	B-24H	R4-H	*Beast of Bourbon.* W/O 19/2/45
42-50476	B-24J	R4-J	—
42-50495	B-24J	R4-V	—
44-50502	B-24	R4-C	—
44-10507	B-24J	R4-	—
42-95507	B-24J	R4-D	Maintenance only. RCM School
42-51546	B-24J	R4-L	*I Walk Alone*
42-50576	B-24	R4-H	—
41-29593	B-24	R4-	
42-7607	B-24H	R4-A	—
44-10609	B-24J	R4-S	—
42-50622	B-24J	R4-N	*This is it Men/Bama Bound-Lovely Libba*
42-50665	B-24J	R4-K	*Lady in The Dark*
42-50671	B-24J	R4-F	*Ramp Rooster*
42-51685	B-24J	R4-R	*Playmate*
42-50750	B-24J	R4-P	—
42-40796	B-24	R4-	—
42-94811	B-24J	R4-I	*Miss-B-Haven*
44-23156	P-38	R4-	—
43-28479	P-38	R4-	Crashed 25/6/45
44-23501	P-38	R4-	—
44-23515	P-38	R4-	MIA

Named aircraft that are unknown

—	B-24	R4-	*Black Magic*
—	B-24	R4-	*The Jigs Up*
—	B-24	R4-	*The Gypsy Jane*

36th Bomb Squadron

Missions

6 June 1944-30 April 1945

JUNE 1944

Date	Sorties
5/6	4
16/17	6
17/18	5
22/23	6
27/28	5
28/29	5

JULY 1944

Date	Sorties
4/5	5
7/8	5
9/10	5
12/13	5
14/15	5
17/18	4
19/20	4
20/21	4
21/22	3
23/24	5
24/25	3
25/26	3
28/29	4
29/30	3

AUGUST 1944

Date	Sorties
4/5	2
6/7	5
7/8	5
8/9	5
9/10	4
10/11	4
11/12	4
12/13	5
13/14	6
16/17	4
17/18	2
18/19	6
25/26	6
26/27	7
27/28	6
29/30	4
30/31	6

SEPTEMBER 1944

Date	Sorties
1/2	4
5/6	4
6/7	4
8/9	4
9/10	4
10/11	3
11/12	5
12/13	6
13/14	6
15/16	7
16/17	5
17/18	6
18/19	7
22/23	4
23/24	6
25/26	3
26/27	4
28/29	5

OCTOBER 1944

Date	Sorties
5/6	5
6/7	7
7/8	6
9/10	7
14/15	7
15/16	6
19/18	7
21/22	8
23/24	6
24/25	6
26/27	6
30/31	7
31/1	7

NOVEMBER 1944

Date	Sorties
1/2	7
2/3	7
4/5	6
6/7	8
9/9	7
10/11	8
11/12	7
15/16	5
18/19	6
20/21	5
21/22	6
23/24	6
25	6
25/26	3
26	6
26/27	3
27	5
27/28	3
28	8
28/29	2
29	7
29/30	2
30	6
30/31	2

DECEMBER 1944

Date	Sorties
1	7
1/2	1
2	6
2/3	2
3	7
4	8
4/5	2
5	9
6	8
6/7	2
7	8
8	10
9	10
9/10	1
10	8
11	9
12	8
12/13	1
13	3
15	6
16	5
17/18	1
18	9
18/19	1
19	8
23	2
24	5
25	8
28	9
30	5
30/31	1
31	7

JANUARY 1945

Date	Sorties
1	7
1/2	1
2	7
2/3	1
3	4
5	10
6	5
7	7
8	6
9	5
10	4
13	6
15	6
16	5
17	7
18	7
20	8
21	6
23	5
24	6
26	3
28	5
29	5
31	7

FEBRUARY 1945

Date	Sorties
1	7
2	6
3	7
5	9
6	8
7	6
8	6
9	6
10	6
11	6
14	7
15	7
16	7
17	6
19	2
20	7
21	7
22	7
23	7
24	7
25	7
26	6
27	6
28	6

MARCH 1945

Date	Sorties
1	6
2	5
3	4
5	2
6	2
7	5
8	5
9	4
10	5
11	5
12	5
14	5
15	5
16	13
17	14
18	13
19	15
20	11
21	11
22	4
23	12
24	9
24	3
25	5
26	4
27	14
30	13
31	3

APRIL 1945

Date	Sorties
2	4
3	5
3	4
4	4
5	4
6	5
7	4
8	4
10	4
11	4
12	4
13	5
16	4
17	4
18	4
19	4
20	4
23	4
25	3

36th Bomb Squadron

Mission Summary

5 June 1944-30 April 1945

TYPE OF OPERATION	MISSIONS	FROM/TO
RAF Radar Screen	97	5/6/44-3/1/45
VHF Screen	122	25/11/44-30/4/45
'Spoof'	3	28/11/44-8/12/44
'Jackal'	5	28/12/44-7/1/45
AAF Radar Screen	10	16/3/44-30/3/45
B-24 Search	16	7/3/45-3/4/45
P-38 Search	8	17/3/45-13/4/45

June 1944			*July 1944*	
Total Missions	6		Total Missions	19
Total Sorties	31		Total Sorties	58
Aborts	3		Aborts	4

August 1944			*September 1944*	
Total Missions	17		Total Missions	18
Total Sorties	79		Total Sorties	87
Aborts	6		Aborts	1

October 1944			*November 1944*	
Total Missions	13		Total Missions	24
Total Sorties	85		Total Sorties	131
Aborts	4		Aborts	4

December 1944			*January 1945*	
Total Missions	32		Total Missions	24
Total Sorties	177		Total Sorties	133
Aborts	8		Aborts	8

February 1945			*March 1945*	
Total Missions	24		Total Missions	28
Total Sorties	156		Total Sorties	202
Aborts	1		Aborts	5

April 1945	
Total Missions	20
Total Sorties	78
Aborts	2

36th Bomb Squadron (RCM)

Letter of Commendation

14 November 1944
TO:
Commanding Officer, AAF Station 113, US Army,
(Attention: Commanding Officer, 36th Bomb Squadron)

1. This Headquarters has received a confidential message D-67417, dated 13 November 1944, from the Commanding General of the Eighth Air Force. This message is quoted below.

'Attention Commanding Officer 36th Bomb Squadron RCM. Jamming, screening, and diversionary efforts of the 36th Bomb Squadron have contributed greatly to the effects of the RAF bombing efforts. Mission of 9/10 November was one of the most effective in confusing the GAF and causing them to assemble in great haste to intercept the bomb stream which was not there, and reflects great credit to the Command and the individuals concerned. Signed Doolittle.'

2. This Command forwards this message from General Doolittle with great pleasure and wishes to add its own commendation for a job extremely well done.

By order of Colonel Webster

(Signed)
Richard N. Ellis,
Lt-Colonel, Air Corps,
Chief of Staff

36th Bomb Squadron (RCM)

Letter of Commendation

23 May 1945
TO:
Commanding Officer, 36th Bomb Squadron (RCM), APO 557,
(Thru: Commanding General, 1st Air Div)

1. The advance of the Allied Ground Forces has exposed the effectiveness of air bombardment activities in the destruction of the fighting potentialities of our enemy. The special operations conducted by the 36th Bombardment Squadron (RCM) cannot be over-emphasized in the contribution of the unit to the striking power of this Air Force.

2. Each individual in the organization expended great effort in extensive training in new equipment which you used operationally for the first time on the night of 5th/6th June 1944. Cooperating with the RAF, they provided an efficient radar screen of the enemy early warning system. Individual activities of every member of your Command combined to effect the greatest possible chance of total success not only for this operation but for all operations to follow.

3. The organization, throughout its relatively short but colourful history, has displayed the highest type of initiative and performance. Lacking the glory of combat over enemy territory, your missions were still carried on under the most hazardous of weather conditions. At times, you were still successfully carrying out your missions when it was necessary to issue orders standing down all combat operations.

4. Yours was the assignment of catching the enemy at his own game, and in effectively accomplishing this task, the whole nature and tactics of your missions changed as the enemy scientists devise methods of overcoming our counter-measures. The complexity of your work included jamming of enemy radar, screening of our bomber VHF channels while bombers were assembling, carrying out 'spoof' raids, jamming enemy tank communications, and performing special electronic search missions as directed by this Headquarters. The material advantage of these operations may never be adequately assessed and it is impossible to fully evaluate the number of air crews, as well as bomber and fighter aircraft, saved when enemy fighters discovered too late the essential interception data.

5. Hardwork, exceptional technical ability and determination to see a job well done enabled the 36th Bomb Squadron (RCM) to successfully carry out this mission and reflected high credit upon the whole Eighth Air Force.

6. It is my desire that this commendation be disseminated to all members of your Command.

(Signed) W. E. Kepner,
Major-General, US Army,
Commanding.

Other Known Unit Aircraft

SERIAL	TYPE	CODE	UNIT/COMMENTS
8th Weather Flight			
42-39871	B-17G	'H'	Crashed St Eval
42-37869	B-17G		Crashed Okehampton
39th Service Group			
43-7482	Cessna UC-78		Bobcat (transport variant)
44-70393	Noorduyn C-64A Norseman		
43-14485	Fairchild UC-61		Forwarder
42-58189	Cessna AT-17 Bobcat (training variant)		Burnt out Cheddington 31/8/44
495th Fighter Training Group			
44-70292	Noorduyn C-64A Norseman		
Courier Squadron			
42-98996	Vultee L-5		
42-98997	Vultee L-5		
42-78998	Vultee L-5		
12/2/4 CRCC			
41-24500	B-17F		Ex-381BG. *Annie Freeze*
42-40801	B-24D		
11 CCRC			
41-2578	B-17E		Ex-97BG. *Butcher Shop*. On first AF mission
41-2628	B-17E		Ex-97BG
41-9013	B-17E		Ex-97BG
41-9021	B-17E		Ex-97BG. *Hangar Queen*. First 8AF mid-air collision
41-9025	B-17E		Ex-97BG. *Little John*
41-9089	B-17E		Ex-97BG. *Johny Reb*. First 8AF fatal
41-9100	B-17E		Ex-97BG. *Birmingham Blitzkreig*
41-9119	B-17E		Ex-97BG
41-9121	B-17E		Ex-97BG. *The Big Bitch*
41-9174	B-17E		Ex-97BG

Composite Command

Airfields

NUMBER	NAME	OPERATIONS
102	Alconbury	Pathfinder
112	Bovingdon	B-17 CCRC
113	Cheddington	B-24 CCRC, Leaflet, RCM, AFCC HQ
172	Snettisham	B-17 Gunnery School
179	Harrington	'Carpetbagger', Leaflet
236	Toome	A-20 CCRC, B-26 CCRC
237	Greencastle	B-24/Anti-Aircraft Gunnery School
238	Cluntoe	B-24 CCRC
342	Atcham	P-47 CCRC, P-38 CCRC
345	Goxhill	P-51 CCRC

Airfield Staffing Levels — August 1944

AAF STN	COMPOSITE COMMAND		OTHER COMMANDS		STUDENTS TRAINING		TOTAL STAFF	
	Off	EM	Off	EM	Off	EM	Off	EM
102	339	1,850	5	234	75	177	419	2,261
112	152	1,257	37	193	579	—	768	1,450
113	371	2,031	25	209	—	—	396	2,240
172	42	585	4	24	—	781	46	1,390
179	461	213	1	4	—	—	462	217
236	110	1,231	1	11	329	333	440	1,575
237	63	1,019	—	—	13	724	76	1,743
238	177	1,072	1	11	335	87	513	1,170
342	132	1,220	2	16	353	—	487	1,236
345	123	1,353	2	20	445	—	570	1,373
TOTAL	1,970	11,831	78	722	2,129	2,102	4,177	14,655

(Note: *Off* = Officers; *EM* = Enlisted Men.)

Unit Staffing Levels — August 1944

UNIT ASSIGNED	AAF STN	TOTAL STAFF
Headquarters & Headquarters Squadron Composite Command	416	416
Headquarters & Headquarters Squadron CCRC Group	451	1,804
Replacement & Training Squadron	303	1,214
Headquarters & Headquarters Squadron Fighter Training Group	224	448
Fighter Training Squadron	603	1,207
Bomb Group Headquarters	178	357
Bomb Squadron	1,480	4,442
Air Division Gunnery School	518	518
Headquarters & Headquarters Squadron Service Group	120	482
Service Squadron	199	1,194
Station Complement Squadron	124	1,120
Military Police Company	85	852
Signal Company	54	491
Ordnance Supply & Maintenance Company	62	564
Quartermaster Company	40	359
Gunnery & Tow Target Flight	23	117
Engineering Fire Fighting Platoon	15	117
Medical Dispensary	19	39
Finance Detachment	12	224
Weather Detachment		

(This table shows the average number of personnel attached to each unit of Composite Command on an airfield, and also the total personnel in the Command.)

Consolidated Aircraft Report — August 1944

TYPE	B-17	B-24	B-26	P-38	P-47	P-51	A-20	Other	TOTAL
On hand	79	94	26	18	71	40	5	63	396
Serviceable	61	71	19	15	57	29	3	48	303
Grounded	18	23	7	3	14	11	2	15	93
GROUNDED									
General maintenance	13	19	5	3	14	9	1	8	72
Parts	2	2	2	0	0	2	1	7	16
Other	3	2	0	0	0	0	0	0	5
% ON HAND									
Serviceable	77	76	73	83	80	73	60	76	77
Grounded	23	24	27	17	20	27	40	24	23
General maintenance	16	20	19	17	20	22	20	13	18
Parts	3	2	8	0	0	5	20	11	18
Other	4	2	0	0	0	0	0	0	1
FLYING HOURS									
Ops	569	3,312	—	—	—	—	—	84	3,965
Non-Ops	3,319	1,374	833	553	7,365	3,951	86	1,443	18,924
Total	3,888	4,686	833	553	7,365	3,951	86	1,527	22,889
AVERAGE	49.1	49.5	32.1	30.4	103.4	98.5	17.1	24.1	57.5

Aircraft Use — August 1944

AAF STATION NUMBER HQ	102	112	113	113	172	179	236	237	238	342	345	TOTAL
On Hand												
10	49	18	16	14	6	64	35	12	32	8	56	320
Serviceable												
7	39	13	10	12	4	52	28	9	18	68	43	303
Grounded												
3	10	5	6	2	22	12	7	34	14	16	13	144
GROUNDED												
General maintenance												
3	8	2	6	2	1	9	5	1	11	16	11	75
For parts												
0	2	2	0	0	1	1	2	2	3	0	2	15
Other												
0	3	0	0	0	0	2	0	0	0	0	0	5

AAF STATION NUMBER													
	HQ	102	112	113	113	172	179	236	237	238	342	345	TOTAL
% ON HAND													
Serviceable	70	80	72	62	86	66	91	80	75	56	81	77	77
% GROUNDED													
General maintenance	30	20	11	38	14	17	14	14	9	34	19	20	18
For parts	0	4	17	0	0	17	2	6	16	10	0	3	4
Other	0	6	0	0	0	0	3	0	0	0	0	0	1
FLYING HOURS													
Operational	—	107	—	500	279	—	3,086	—	—	—	—	—	3,972
Non ops	340	2,755	439	32	117	266	905	1,123	192	702	7,358	4,695	18,924
TOTAL	340	2,862	439	532	386	266	3,991	1,123	192	702	7,358	4,695	22,896

Aircraft Allocation — August 1944

AIRCRAFT TYPE					AAF STATION NUMBER							TOTAL
	HQ	102	112	113	172	179	236	237	238	342	345	
B-17	1	45	12	13				2	7			80
B-24		1	2	21		2			16			42
B-26							25					25
P-38										18		18
P-39			1									1
P-47	1	1	1							68		71
P-51											4	4
A-20								1				1
Havoc								1				1
RB 25			1									1
L-4B			1				1	1	1	1	1	6
Oxford	3		1		1					1		6
UC-61A	2	1	1		1							5
UC-64A			1									1
UC-78A	1									1		2
C-47					4							4
AT-6										3	1	4
AT-16	1										2	3
AT-23	1					9						10
RA-35	1			5					8	6		20
YC-108			1									1
TOTAL	11	49	21	34	5	8	35	13	30	91	9	306

Total aircraft on hand with Composite Command August 1944

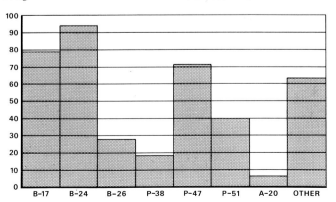

Aircraft Accident Summary — August 1944

TYPE	P-47	P-38	P-51	B-26	B-24	B-17	OTHER	TOTAL
TOTAL	17	6	19	3	3	0	6	54
FATAL	3	0	3	0	1	0	1	8
CAUSE								
Technique	10	3	11	1	0	0	2	27
Judgement	1	1	2	0	0	0	1	5
Careless	1	1	0	0	0	0	0	2
3rd Party	2	0	2	1	0	0	0	5
Airframe	3	1	3	1	2	0	2	12
Unknown	0	0	1	0	1	0	1	3
TOTAL	17	6	19	3	3	0	6	54
OCCURRED								
Taxying	1	1	4	0	0	0	1	7
Take-off	1	0	1	1	0	0	0	3
Flight	12	1	4	2	2	0	2	23
Landing	2	3	9	0	1	0	1	16
Emergency	1	1	1	0	0	0	2	5
TOTAL	17	6	19	3	3	0	6	54
DAMAGE								
Minor	0	0	0	1	0	0	0	1
Major	6	2	13	1	1	0	4	27
Wreck	8	4	6	1	2	0	2	23
TOTAL	14	6	19	3	3	0	6	51

CCRC Training — 1944

	MARCH	APRIL	MAY	JUNE	JULY	AUGUST
Graduated AAF STN 112 (B-17)	251	351	353	475	398	422
By-Passed CCRC	63	213	84	77	268	64
Arrived Stone Depot	315	544	579	417	680	486
Overall Attrition	353	350	372	285	296	364
Graduated AAF STN 236 (B-26)	28	97	62	69	62	116
Arrived Stone Depot	255	75	53	127	131	102
Graduated AAF STN 236 (A-20)	11	11	43	60	20	42
Arrived Stone Depot	11	45	103	35	65	33
Graduated AAF STN 238 (B-24)	49	116	224	328	382	315
By-Passed CCRC	27	—	92	10	12	19
Arrived Stone Depot	156	149	320	427	382	283
Overall Attrition	160	177	160	210	282	308
Graduated AAF STN 342 (P-47)	15	330	275	610	247	310
Arrived Stone Depot	141	487	494	250	342	328
Overall Attrition	92	99	124	131	209	86
Graduated AAF STN 342 (P-38)	51	99	156	144	114	51
Arrived Stone Depot	107	158	145	116	56	84
Overall Attrition	35	47	67	220	71	13
Graduated AAF STN 345 (P-51)	70	152	89	212	241	212
Arrived Stone Depot	80	190	192	108	340	451
Overall Attrition	100	129	134	168	99	220

Miscellaneous Training — 1944

STN	TRAINING SCHOOL	MARCH	APRIL	MAY	JUNE	JULY	AUGUST
237	Anti-Aircraft Gunnery School	689	843	868	862	480	287
237	B-24 Gunnery School	—	—	1,075	1,631	1,947	1,657
172	B-17 Gunnery School	1,528	1,146	2,169	2,432	2,031	2,929
102	Pathfinder Navigator School	39	65	75	66	80	74
113	Radar School	44	39	42	87	76	20
113	Personnel Equipment School	—	—	119	105	173	120

(Note: B-17/B-24 Gunnery Schools operated as an annexe to Stations 112 and 238.)

IN MEMORY

Interments at Cambridge Cemetery

RANK	NAME	UNIT	CAUSE OF DEATH
LCol	Earle Aber	406BS	*Hit by Allied anti-aircraft fire*
2Lt	Gilman Blake	406BS	*Struck aircraft after bailing out*
SSgt	Albany Blanchard	8AF WX	*Hit hill in Devon*
Sgt	Leslie Cazzell	856BS	*Crashed Oulton*
FO	Gerben Coehoorn	406BS	*Crashed Harrington*
2Lt	Maurice Harper	406BS	*Hit by Allied anti-aircraft fire*
2Lt	Cressy Kingery	406BS	*Crashed Madley*
2Lt	Walter Lamson	36BS	*Take-off crash*
Cpl	Dale Patterson	406BS	*Crashed Madley*
2Lt	Jarome Pfullman	406BS	*Take-off crash*
TSgt	Sherwood Renner	8AF WX	*Hit hill in Devon*
Sgt	William Repp	406BS	*Take-off crash*
Cpl	Maurice Rushing	406BS	*Crashed Madley*
PFC	Leonard Smith	36BS	*Take-off crash*
Cpl	Clarence Spect	406BS	*Crashed Madley*
Maj	Seymore Winslow	8AFCC	*Took own life with pistol*

Missing in Action

RANK	NAME	UNIT	CAUSE OF DEATH
Sgt	Robert Brass	36BS	*MIA North Sea*
SSgt	Ray Brecht	36BS	*MIA North Sea*
SSgt	Galen Brooke	36BS	*MIA North Sea*
SSgt	Arthur Clemens	36BS	*MIA Irish Sea*
Sgt	Charles Dautel	36BS	*MIA Irish Sea*
Sgt	Harold Eckert	36BS	*MIA North Sea*
SSgt	Jamie Forseca	36BS	*MIA Irish Sea*
Sgt	Paul Frantz	36BS	*MIA North Sea*
TS	Roger Gagne	36BS	*MIA Irish Sea*
Sgt	Bruce Gist	36BS	*MIA North Sea*
2Lt	Eugene Junkin	36BS	*MIA North Sea*
2Lt	William Lehner	36BS	*MIA Irish Sea*
SSgt	Francis Lynch	36BS	*MIA Irish Sea*
2Lt	John McKibben	36BS	*MIA North Sea*
2Lt	Gaylord Moulton	36BS	*MIA North Sea*
SSgt	Harvey Nystrom	36BS	*MIA Irish Sea*
SSgt	Andrew Zapotochy	36BS	*MIA North Sea*
Sgt	Max Oeitle	36BS	*MIA North Sea*

Interments Elsewhere

RANK	NAME	UNIT	CAUSE OF DEATH
2Lt	Gene Anderson	406BS	*Take-off crash*
Pte	Fred Becker	36BS	*Take-off crash*
1Lt	Fred Bofink	856BS	*Crashed Oulton*
1Lt	Chester Cherrington	406BS	*Crashed Madley on cross-country*
Sgt	William Daugherty	CCRC	*Bomb explosion Cheddington*
TSgt	Gordon Elmore	856BS	*Crashed Oulton*
2Lt	William Ferguson	406BS	*Hit by flak in France*
Cpl	Elmer Frieder	406BS	*Crashed Madley*
2Lt	Fred Gray	36BS	*Hit by flak in France*
Pte	Fred Haley	36BS	*Take-off crash*
SSgt	George Hawkes	406BS	*Take-off crash*
2Lt	Ray Hendrix	406BS	*Take-off crash*
2Lt	Walter Lawson	36BS	*Take-off crash*
1Lt	Fred Lemke	856BS	*Crashed Oulton*
SSgt	Carl Lindquest	36BS	*Take-off crash*
Sgt	Ray Mears	36BS	*Hit by flak in France*
2Lt	Charles Miller	406BS	*Take-off crash*
2Lt	Vincent Murphy	406BS	*Take-off crash*
2Lt	Richard Neary	8AF WX	*Hit hill in Devon*
SSgt	Marcia Panteei	8AF WX	*Hit hill in Devon*
SSgt	Garrett Parnell	856BS	*Crashed Oulton*
2Lt	Robert Preston	406BS	*Crashed Madley*
Sgt	Frank Bartho	36BS	*Hit by flak in France*
Cpl	Doug Reseigh	406BS	*Crashed Madley*
1Lt	James Rush	406BS	*Take-off crash*
Sgt	Sam Schaffer	406BS	*Take-off crash*
1Lt	Louis Sherman	CCRC	*Bomb explosion Cheddington*
Sgt	Blyth Smyth	406BS	*Take-off crash*
Sgt	Edmond Szymczak	406BS	*KIA oxygen loss*
Cpl	Robert Waite	406BS	*Crashed Madley*
Sgt	Josef Weik	406BS	*Take-off crash*
Sgt	John Wheatley	406BS	*Take-off crash*
2Lt	Donald Wilson	406BS	*Crashed Madley*
2Lt	Herman Wolters	36BS	*Electrical fault Belgium*

We Will Remember Them

OMUR OCT 2021

OMUR OCT 2021

The Complete
Beginner's Guide to
Knitting

sona
BOOKS

sona
BOOKS

First published in the UK 2019 by Sona Books
an imprint of Danann Publishing Ltd.

CAT NO: SON0438
ISBN: 978-1-912918-02-7

Made in the EU.

Welcome to

The Complete
Beginner's Guide to

Knitting

In recent years we have seen a popularity boom surrounding all kinds of crafts. Once the reserve of older generations, hand-knitting skills have taken on a new life as a modern art form and relaxing pastime. So, from lavish fashion trends to homemade gifts, add a hand-crafted touch to your garments, gifts and decorations with the help of *The Complete Beginner's Guide to Knitting*. Start by choosing your yarn and needles before getting to grips with casting on, knitting, purling, ribbing and casting off again. Once you've mastered the essentials, find out how to finish projects with finesse. Next you'll put your newfound skills into practice with a range of creative project patterns that are perfect for newbie knitters. So pick up your needles today, and you'll be an expert in no time at all!

Contents

Getting started

Star rating explained
All of the patterns in this book are suitable for new knitters. A higher rating simply denotes that more advanced skills within this book are required to complete the pattern.

82

126

Getting Started

Get to grips with the basics of knitting

Yarns

From chunky wool to 4-ply acrylic, there is a wide variety of yarns with which you can knit

To begin knitting, it's pretty straightforward, as all you need are two things: a pair of knitting needles and a ball of yarn. The yarn that you decide to use will play a part in determining which needles you work with, so let's start by looking at the many types of yarn available to you.

Yarns are made with a wide variety of fibres; most are natural, some are synthetic, and others blend different fibres together. All yarns have different textures and properties, and will affect the look and feel of your finished project. For example, wool is stretchy and

tough, alpaca is soft and luxurious, and natural and synthetic blends are durable with other enhanced properties.

When choosing a yarn you also need to consider its thickness, usually called its weight. Different weights affect the appearance of your project and the number of stitches needed.

When learning to knit, it's a good idea to start with a medium-weight yarn that feels comfortable in your hand and is smooth but not too slippery. A yarn described as worsted, Aran or 10-ply in wool or a wool blend is ideal.

Wool
Wool is very warm and tough, which makes it great for winter wear. It can be fine and soft or rough and scratchy, but will soften with washing. It's mostly affordable, durable and a good choice for the new knitter.

Cotton
This natural vegetable fibre is typically less elastic than wool, and is known for its robustness and washability. Cotton has a lovely stitch definition when knitted, and is good for homewares and bags. However, it can be a bit hard on the hands.

Mohair
Mohair is a silk-like fibre that comes from the Angora goat. It's a yarn that dyes particularly well and is commonly blended with other fibres. It makes for fantastic winter garments as it is warm and durable.

Acrylic
Made from polyacrylonitrile, acrylic yarn is both affordable and also washable. This synthetic yarn is very soft to the touch and comes in a wide variety of colours and textures. Acrylic is commonly blended with other yarns in order to add durability.

Alpaca
With long and fine fibres, alpaca yarn can sometimes be hairy looking, but it is one of the warmest and most luxurious wools out there. It is also incredibly soft, and comes in varieties such as baby and royal, which are even softer.

Natural and synthetic blends
Blending natural and man-made fibres often creates yarns that are stronger and more versatile. It can also enhance their appearance, making them shinier or more vibrant. Blended yarns are often washable, making them great for garments for children.

Did you know?

Every ball of yarn comes with a recommended needle size, which is printed on the label. Use bigger needles than this to make a more open stitch, and smaller ones to make a tighter, more compact fabric.

Yarn Weights

Yarn weight	Properties	Ideal for	Recommended needle sizes		
			Metric	US	Old UK
Lace, 2-ply, fingering	Extremely light, Lace yarn produces a very delicate knit on 2mm (US 0) needles. Bigger needles will produce a more open fabric.	Lace	2mm 2.25mm 2.5mm	0 1	14 13
Superfine, 3-ply, fingering, baby	Using very slim needles, Superfine yarn is perfect for lightweight, intricate lace work.	Fine-knit socks, shawls, babywear	2.75mm 3mm 3.25mm	2 3	12 11 10
Fine, 4-ply, sport, baby	Fine yarn is great for socks, and can also be used in items that feature slightly more delicate textures.	Light jumpers, babywear, socks, accessories	3.5mm 3.75mm 4mm	4 5 6	 9 8
Double knit (DK), light worsted, 5/6-ply	An extremely versatile weight yarn, DK can be used to create a wide variety of things and knits up relatively quickly.	Jumpers, light-weight scarves, blankets, toys	4mm 4.5mm	7	7
Aran, medium worsted, Afghan, 12-ply	With many yarns in this thickness using a variety of fibres to make them machine washable, Aran yarn is good for garments with thick cabled detail and functional items.	Jumpers, cabled garments, blankets, hats, scarves, mittens	5mm 5.5mm	8 9	6 5
Chunky, bulky, craft, rug, 14-ply	Quick to knit, chunky yarn is perfect for warm outerwear. Often made from lightweight fibres to prevent drooping.	Rugs, jackets, blankets, hats, legwarmers, winter accessories	6mm 6.5mm 7mm 8mm	10 10.5 11	4 3 2 0
Super chunky, super bulky, bulky, roving, 16-ply and upwards	Commonly used with very large needles, Super chunky yarn knits up very quickly. Good for beginners as large stitches make mistakes easy to spot.	Heavy blankets, rugs, thick scarves	9mm 10mm	13 15	00 000

Knitting needles

The tools of the trade, choosing your needles will ultimately depend on your project, yarn and, of course, personal preference

Knitting needles come in many types, sizes and materials. Once you become more familiar with knitting, you may find that you prefer one type over another, but the variations are designed with different patterns and yarns in mind. This guide will explain the features of each, but the best way to decide which needles suit you is to practise and find the ones that feel most comfortable.

Learning to knit on bent, dull or rough needles will be a frustrating process, so it's worth investing in a good pair that feel nice in your hands to get started. To practise knitting, it's better to work with thick yarn as this will make it easier to spot mistakes. If you're getting started with yarn that is Aran weight or thicker, your first pair of needles should be at least 5mm (US 8) in diameter.

Straight needles

Pointed at one end with a stopper at the other, straight knitting needles come in pairs and a variety of lengths. Short needles are best for small projects and long needles are recommended for wider projects, such as blankets. When you're new to knitting, it's best to start with long, straight needles, as they have more length to hold on to and give the most support to the hand.

Metal needles

Strong and not prone to bending, metal needles are good for all types of yarns, especially wool, wool blends and acrylic. Stitches move quickly on the polished surface of metal needles, which makes them quick to knit with but also unsuitable for beginners, as stitches can easily slip off the needle's tip. Metal needles of more than 8mm (US 11) in diameter can be heavy and difficult to work with.

Plastic needles

Lightweight and flexible, plastic needles can be used with all types of yarns. The smooth surface of plastic needles allows stitches to move quickly, but not as quickly as on metal needles, so the risk of stitches slipping off the needle is reduced. Larger needles are commonly made of plastic in order to reduce their weight.

Bamboo needles

Bamboo needles are strong and tend to be lighter than metal needles. The bamboo has a slight grip, which helps to keep stitches regularly spaced, creating an even knit. This also minimises the risk of stitches slipping off the needle's tip, making them an excellent choice for beginners. Bamboo needles are also recommended for arthritis sufferers, as they are warm to the touch and can warp slightly to fit the curvature of the hand.

Square needles

Although most needles are cylindrical, square needles with four flat sides make a more consistent stitch and require less hand tension to maintain in position. This makes them good for beginners and arthritis sufferers.

Image credit: KnitPro

Double-pointed and circular needles

In order to produce a tube of knitting without a seam, such as a sock or cowl, you will need to knit in the round using double-pointed or circular needles. Choosing which to use will often depend on the length of your project. Double-pointed needles (DPNs) can knit a very narrow tube, whereas circular needles are better for larger projects.

Double-pointed needles

Usually sold in sets of four or five, double-pointed needles (DPNs) have points at both ends. They are typically quite short and do not hold a lot of stitches, so are best for smaller projects, such as socks.

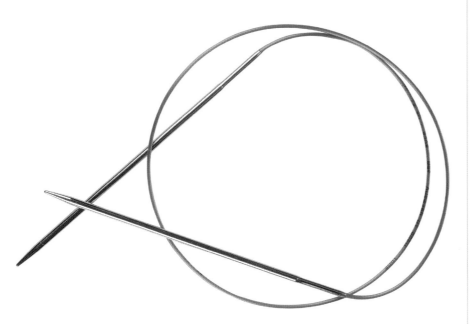

Circular needles

These are two straight needles connected with a flexible plastic cord. The cord can come in many different lengths, from 30-152cm (12-60in), and it is important to choose a length that is appropriate for your project. A good rule of thumb is to use a cord that will match or be slightly smaller than the circumference of the piece you are knitting.

Size

Knitting needles come in a variety of diameters, from as small as 1.5mm (US 000 / 00) up to 25mm (US 50). The size of the needle that you use will determine the size of the stitch you create, and most yarns will come with a recommended needle size.

There are three common needle-sizing systems: European metric, old British and American. Use this chart to convert between sizes. If your needles are not labelled by diameter, you may need to buy a needle size gauge to establish their size.

Metric (mm)	US	Old UK
1.5	000 / 00	N/A
2	0	14
2.25 / 2.5	1	13
2.75	2	12
3	N/A	11
3.25	3	10
3.5	4	N/A
3.75	5	9
4	6	8
4.5	7	7
5	8	6
5.5	9	5
6	10	4
6.5	10.5	3
7	N/A	2
7.5	N/A	1
8	11	0
9	13	00
10	15	000
12	17	N/A
15	19	N/A
20	35	N/A
25	50	N/A

Knitting kit bag

Although you can quite easily start knitting with just a pair of needles and a ball of yarn, there are lots of other useful tools available

Needle organiser

When you've built up a collection of needles of all different sizes and types, storing them can become tricky. A needle organiser keeps them all in one place and protected against damage. Depending on your preference, you can get either a needle roll or a bag, which is like a long pencil case.

Row counter

Used to keep track of how many rows you've knitted, this is another helpful tool that will save you from counting the stitches in your work. There are different types of counters available; some sit on the end of your needle and can be turned at the end of each row, while others are available as a clicker.

Pins

Useful for pinning pieces of knitting together when sewing up or pinning out to get measurements, pins with large heads are ideal, as they won't get lost in your work.

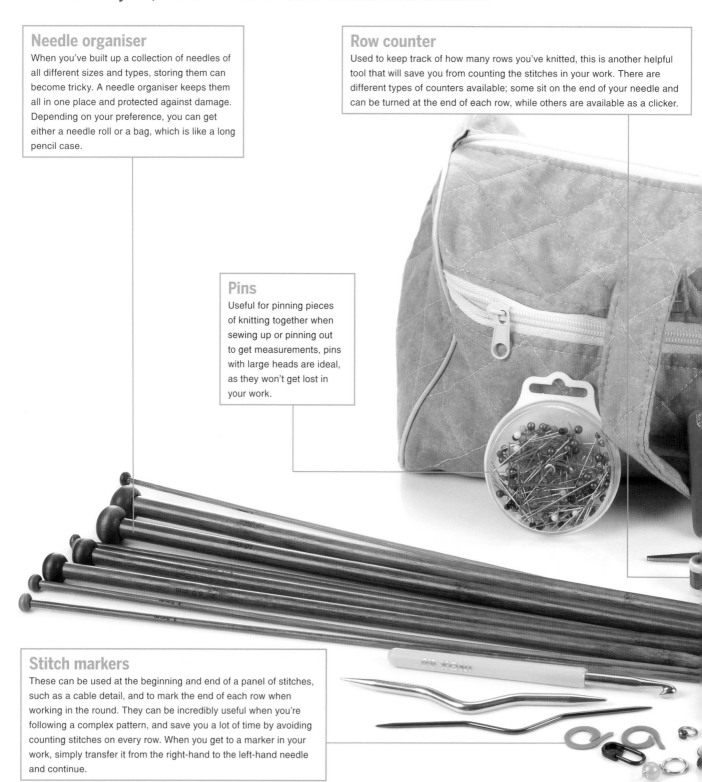

Stitch markers

These can be used at the beginning and end of a panel of stitches, such as a cable detail, and to mark the end of each row when working in the round. They can be incredibly useful when you're following a complex pattern, and save you a lot of time by avoiding counting stitches on every row. When you get to a marker in your work, simply transfer it from the right-hand to the left-hand needle and continue.

Knitting bag

Available at most craft stores, knitting bags come with many compartments for storing all your tools and materials. They are usually made of sturdy material that won't be damaged by the sharp points of your needles.

Did you know?

Knitting is actually good for your health. Studies have proven that knitting can help reduce blood pressure, decrease heart rate, and provide many benefits for those suffering with mental health issues.

Point protectors

These will prevent the points of your needles from being damaged, as well as other things being damaged by them. Sharp needles will easily puncture bags, and fragile tips can be rather prone to breaking while being transported. Point protectors will also prevent unfinished work from slipping off the ends of your needles while you are not working on your project.

Knitting needle gauge

It's essential to know what size of needle you're knitting with. If you're unsure, either because the needle has no marking or it has been rubbed off, a needle gauge will be able to tell you. All you need to do is poke the needle through the holes to find the best fit. Most will also feature a ruler to measure tension squares.

Scissors

You will need a pair of scissors for cutting off yarn and trimming edges. It's best to use a good-quality pair with sharp, short blades that will allow you to snip close to the work for a clean finish.

Stitch holders

Available in many different sizes, these are used to hold stitches that you will return to later. You can even make your own from a length of thin yarn or a safety pin.

Tape measure

A handy tool when you're knitting to exact measurements, you should always keep a tape measure nearby. Not only can you use it to measure the person you are knitting for, but also to check your tension and the size and progress of your piece of knitting.

Making a slip knot
Almost every piece that you knit will begin with this simple knot, which creates your first stitch

This is an easy and quick-to-learn knot. The slip knot is, in fact, the first loop you will place on the needle when you begin a piece of knitting, and it will form the first stitch.

There are many ways to create a slip knot, and as you practise making it, you might find that you develop your own technique. Here is just one way.

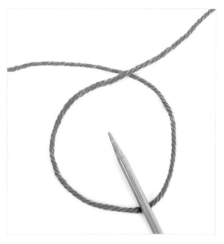

01 Make a circle
Lay out a length of yarn. Pick it up close to the ball and cross it over the yarn end (called the tail) to make a circle.

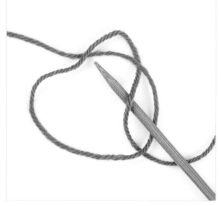

02 Bring the yarn through
Insert the tip of a needle through the circle of yarn and underneath it, then over the piece of yarn coming from the ball end. Pull this bit of yarn through the circle.

03 Knot and loop
This forms a loop on the needle and a loose knot below, as shown in the image above.

04 Tighten
With the needle in one hand, pull both ends of the yarn firmly in order to tighten the knot and the loop.

05 Check tension
Ensure the slip knot is tight enough that it won't fall off the needle or fall apart but not so tight that you can't move it along the needle.

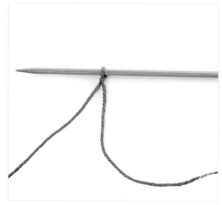

06 Assess the tail
The tail end of your yarn should be at least 10-15cm (4-6in) long so it can be woven in later. Some patterns will instruct that you leave a longer tail (called a long loose end) to use for seams or something else at a later stage.

Holding yarn & needles

Picking up your needles and yarn together for the first time might feel a bit awkward and unnatural, but it will soon become second nature

It will take practice to hold needles and yarn comfortably. You'll mostly hold the yarn and a needle in one hand at the same time, which can be complicated. For now, do what feels comfortable. As you improve, you will find a technique that works for you.

There are two styles of knitting: holding the yarn in the right hand is called English style and holding it in the left hand is called Continental style. However, knitting is ambidextrous, so whether you're right or left handed, try both to see which you prefer. technique. Here is just one way.

English style

01 Position the yarn
With your palm facing you, wrap the yarn around your little finger on your right hand. Take it across your next two fingers then under your index finger. You need to control the yarn firmly but with a relaxed hand, so that the yarn will flow through your fingers as you knit.

02 Alternative technique
If you can't get comfortable, try this technique, or any other that you prefer, instead. The main thing you need to make sure of is that the tension is enough to create even loops that are not too loose or too tight. Keep this in mind the whole time.

03 Hold the needles
Once your yarn is in position, grab your needles. The needle with the stitches about to be worked needs to be in the left hand, and the other in the right. Use the right index finger (or middle finger if you prefer) to wrap the yarn around the needle.

Continental style

01 Position the yarn
Wrap the yarn around your little finger with your palm facing you. Then take it over the next two fingers to lace it underneath your index finger. Check your tension: not too loose and not too tight.

02 Alternative technique
If that does not feel comfortable, try wrapping the yarn around a different finger. You can also try wrapping the yarn twice around the index finger, which will help you tighten the tension if you need to.

03 Hold the needles
As with English-style knitting, hold the needle with the stitches to be worked in the left hand and the other in the right. Use your left index finger to wrap the yarn around the right-hand needle when working a stitch.

Casting (binding) on

Now you're comfortable holding your needles and yarn, it's time to get knitting. The first step is casting on

TOP TIP

Don't forget that the slip knot makes your first stitch, so you need to include it when you're counting how many stitches are on your needle.

To get started, you must cast (bind) on. This creates a row of loops that will be the foundation for your knitting. There are many methods. Single-strand cast (bind) ons are simple and soft; they can be created using one or two needles. Two-strand cast (bind) ons mostly use one needle and are strong, elastic and versatile.

Here, we are going to showcase three of the most common cast (bind) ons, but there is an abundance of others with different properties that you can also use, and which will affect the look of your knitting. Don't forget to create your first stitch with a slip knot — turn back to page 16 if you need a reminder on how to do this.

01 Make a loop around your thumb
This is the simplest cast (bind) on, and is quick and easy to get on the needle. With the needle that has the slip knot on it in your right hand, wrap the working yarn around your left-hand thumb (and index finger if it's more comfortable). Hold the yarn in place in your palm.

02 Collect the loop
Put the needle tip near the crook of your thumb and underneath the yarn that is closest to you. Pull it up so that the yarn is on the needle.

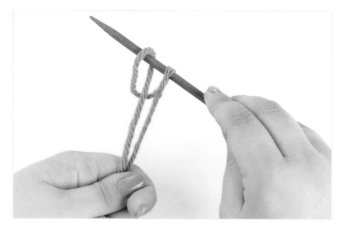

03 Tighten the stitch
Pull the loop off your thumb (and index finger if necessary) with the needle, but keep hold of the yarn in the palm of your hand. Lift the needle or pull on the yarn to tighten the stitch.

04 Repeat the process
Wrap the yarn around your left-hand thumb again and continue making loops until you have the desired number on your needle.

Cable cast (bind) on
Master this casting (binding) on alternative

01 Begin to knit

Holding the yarn in either English or Continental style, place the needle with the slip knot in your left hand. Put the tip of the right-hand needle through the loop on the left needle.

02 Make a loop

With the yarn behind the needles, wrap it under and around the right needle. With the tip of the right needle, carefully pull the yarn through the loop on the left needle.

03 Transfer to the needle

To move the loop from the right needle to the left, insert the tip of the left needle from right to left through the front of the loop. Tighten the loop by pulling both yarn ends.

04 Insert the needle

Put the tip of the right needle between the two loops on the left needle. Then, you must wrap the yarn under and around the tip of the right needle.

05 Pull the loop through

Now you need to draw the yarn through very carefully with the tip of the right needle. You should find that you have a loop on the right-hand needle.

06 Continue

Move the loop on the right needle to the left as you did in step 3. Continue, being sure to insert the needle between the first two loops on the left needle.

Long tail cast (bind) on
Create an even, stretchy edge with this cast (bind) on

01 Leave a tail
This cast (bind) on is a bit harder, as it uses two yarn strands (the working yarn and the tail) at the same time. You will need to use a long tail, one that is approximately four times as long as the desired width of your cast (bind) on. Start by holding the needle with the slip knot in your right hand. In your left hand, hold the tail going over your thumb and the working yarn over your index finger. Hold both strands in your palm.

02 Pick up the loop
Insert the tip of the needle under the loop on your thumb, much the same as when making the single cast (bind) on.

03 Go over the back
While keeping the yarn on your thumb, wrap the tip of the needle around the loop on your index finger.

04 Form the first stitch
Pull the yarn through the space next to your thumb and then up to form a stitch.

05 Tighten the stitch
Release the yarn from your thumb and pull both ends to tighten the stitch on the needle.

06 Continue the process
Loop the strands of yarn around your thumb and index finger again, and repeat the steps until you have the desired number of stitches.

Did you know?

If you have wooden knitting needles, it's very important to clean and moisturise them once or twice a year using natural wax wood cleaners.

Did you know?

The word 'knit' comes from the Old English word 'cnyttan', which literally means 'knot'.

The knit stitch

Learn the foundation stitch of knitting with this simple tutorial and you'll be making scarves, tea cosies and more in next to no time

The knit stitch (abbreviated as K in patterns) is the very first stitch that you'll learn. It is the most important stitch and even when it's used on its own you can still create great pieces from scarves to tea cosies. Now that you've learnt how to cast (bind) on — we recommend that you start off with cable cast (bind) on (page 19) — you're more than 80 per cent of the way there with knit stitch.

Working the knit stitch (K) every row is called garter stitch (g st), the result is a flat fabric with horizontal ridges of V stitches and bumps, this somewhat corrugated finish is great for making warm garments as the rows of bumps hold in warm air. Garter stitch is also often worked on the edges of flat pieces of stocking

(stockinette) stitch (st st) knitting to prevent it from curling. Once you've followed the steps and mastered the stitch, have a go at the garter stitch scarf.

> *"It's the most important stitch — even when it's used on its own you can still create great pieces"*

Knit stitch
Discover how to master the knit stitch

01 Use the cable cast (bind) on method
Following the cable cast (bind) on method on page 19, cast (bind) on a manageable 20 stitches. Hold the needle with your stitches in your left hand and with your right hand hold the yarn at the back of your needles, insert the point of right-hand needle into the left side of first stitch (loop) on the left-hand needle.

02 Maintain an even tension (gauge)
With the yarn guided by your index finger, wind it under and around the point of the right-hand needle, in an anti-clockwise direction. Keep the yarn in your right hand relatively taut, this will help to keep your work stable and maintain an even tension (gauge).

04 Finish the stitch
Move the right-hand needle little further through the stitch that you have just created, then gently pulling the right needle to your right, you can let the stitch from the left needle drop off. You have now worked one knit (K) stitch. Continue for the rest of the row. When you've worked all the stitches, swap the needles into the other hands and start again.

03 Thread the needle through the loop
With a firm hold of the left-hand needle, carefully move the right-hand needle so that you bring the tip through the loop on the left-hand needle, catching the yarn that you wound round the needle in step 1.

Cast (bind) off knitwise
Learn how to cast off kwise

01 Begin to cast (bind) off

With the yarn at the back of the work knit the first two stitches as you would normally do. Then insert the tip of the left-hand needle into the right side of the first stitch on the right-hand needle.

02 One stitch at a time

Lift the stitch over the second stitch and the tip of the right-hand needle then drop from the left needle. You have cast (bind) off one stitch. Knit the next stitch and repeat to the end of the row.

03 Loop and pull

At the end of the row you will be left with one stitch on the right needle. Cut your yarn to leave a tail of approximately 15cm (8in) and enlarge the last stitch and feed the end of the yarn through the loop and pull tightly.

Garter stitch scarf

Pick an interesting yarn with texture and colour variations in order to make a creative garter stitch scarf

While garter stitch is a simple stitch, it looks most effective when worked in an interesting yarn. Here we've chosen a super snuggly, super chunky weight yarn that has texture and subtle colour differences.

Difficulty ★☆☆☆☆

Skills needed
Knitting in rows

Finished measurements
152cm (60in)

Yarn
For this pattern you will need a super chunky yarn. In the example Sirdar Bohemia was used in Ombre. You will need approximately 135m (147yd) for the main body of the scarf, plus more for tassels.

Tension (Gauge)
7 stitches and 10 rows = 10x10cm (4x4in) in garter stitch using 15mm (US 19) needles, or size required to obtain correct tension (gauge).

Needles
15mm (US 19) needles

Other supplies
Crochet hook for tassels

Construction notes
You'll need to add in new balls of yarn for this project. Turn to page 34 to see how to do this, then turn to page 83 to find out how to darn in the ends.

Garter stitch scarf
Using 15mm needles, cast (bind) on 14 sts leaving a long tail.

Row 1: Knit.

Continue to knit every row until you have worked all three balls of yarn leaving enough to cast (bind) off or have a scarf the length that you require.
   Add your new balls at the start of the row.
   Cast (bind) off knitwise and cut the yarn leaving a long tail.

Note: If you prefer a narrower scarf, cast (bind) on fewer stitches. Similarly, to make a wider scarf, cast (bind) on more stitches.

Making up
Darn in yarn tails, however if you are adding tassels to your scarf, there is no need to darn in the cast (bind) on and cast (bind) off tails of yarn.

Making tassels

01 Wind your yarn loosely around an object to obtain the length you require.

02 Cut the yarn along the bottom edge. You will now have lengths of yarn. Be careful to keep them all the same length.

03 Taking two strands of yarn, insert your crochet hook into the end of the scarf, catch the middle of the yarn on the hook and pull through the knitting to make a loop.

04 Feed the four yarn ends through the loop and pull tight. Repeat this to add more tassels at equal intervals along both ends of the scarf. Once you have added all the tassels, cut all to the same length.

The purl stitch

Now that you have mastered the knit stitch, it's time to learn how to work its partner the purl stitch — you'll find it's not all that different

There are only two main stitches to the art of knitting. The first is knit (K), which you will have now mastered; the second is purl (P), which we will show you how to work here. When worked together with subtle variations, you will be able to make anything!

Purl stitch is effectively the reverse way to work a knit stitch. If you were to purl every row, you would end up with a piece of fabric identical to a garter stitch (g st) (knit stitch every row). However, when you work a row of knit stitches followed by a row of purl stitches and repeat these two rows, you will have a piece of fabric that has smooth 'Vs' on one side and rugged 'bumps' on the other. This is called a stocking (stockinette) stitch (st st), and you will recognise this as the standard knit fabric. Usually the 'V' side is called the right side (RS), and when this faces you on the left needle, it indicates that you knit the next row. The wrong side (WS) has bumps and indicates that you purl the next row.

When you knit a sample of stocking (stockinette) stitch, it has a tendency to curl on itself, so it is often worked alongside garter stitch (see page 22) for flat pieces and rib stitch (see page 30) for garments.

> ### "The WS has bumps and indicates you purl the next row"

01 Set up the needles
With the needle holding the unworked stitches in your left hand (LH) and the empty needle in your right hand (RH), hold the yarn at the front of your work. Insert the tip of the right-hand needle into the first stitch entering the loop from left to right.

02 Wind the yarn
Wind the yarn around the tip of the right needle, moving it from right to left in an anticlockwise direction, ensuring that you're keeping a tension on the yarn as it moves through your fingers.

> ### "When worked together with subtle variations, you will be able to make anything!"

03 Work the stitches
Work the tip of the right-hand needle through the stitch on the left needle, catching the yarn as you go and drawing it through.

Reverse stocking stitch
While on the majority of patterns, a stocking stitch (st st) shows the 'V' side as the right side of your work, sometimes reverse stocking (stockinette) stitch is called for in the design. This is simply where the 'bumpy' side becomes the right side.

04 Drop off and continue
Move the right-hand needle a little further through the stitch that you have just created, then gently pulling the right needle to your right, you can let the stitch from the left needle drop off. You have now worked 1 purl (P) stitch. Continue for the rest of the row.

Cast (bind) off purlwise (p-wise)
Sometimes a pattern will ask you to cast (bind) off on a purl row

01 Purl the first 2 stitches
With the yarn at the front of the work, purl (P) the first 2 stitches as you would normally do. Then, insert the tip of the left-hand needle into the right side of the first stitch on the right-hand needle.

02 Cast and purl
Carefully lift the stitch over the second stitch and the tip of the right-hand needle, and drop from the left needle. You have cast off 1 stitch. Purl the next stitch and repeat this method to the end of the row.

03 Cut and enlarge
At the end of the row, you will be left with 1 stitch on the right needle. Cut your yarn to leave a tail of approximately 15cm (8in). Enlarge the last stitch, feed the end of the yarn through the loop and pull tightly.

Simple cushion

This stocking stitch cushion project will help you to learn the feel of the yarn and needles as well as giving you the opportunity to grasp the technique and create an even tension (gauge)

Difficulty ★☆☆☆

Skills needed

Knitting in rows
Stocking (stockinette) stitch
Seaming

Finished measurements

Cushion covers measures 33 x 33cm (13 x 13 in) for a 36 x 36 cm (14 x 14 in) cushion pad.

Yarn

For this project you will need a DK yarn. In this example, Adriafil, Knitcol has been used in Pascal Fancy. You will need approximately 250m (274 yd).

Tension (Gauge)

18st and 25 rows = 10cm (4in) in st st using 4.5mm (US 7) needles, or size required in order to obtain the correct tension (gauge).

Needles

4.5mm (US 7) needles

Other supplies

Tapestry needle

Simple cushion

Cast (bind) on 60 stitches.
Row 1 (RS): Knit.
Row 2: Purl.
   Repeat these 2 rows until knitting measures 66cm (26in).
   Cast (bind) off.

Making up

Darn in all ends. Fold your knitted piece in half lengthways, with right sides facing each other. Sew together the two side edges. Turn the cover right side out and insert the cushion pad and sew the opening closed using mattress stitch.

TOP TIP

Why not add further interest to your cushion by making tassels and attach them to the corners.

For more confident knitters

If you're feeling more confident, start and end with 5cm (2in) of rib stitch with 66cm (26in) of stocking (stockinette) stitch in between. When making up, fold your knitting with the right sides facing so that one of the rib sections overlaps the other rib section plus 5cm (2in) of the st st to make an envelope for easy cushion pad removal.

Slipping stitches

Slipping your stitches in the correct way is a technique that is important to master, because it will ensure that your knitting looks neat and professional

To slip stitches (sl st), you must displace stitches from one needle to the other. Whether it's to decrease stitches, transfer stitches to cable needles and stitch holders, or add detail in a lace pattern, you'll use this method a lot. The result is an elongated stitch with a bar across it. Depending on whether your yarn is at the front of the work before slipping the stitch will determine whether the bar is in front or behind the slipped stitch. Unless the pattern tells you to bring the yarn to the front (yf), or take it to the back (yb), leave it where it is.

There are two ways of slipping stitches: knitwise (kwise) or purlwise (pwise). Unless the pattern instructs otherwise, slip the stitch purlwise.

Slip stitches purlwise
Master this default method

01 Prepare to purl
On both right and wrong side rows, insert the tip of the right-hand needle into the first stitch (unless otherwise stated) as if to purl the stitch.

02 Work the stitches
Drop the stitch from the left needle by sliding it onto the right. Work the next stitch as instructed, being careful not to pull the yarn too tightly.

Slip stitches knitwise
For when you are instructed

01 Prepare to knit
Slip knitwise only when instructed, as this will twist the stitch. On both right and wrong side rows, insert the tip of the right-hand needle into the first stitch (unless otherwise stated) as if to knit the stitch.

02 Work the stitches
The next part of the method is the same as if you were purling. So, drop the stitch from the left needle by sliding it onto the right. Work the next stitch as instructed, being careful not to pull the yarn too tightly.

Rib stitch

Rib is an elastic stitch that is most commonly used for welts and cuffs of garments, but used in its own right can be very useful

Rib stitch gets its name from the vertical raised and indented ridges of the worked fabric. When alternate stitches of knit (K) and purl (P) are worked along a row, you will notice that it is narrower than a piece of stocking stitch (st st) worked over the same number of stitches. This is because the fabric 'draws in', resulting in an elasticity that is perfect for cuffs and waistbands.

Most often, a garment project will ask for a section of 1x1 rib at the start of all pieces; the term 1x1 simply means that you will work a regular rib section of knit 1 (K1) stitch, then purl 1 (P1) stitch all the way across the row. In the same way a double or 2x2 rib would be worked by knitting 2 (K2) stitches, then purling 2 (P2) stitches. An irregular rib pattern will often be used for a more decorative piece of knitting, such as the tube socks on page 114 (2x1 rib).

> **"A garment project will ask for a section of 1x1 rib at the start"**

01 Knit 1 stitch

Cast (bind) on the required number of stitches as stated in the pattern, or for practice purposes, cast (bind) on 20 stitches. With yarn at the back of the work and cast (bind) on stitches on the needle in your left hand, knit 1 (K1) stitch.

TOP TIP
When working a 1x1 rib on an even number of stitches, you will always work a K st first on every row. An odd number of stitches will mean you have to alternate between K and P stitches at the start of each row.

02 Work all the stitches

Your next stitch is a purl stitch, but your yarn is at the back of your work, so bring the yarn between your needles so that it is now at the front of your work. Purl (P) the next stitch. Now take the yarn back through your needles and knit the next stitch. Continue in this way until you have worked all the stitches.

03 Look for 'Vs' and 'bumps'

Now that you have worked your first row, when you turn your knitting to work the next row, you will notice that you have alternate 'Vs' and 'bumps' below the stitches on the needle. These are handy guides to know what stitch to work next. If there is a 'V', knit (K) the stitch, and if there is a 'bump', purl (P) the stitch. After a few rows you will notice columns of alternate stitches.

Ribbed gadget cosies

Keep your technology safe in these simple-to-knit cosies. Due to its stretchy nature, rib stitch is perfect for these holders, and the raised texture will help to protect screens

TOP TIP

These make quick and easy gifts for loved ones. You could use several colours and even work in stripes. See how to do this on page 34.

Difficulty ★☆☆☆☆

Skills needed

Knitting in rows
Rib stitch
Cast (bind) off in rib

Finished measurements

Smart phone cosy:
To fit phone width 6-8cm (2.5-3in) snuggly
Tablet cosy:
To fit tablet width 13-18cm (5-7in) snuggly

Yarn

For this pattern you will need a DK yarn. In the example, Woolyknit.com Countryside Tweed has been used in Cheviot. One ball is enough to make both cosies.

Tension (Gauge)

29 sts and 28 rows = 10x10cm (4x4in) in rib stitch using 4mm (US 6) needles.

Needles

4mm (US 6) needles

Other supplies

Tapestry needle

Ribbed smartphone and tablet cosies

Cast (bind) on 32 sts for the smartphone cosy, or 64 sts for the tablet cosy.
Row 1: *Knit 1, purl 1, rep from * to end of row.
Repeat row 1 until knitting measures for your desired length to fit your device.
Cast (bind) off stitches in the K1, P1 rib pattern.

Making up

Darn in ends. Fold knitting in half width-wise and join seams along the cast (bind) on edge, and then down the long side of the cosy. Turn right side out and your cosy is ready to use.

Cast off in single rib

If you've been working a pattern in rib, you'll want to cast off in rib too. This is as simple as keeping to the pattern you've been working while you cast (bind) off. To do so in single ribbing, K1, P1, then remove the first stitch from the needle as you would for a standard cast off. Always move the working yarn to the back of the work before removing a stitch.

Moss (seed) stitch

Combining knit and purl stitches can create a pretty moss (seed) stitch which, when worked in conjunction with stocking stitch, looks great

Moss (seed) stitch, which is also known as seed stitch in the US, uses alternate knit (K) and purl (P) stitches to create a textured fabric. While it looks rather complicated, this is a very easy stitch to work and looks effective when worked in between sections of stocking stitch.

If you have mastered rib stitch, then the mechanics of working moss (seed) stitch is not too dissimilar. You simply alternate between knit and purl stitches along the row, then on the next row you knit above a 'bump' and purl above a 'v'. While it is worked in a similar way to rib stitch, moss (seed) stitch actually produces a flat fabric, which does not have an elastic quality, so it would not be good to use for welts or cuffs, unless a loose finish is required.

Garments worked in moss (seed) stitch tend to be a little bulkier due to the raised 'purl' bumps, making them the perfect cover-up for a cool day. Why not work up squares of the same stitch and row count in moss (seed) stitch in different colours, and join them together to make a cot blanket, or something larger if you're feeling ambitious?

> *"Garments worked in moss (seed) stitch are a little bulkier due to the raised 'purl' bumps"*

02 Knit and purl stitches

When you swap needles so that the stitches to be worked are in your left hand, you will notice alternate 'v' and 'bump' stitches. You have an even number of stitches to work so row 2 and all even numbered rows of moss (seed) stitch you will start with a purl stitch, then alternate between knit and purl stitches to the end of the row. So effectively you purl when there is a 'v' and knit when there is a 'bump'. When you have finished, cast (bind) off your work using the rib cast (bind) off (see page 30) following the pattern set.

01 Mimic the rib stitch

Cast (bind) on 20 stitches. Start your first row as you would with rib stitch: K1 stitch, P1 stitch, remembering to bring your yarn back and forth through the needles between stitches, all the way to the end of the row. (Do not take yarn over the needles, otherwise you will create extra stitches and holes in your work.)

Variations

A 2x2 moss (seed) stitch is where you K2 sts, then P2 sts along the row. The next row K the K (v) stitches, and P the P (bump) stitches. On the third row alternate the stitches, so K the P sts and P the K stitches. On the fourth row you K the K (v) stitches, and P the P 'bump' stitches again. Repeat these 4 rows for chequerboard-effect fabric.

Textured draught excluder

Keep your rooms nice and cozy with this textured Moss (seed) stitch draught excluder

Difficulty ★★ ☆ ☆

Skills needed

Rib stitch
Stocking (stockinette) stitch
Moss (seed) stitch
Knitting in rows
Seaming
Cast (bind) off in rib

Finished measurements

66.5cm (26in). This will fit a standard door width, but if you wish to make a longer draught excluder, work the pattern shown between ** and ** again to add a further 17cm (18in).

Yarn

For this pattern you will need an Aran weight yarn. In this example we have used Sirdar, Hayfield Bonus Aran in Petrol. You will need approximately 210m (230yd) or more if you want to make a longer draught excluder.

Tension (Gauge)

Work 18 sts and 22 rows in st st stitch to measure 10x10cm (4x4in) using 5mm (US 8) needles, or the size required to obtain the correct tension.

Needles

5mm (US 8)

Other supplies

Tapestry needle
Toy stuffing (old tights or old, cut-up t-shirts work equally well)

Textured draught excluder

Cast (bind) on 50 sts.
Row 1: *K1, P1, rep from *.
Rep row 1 a further 9 times.
***Next row (RS):* Knit.
Next row (WS): Purl.
Rep last 2 rows 12 more times ending with RS facing for next row.
Next row: *K1, P1, rep from * to end.
Next row: *P1, K1, rep from * to end.

These 2 rows form the moss (seed) stitch. Cont in moss (seed) stitch as set for a further 14 rows ending with RS facing for next row **.
Rep between ** and ** twice more.
Next row: Knit.
Next row: Purl.
Rep last 2 rows 12 more times.
Row 1: (K1, P1) to end of row.
Rep row 1 a further 9 times.
Cast (bind) off in rib pattern.

Making up

Darn in ends. With right sides facing, fold the knitting in half lengthways. Join the side edges to create a tube using a mattress stitch (see page 100). With side edges joined and the draught excluder inside out, flatten the tube, so that the join is in the middle. Now join one of the ribbed openings. Turn out the right way, stuff with preferred material, and close final end by oversewing the seams.

Joining a new yarn

If your project is going to use up more than one ball of yarn, then you will need to join the next as seamlessly as possible

There are many things that you may like to knit in one colour that, because of their size, will need more than one ball of yarn. Joining a new ball of yarn to your existing work is very simple to do and if done well can make a seamless transition — even you won't be able to tell where you made the change.

At the beginning of a row
Add a new ball of yarn to your knitting

01 Knit with the new yarn
The simplest way to join a new ball of yarn is at the beginning of a row. All you need to do is drop the old yarn and start knitting with the new. After a few stitches, tie the ends together. When you've finished the piece, darn the ends in.

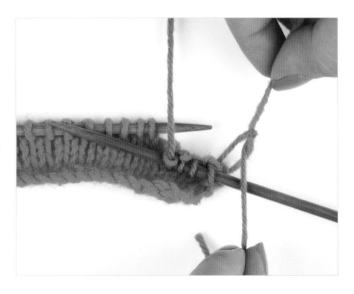

In the middle of a row
Seamlessly change yarn

01 Drop the old
Sometimes it won't be possible to join the new yarn at the end of the row. If you need to join your new yarn in the middle of a row, drop the old yarn so that it rests down the back of the piece.

02 Pick up the new
In the same way as you would at the end of a row, simply start knitting with the new yarn, and after a few stitches, tie the ends together to secure them. Weave the ends in using duplicate stitch weaving when you're finished.

Felted join
Join the same colour together first

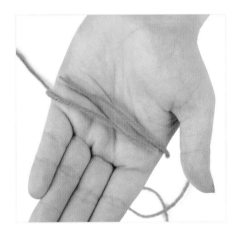

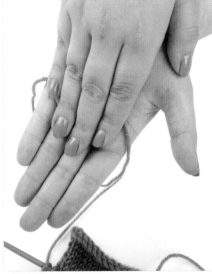

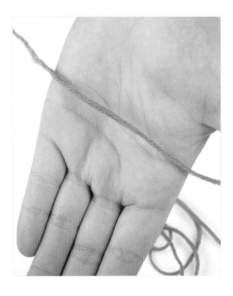

01 Pick up the ends
Although this method only works with feltable animal fibres, it will produce an almost seamless join that can be used anywhere in the row. Start by picking up the two ends of the old and new yarn and placing them in your palm, parallel to each other and heading in opposite directions. Moisten the ends with water, or simply licking your palms will do.

02 Rub them together
Between your palms, rub the two ends together firmly, but gently. The idea is to felt the fibres together using pressure, moisture and heat.

03 Knit away
The two ends will be joined. There will be a light bulge where the two have become one, but this should be barely recognisable once it is knitted into the fabric.

> *"This method (at the beginning of the row) can also be used to simply join a different coloured yarn, for example to incorporate a stripe along the rows."*

Graduating stripes table mat

Joining a new yarn is handy in all projects, but doing so neatly when incorporating stripes into your project is paramount!

Difficulty ★☆☆☆☆

Skills needed

Moss (seed) stitch
Knitting in rows
Buttonhole

Finished measurements

Approximately 23.5cm (9.25in) long and 31.5cm (12.5in) wide.

Yarn

For this project you will need a Aran weight yarn in various colours. In this example the colours Teal, Light Grey and White have been used. To make two mats, you will need one ball of each colour.

Tension (Gauge)

18 sts and 32 rows = 10cm (4in) in moss (seed) stitch on 4mm (US 6) needles.

Needles

4mm (US 6) needles

Other supplies

2 x 1.4mm buttons
Sewing needle and thread

Moss (seed) stitch pattern

Row 1: *K1, P1; rep from * to the last st, K1
Rep Row 1 as many times as stated.

Place Mat 1: Colour Variation 1 (Worked from the bottom up)

Using col 1, cast (bind) on 57 sts.
Rows 1-12: Work 12 rows in moss (seed) stitch. Change to col 2.
Row 13: Knit.
Rows 14-24: Work 11 rows in moss (seed) stitch. Change to col 3.
Row 25: Knit.
Rows 26-36: Work 11 rows in moss (seed) stitch. Change to col 1.
Row 37: Knit.
Rows 38-46: Work 9 rows in moss (seed) stitch. Change to col 2.
Row 47: Knit.
Rows 48-56: Work 9 rows in moss (seed) stitch. Change to col 3.
Row 57: Knit.
Rows 58-66: Work 9 rows in moss (seed) stitch. Change to col 1.
Row 67: Knit.
Rows 68-74: 7 rows in moss (seed) stitch.

Making up

Cast (bind) off purlwise. Darn in ends.

Note: If desired, pin out your table mat onto a flat surface to straighten the sides then spray with cold water. Leave to dry completely.

Place Mat 2: Colour Variation 2

Using col 2, cast (bind) on 57 sts.
Rows 1-12: Work 12 rows in moss (seed) stitch. Change to col 3.
Row 13: Knit.
Rows 14-24: Work 11 rows in moss (seed) stitch. Change to col 1.
Row 25: Knit.
Rows 26-36: Work 11 rows in moss (seed) stitch. Change to col 2.
Row 37: Knit.
Rows 38-46: Work 9 rows in moss (seed) stitch. Change to col 3.
Row 47: Knit.
Rows 48-56: Work 9 rows in moss (seed) stitch. Change to col 1.
Row 57: Knit.
Rows 58-66: Work 9 rows in moss (seed) stitch. Change to col 2.
Row 67: Knit.
Rows 68-74: 7 rows in moss (seed) stitch.

Making up

Cast (bind) off purlwise. Darn in ends.

Strap

MAKE ONE PER TABLE MAT
If you wish to make a strap with button hole, you can find the technique needed on page 84.
Using col 3, cast (bind) on 35 sts.
Row 1 (WS): Purl.
Row 2: K3, yo (to create a stitch, which becomes the buttonhole), then k2tog, K to end.
Cast (bind) off.

Making up

Darn in ends.

For each mat: Roll up your table mat and place the strap around the mat to position the button. Stitch the button in place and fasten the strap around the mat

Simple increases

Not all knitting is worked straight; for garments and some other projects you will need to increase the number of stitches you work

In order to change the shape of your knitting, you'll need to increase and decrease the number of stitches that you work. Here we will focus on increasing (inc) stitches. There are many ways to increase stitches, and some are more decorative than others. We will show you some of the most common ways to increase the number of stitches that you work. Once you become more experienced in knitting techniques, you'll be able to understand the directions on patterns that instruct you to increase in alternative ways.

Most increases add one or two stitches at a time, and usually at the end of rows. In order to keep a neat selvedge, you will usually perform an increase one stitch in. You'll notice that the shaping will travel diagonally, and sometimes the increase stitch will form part of the design.

If you have to work increases on multiple rows, it's a good idea to keep a notebook and pen to hand; this way you can note down how many increases you have worked either by tally charts or any other method that will help you remember. You'll find this particularly helpful if you have to leave your knitting at some point.

TOP TIP
If you have to make several increases across the row for a designated number of rows, use stitch markers on your needle so that the increase positions are easily seen.

Knit into front and back of stitch (kfb)
When you work this increase, it forms a bar effect, giving it the alternative name of bar increase

01 Knit the stitch
Knit (K) the next stitch, but don't drop the working loop off the left-hand needle. Insert the tip of the right needle into the back of the loop on the left needle.

02 Wind the yarn
Wind the yarn around the tip of the right needle as if working a knit stitch (K), catch the yarn and pull it through the loop, dropping the stitch off the left needle.

03 Continue
You have now created an extra stitch. Continue to work the rest of the row as instructed in your pattern.

Purl into front and back of stitch (pfb)

Increasing on a purl row is rare, but there may be occasions when you need to do so

01 Purl the next stitch

Purl (P) the next stitch, but don't drop the working loop off the left-hand needle. Insert the tip of the right needle into the back of the loop on the left needle from left to right.

02 Wind the yarn

Wind the yarn around the tip of the right needle as if working a purl stitch, catch the yarn and pull it through the loop, dropping the stitch off the left needle.

03 Continue

You have now created an extra stitch. Continue to work the rest of the row as instructed in your pattern.

Make 1 Knitwise (M1 or M1K)

Favoured for increases in the middle of a row, as it's almost invisible

01 Knit to increase

Knit (K) to the point in the pattern that instructs you to increase (inc). Guide the tip of the left needle and insert it under the horizontal strand between the previous and next stitch.

02 Wind the yarn

Insert the tip of the right needle into the back of the raised strand, wind yarn around needle tip as if to knit (K) the stitch, and draw the yarn through.

03 Drop the loop

Drop the loop from the left needle. You have now 'made' another stitch. If you didn't work into the back of the loop, you would create a hole in your work.

Make 1 Purlwise (M1 or M1P)

Perfect for toy making and increasing in the middle of a row

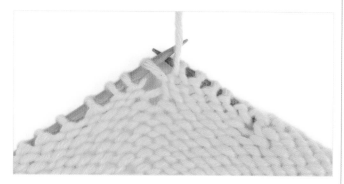

01 Work to increase

Work to the point in the pattern that instructs you to increase. Guide the tip of the left needle and insert it from front to back under the horizontal strand between the previous and next stitch.

02 Wind the yarn

Insert the tip of the right needle into the back of the raised strand from left to right, wind the yarn around the needle tip as if to purl the stitch, and draw the yarn through.

03 Drop the loop

Drop the loop from the left needle. You have now 'made' another stitch. If you didn't work into the back of the loop, you would create a hole in your work.

Simple purse

It's now time to put everything you've learned into practice and make a simple but attractive purse to carry your coins

Difficulty ★★☆☆☆

Skills needed

Increasing
Decreasing (see page 42)
Knitting in rows
Seaming

Finished measurements

Purse measures approx 12.5cm (5in) at widest part x 8cm (3¼in) measured laid flat.

Yarn

For this project you will need a DK yarn. In this example we have used Patons Diploma Gold DK in Violet. You will need one ball of your chosen yarn.

Tension (Gauge)

22st and 30 rows = 10cm (4in) in st st using 4mm needles — tension is not critical for this project.

Needles

4mm (US 6) needles

Other supplies

Tapestry needle
2 press studs (poppers)

Did you know?

Early knitting needles were crafted out of bone, ivory, wood and even tortoise shell!

"If you didn't work into the back of the loop, you would create a hole in your work"

Simple purse

Cast (bind) on 20 sts.

Knit 3 rows.

Start increases

Row 1 (RS): K2, kfb, K to last 3 sts kfb, K2.
Row 2: K2, P to last 2 sts, K2.

Rep these 2 rows until you have 30 sts.

Next row: Knit.
Next row: K2, P to last 2 sts, K2 (28 sts).

Rep last 2 rows 4 more times.

Create fold

Next row (RS): Purl.
Next row (WS): Knit.

Next row: Knit.
Next row: K2, P to last 2 sts, K2.

Rep last 2 rows 4 more times.

Start decreases

Row 1: K2, ssk, K to last 3 sts k2tog, K2.
Row 2: K2, P to last 2 sts, K2.

Rep last 2 rows until 20 sts rem.

Work Row 1 again.

Create flap fold

Next row (WS): Knit.

Flap

Row 1: K2, ssk, K to last 3 sts k2tog, K2
(18 sts).
Row 2: K2, P to last 2 sts, K2.

Rep these 2 rows until 10 sts rem.

Knit 2 rows.
Cast (bind) off knitwise.

Making up

Darn in the ends and block them with a hot
iron and damp tea towel with the wrong side
facing up, being careful not to press the garter
stitch edges.

With right sides facing, join the sides of the
purse. Sew on the press studs to the corners
of the underside of the flap and corresponding
places on the body of the purse.

Decorative increases

The stitches used here may also be used
to create decorative effects, for example
in ripple stitch techniques (page 42) or in
lace garments (page 46). When a variety
of increase and decrease methods
are worked together the results can be
beautiful and intricate. Don't shy away
from these types of patterns; you have
mastered knit and purl, and they are your
foundations to make anything.

Simple decreases

Use these simple stitches to shape your work or pair them with increases to create texture and lace patterns

If you're creating a garment that needs to get smaller as it goes along, for example a hat, then you will need to use decreases (dec) to reduce the number of stitches on your needles, and therefore the size of your piece. Decreases can also be used together with increases (inc) to add decorative elements to your work. Knitting or purling two stitches together (k2tog or p2tog) is one of the simplest decreases, and will cause your work to lean to the right. In order to make your work lean to the left, you will need to use a different decrease (see slip slip knit (ssk) on page 51). These decreases can be used together to create interesting shapes and textures in your work. These stitches can also be adapted to decrease by more than one stitch at a time by knitting/purling more than two together at a time.

Knit two together (k2tog)
Check out the knitting way

01 Needle through two
Insert the right-hand needle through the second and then the first stitch on the right needle, from left to right, as if to knit.

02 Make a new stitch
Knit (K) into the two stitches by wrapping the working yarn around the tip of the right-hand needle, then pull it through both loops to create the new stitch. Drop both of the old stitches off the left-hand needle

03 Slant to the right
Your stitch count will now be reduced by one, because two stitches have been turned into one. You will see that your decrease (dec) slants to the right.

Purl two together (p2tog)
Now try the purling way

01 Needle through two
Insert the right-hand needle through the first and then the second stitch on the right needle, from right to left, as if to purl.

02 Make a new stitch
Purl (P) into the two stitches by wrapping the working yarn around the tip of the right-hand needle, then pull it through both loops to create the new stitch. Drop both of the old stitches off the left-hand needle

03 Slant to the right
Your stitch count will be reduced by one as you've joined two together. You will see that your decrease (dec) slants to the right.

Bobbles tea cosy

It's undoubtedly one of the most rewarding items to knit! Learn how to make the perfect tea cosy, ready to keep your hot drinks hot

Difficulty ★★★☆☆

Skills needed

Decreasing
Knitting in rows
Bobbles
Seaming
Pompom

Finished measurements

23cmx21cm (9x8in) laid flat

Yarn

For this project you will require an Aran weight yarn. In the shown example, Drops Alaska and Drops Nepal were used. The Alaska is 100% wool, while the Nepal is 65% wool and 35% alpaca.
Colour 1: Off White; 2 x balls
Colour 2: Grey Pink; 1 x ball
Colour 3: Goldenrod; 1 x ball
Colour 4: Light Olive; 1 x ball
Colour 5: Cerise; 1 x ball

Tension (Gauge)

18 sts and 24 rows = 10cm (4in) in stocking stitch

Needles

5mm (US 8) needles

Other supplies

Tapestry needle

Pattern notes

To make the bobbles:
K into front, back and front of next st, turn and K3, turn and P3, turn and K3, turn and sl1, k2tog, psso.
On the sample, 16 bobbles in four different colours are worked on each side.

Bobbles tea cosy

Make 2 pieces.
With col 1, cast (bind) on 45 sts.
Knit 4 rows.
Starting with a purl row, work in stocking stitch until work measures 13cm (5in), adding bobbles in multiple colours randomly, working bobbles on any knit row.

Top shaping

Continuing to add bobbles on knit rows, shape as follows, starting with a knit row.

Row 1 (dec): K7, k2tog *K6, k2tog * work from * to * to last 4 sts, K4 — 40 sts.
Row 2 and every following alternate row: Purl.
Row 3 (dec): K6, k2tog, *K5, k2tog*, work from * to * to last 4 sts, K4 — 35 sts.

Row 5 (dec): K5, k2tog, *K4, k2tog*, work from * to * to last 4 sts, K4 — 30 sts.
Row 7 (dec): K4, k2tog, *K3, k2tog*, work from * to * to last 4 sts, K4 — 25 sts.
Row 9 (dec): K3, k2tog, *K2, k2tog, work from * to * to end — 19 sts.
Row 11 (dec): K2, k2tog, *K1, k2tog,* work from * to * to end — 13 sts.
Row 13 (dec): K2tog to last st, K1 — 7 sts.

Row 15 (dec): Cast off remaining sts.
Rep for second piece.
Press edges under a damp cloth.
Pin onto teapot to mark where gaps for handle and spout need to be. Sew up seams, leaving gaps for handle and spout.

Pompom

Using col 2, make pompom. Trim and sew onto top centre, secure.

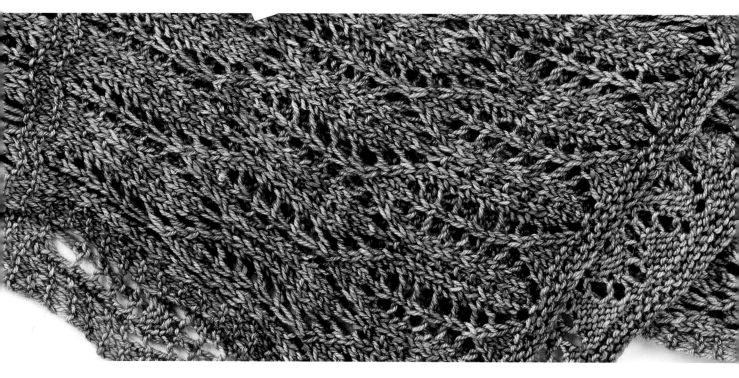

Yarn-over increases

A more decorative method than practical increases, yarn overs add stitches, but also create a hole

Common in lace work and often used for making eyelets, a yarn-over increase is made by looping the yarn around the right-hand needle before making the next stitch. It is important that the loop is wrapped around the needle in the correct way or it will become crossed when worked in the next row, which closes the hole. Yarn overs are normally worked in between two stitches as opposed to at the beginning or end of a row in order to create decorative holes and gaps in the knit.

TOP TIP

As yarn-over increases are mostly used to add decorative holes to knitting, they will often be paired with a decrease. Pair a double yarn over with a k2tog before the increase and a ssk immediately after for a pretty flower bud effect.

Yarn over between knit stitches
Add decorative holes

01 Bring the yarn over
In between two stitches, bring the yarn forward (yf) and wrap it over the top of the right-hand needle. Then work the next knit stitch in the usual way.

02 Check stitch
When you have completed the knit stitch, you will see that the yarn-over increase (yo) is correctly formed on the right-hand needle with the right leg of the loop in front

03 Purl as usual
When you reach the yarn over (yo) on the next row, purl it through the front of the loop in the usual way. This will ensure it creates the open stitch below.

Yarn over between purl stitches
Make decorative holes between purl stitches

01 Bring the yarn over
In between two stitches, bring the yarn backwards and wrap it over the top of the right-hand needle. Work the next stitch as usual.

02 Check stitch
When you have completed the purl stitch, you will see that the yarn-over increase (yo) is correctly formed on the right-hand needle with the right leg of the loop in front.

03 Knit as usual
When you reach the yarn over (yo) on the next row, knit it through the front of the loop in the usual way. This will ensure it creates the open stitch below.

Double yarn over
A bigger hole, great for buttonholes

01 Bring the yarn over twice
In between two knit stitches, bring the yarn forward (yf) and wrap it over the top of the right-hand needle. Then bring it to the front between the needles and wrap it over the top of the right-hand needle again.

02 Knit the next stitch
With the yarn in the back, knit the next stitch in the usual way. This creates two new loops on the right-hand needle.

03 Purl then knit
When you reach the yarn overs on the next row (a purl row), purl the first and then knit the second. This creates a bigger hole than a single yarn over that is great for buttonholes.

Simple lace scarf

Combine the increase and decrease techniques to create a feminine and pretty lace scarf

Difficulty ★★★☆☆

Skills needed

Increasing
Decreasing
Lace
Knitting in rows
Working from a chart or written directions

Finished measurements

Approximately 22x160cm (9x63in)

Yarn

For this project you will need a 3-ply yarn. In the example, Malabrigo Sock yarn was used, it is 100% wool. It uses the Aguas shade. You will need a total of 402m (440yd).

Tension (Gauge)

25 sts and 26 rows = 10cm (4in) in Lace Pattern 2

Needles

4mm (US 6) needles

Other supplies

2 removable stitch markers
Tapestry needle

Notes

If you find charts difficult to work with, don't despair. Many designers usually provide written versions of stitch patterns for those knitters who prefer to use them. If not, it is very easy to create your own. All you need to do is write down the stitches in each row, remembering to read right side (RS) rows from right to left and wrong side (WS) rows from left to right.

Janine Le Cras

Janine is a lifelong knitter who learned to knit at her grandmother's knee. After a break she discovered the world of knitting on the web, which had a new and vibrant image, and was re-inspired to pick up her needles.

Note: Find out how to read stitch symbol charts by turning to page 153.

Simple lace scarf

Cast (bind) on 55 sts.
Knit 4 rows.

Next row: K3, PM, following the chart or written instructions, work Lace Pattern 1, working the sts enclosed by the red lines 6 times in total, PM, K3.

Note: The markers are there to remind you that the three stitches at either edge are to be worked in garter stitch as a border. Garter stitch is great for borders on scarves and shawls as it prevents the edges of the work from curling in.

You might want to add more markers in different colours from the edging markers between each repeat of the lace pattern across your scarf to help you keep track of where you are in the pattern. To do this, add a marker to your needle between every set of 8 stitches (not including the edging stitches).
Continue following the chart or written directions for Lace Pattern 1, using the key to identify the different stitches used, until you have completed all 16 rows shown. Then repeat those 16 rows a further 2 times.
Knit 4 rows.

Next row: K3, sm, following the chart or written instructions, work Lace Pattern 2, working the sts enclosed by the red lines 6 times in total, sm, K3.

Note: If you used extra stitch markers to divide up your repeats of the lace pattern, you need to remove these and reposition them as Lace Pattern 2 has a different number of stitches in each repeat than Lace Pattern 1. Lace Pattern 2 has 6 stitches in a repeat, so you need to place a stitch marker between each set of 6 stitches (not including the edging stitches). Note that on the chart there is a single stitch after the border sts, but before the first pattern repeat, so you might want to place a stitch marker after that stitch to remind you where your first pattern repeat begins.

Continue following the chart or written directions for Lace Pattern 2 until you have completed all 12 rows of the chart. Then repeat those 12 rows a further 21 times.
Knit 4 rows.

Next row: K3, sm, following chart or written instructions, work Lace Pattern 3, working the sts enclosed by the red lines 8 times in total, sm, K3.

Note: If you are using the optional stitch markers, you need to move them to 8-stitch intervals as for the first chart.

Continue following the chart or written directions for Lace Pattern 3 until you have completed all 16 rows of the chart. Then repeat those 16 rows a further 2 times.
Knit 4 rows.
Cast (bind) off.

Making up

Lace always needs to be blocked to bring out its best qualities. Simply soak the scarf in water with a little wool wash added, rinse it, and squeeze out as much water as possible. Wrapping it in a towel and then treading all over it is a pretty good way to get the most water out of it once you have squeezed out as much as you can by hand. Don't wring your knitting, just squeeze it firmly. You don't want to felt it!

Once you have removed as much water as possible, pin out the scarf to the dimensions given in the pattern on a soft surface such as blocking mats. If you don't have blocking mats, a carpet or a spare bed works just as well.

As you pin out the scarf, you will see that the lace opens out so that you can see the pattern created by all those decreases and yarn overs.

Try to keep the edges of the scarf straight either by using blocking wires threaded through or lots of pins short distances apart so as not to make scalloped edges down the sides.

Leave the scarf pinned out until it is completely dry, then unpin, sew in any ends and wear with pride!

Lace pattern 1

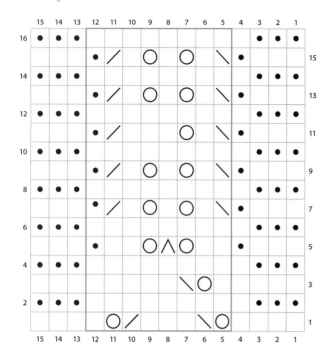

Row 6 (WS): K3, sm, P to last 3 sts, sm, K3.
Row 7 (RS): K3, sm, P1, (ssk, [K1, yo] 2 times, K1, k2tog, P1), work sts in brackets 6 times in all, sm, K3.
Row 8 (WS): K3, sm, P to last 3 sts, sm, K3.
Row 9 (RS): K3, sm, P1, (ssk, [K1, yo] 2 times, K1, k2tog, P1), work sts in brackets 6 times in all, sm, K3.
Row 10 (WS): K3, sm, P to last 3 sts, sm, K3.
Row 11 (RS): K3, sm, P1, (ssk, [K1, yo] 2 times, K1, k2tog, P1), work sts in brackets 6 times in all, sm, K3.
Row 12 (WS): K3, sm, P to last 3 sts, sm, K3.
Row 13 (RS): K3, sm, P1, (ssk, [K1, yo] 2 times, K1, k2tog, P1), work sts in brackets 6 times in all, sm, K3.
Row 14 (WS): K3, sm, P to last 3 sts, sm, K3.
Row 15 (RS): K3, sm, P1, (ssk, [K1, yo] 2 times, K1, k2tog, P1), work sts in brackets 6 times in all, sm, K3.
Row 16 (WS): K3, sm, P to last 3 sts, sm, K3.

Written Versions of the Lace Patterns

Row 1 (RS): K3, sm, K1, (yo, ssk, K3, k 2tog, yo, K1), work sts in brackets 6 times in all, sm, K3.
Row 2 (WS): K3, sm, P to last 3 sts, sm, K3.
Row 3 (RS): K3, sm, K1, (K1, yo, ssk, K1, k2tog, yo, K2), work sts in brackets 6 times in all, sm, K3.
Row 4 (WS): K3, sm, P to last 3 sts, sm, K3.
Row 5 (RS): K3, sm, P1, (K2, yo, sl1, k2tog, psso, yo, K2, P1), work sts in brackets 6 times in all, sm, K3.

Lace pattern 2

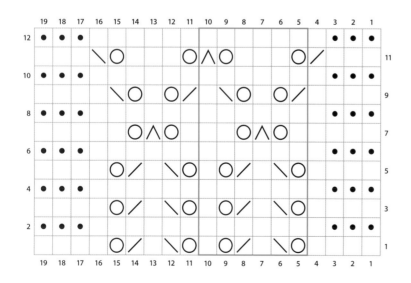

Written Versions of the Lace Patterns

Row 1 (RS): K3, sm, K1 (yo, ssk, K1, k2tog, yo, K1), work sts in brackets 8 times in all, sm, K3.
Row 2 (WS): K3, sm, P to last 3 sts, sm, K3.
Row 3 (RS): K3, sm, K1 (yo, ssk, K1, k2tog, yo, K1), work sts in brackets 8 times in all, sm, K3.
Row 4 (WS): K3, sm, P to last 3 sts, sm, K3.
Row 5 (RS): K3, sm, K1 (yo, ssk, K1, k2tog, yo, K1), work sts in brackets 8 times in all, sm, K3.
Row 6 (WS): K3, sm, P to last 3 sts, sm, K3.
Row 7 (RS): K3, sm, K1, (K1, yo, sl1, k2tog, psso, yo, K2), work sts in brackets 8 times in all, sm, K3.
Row 8 (WS): K3, sm, P to last 3 sts, sm, K3.
Row 9 (RS): K3, sm, K1, (k2tog, yo, K1, yo, ssk, K1), work sts in brackets 8 times in all, sm, K3.
Row 10 (WS): K3, sm, P to last 3 sts, sm, K3.
Row 11 (RS): K3, sm, K1, (yo, K3, yo, sl1, k2tog, psso), work sts in brackets 8 times in all, sm, K3.
Row 12 (WS): K3, sm, P to last 3 sts, sm, K3.

Lace pattern 3

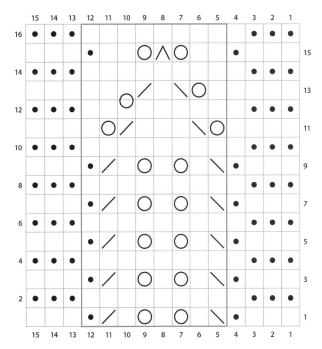

Written Versions of the Lace Patterns

Row 1 (RS): K3, sm, P1, (ssk, [K1, yo] 2 times, K1, k2tog, P1), work sts in brackets 6 times in all, sm, K3.
Row 2 (WS): K3, sm, P to last 3 sts, sm, K3.
Row 3 (RS): K3, sm, P1, (ssk, [K1, yo] 2 times, K1, k2tog, P1), work sts in brackets 6 times in all, sm, K3.
Row 4 (WS): K3, sm, P to last 3 sts, sm, K3.
Row 5 (RS): K3, sm, P1, (ssk, [K1, yo] 2 times, K1, k2tog, P1), work sts in brackets 6 times in all, sm, K3.
Row 6 (WS): K3, sm, P to last 3 sts, sm, K3.
Row 7 (RS): K3, sm, P1, (ssk, [K1, yo] 2 times, K1, k2tog, P1), work sts in brackets 6 times in all, sm, K3.
Row 8 (WS): K3, sm, P to last 3 sts, sm, K3.
Row 9 (RS): K3, sm, P1, (ssk, [K1, yo] 2 times, K1, k2tog, P1), work sts in brackets 6 times in all, sm, K3.
Row 10 (WS): K3, sm, P to last 3 sts, sm, K3.
Row 11 (RS): K3, sm, K1, (yo, ssk, K3, k2tog, yo, K1), work sts in brackets 6 times in all, sm, K3.
Row 12 (WS): K3, sm, P to last 3 sts, sm, K3.
Row 13 (RS): K3, sm, K1, (K1, yo, ssk, K1, k2tog, yo, K2), work sts in brackets 6 times in all, sm, K3.
Row 14 (WS): K3, sm, P to last 3 sts, sm, K3.
Row 15 (RS): K3, sm, P1, (K2, yo, sl1, k2tog, psso, yo, K2, P1), work sts in brackets 6 times in all, sm, K3.
Row 16 (WS): K3, sm, P to last 3 sts, sm, K3.

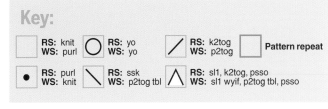

Key:

| | RS: knit / WS: purl | ○ | RS: yo / WS: yo | ╱ | RS: k2tog / WS: p2tog | | Pattern repeat |
| • | RS: purl / WS: knit | ╲ | RS: ssk / WS: p2tog tbl | ⋀ | RS: sl1, k2tog, psso / WS: sl1 wyif, p2tog tbl, psso | | |

Textural decreases

Use these decreases in order to add texture and direction to your shaped knitting

TOP TIP

Placing a stitch marker on your needle at the point where you need to decrease, if you are carrying out decreases on multiple rows will help you keep your place.

In the same way that patterns call for stitches to be increased (inc), you will sometimes need to decrease (dec) the number of stitches you work in order to create different shapes.

The guides on page 42 have already explained the basic decreases of knit two stitches together (k2tog), and purl two stitches together (p2tog), and while these are the most commonly used, the four decreases on this page can offer a more subtle decorative stitch to your knitting. For example, slip, slip, knit (ssk) is a common decrease on sock designs to ensure that the stitches on one side of the toe slant in the right direction. Also see the bunting pattern on page 116, ssk is used on right side of the triangle to follow the contour of the shape to the bottom point, it is coupled with k2tog ,which slants to the right on the other end of the row. A variety of decrease stitches are also used in lacework patterns, usually just before or just after a yarn-over increase to create pretty textural patterns.

> "A variety of decrease stitches are also used in lacework to create pretty textural patterns"

Slip 1, knit 1, pass slipped stitch over (sl1, K1, psso)
This decrease stitch will slant to the left of your knitting, so is worked on the right edge

01 Drop a stitch
Insert the tip of the right needle into the next stitch on the left needle as if to knit it, but instead slip it off the left needle without working it, then knit the next stitch.

02 Pick up the stitch
With the tip of the left needle, insert it from left to right into the front of the slipped stitch.

03 Lift it up and over
Lift the slipped stitch up and over the knitted stitch, in much the same way as you would do for casting off. You have now passed the slipped stitch over the knitted stitch and decreased the number of stitches by one.

Slip, slip, knit (ssk)
Often used in sock design

01 Slip it without working
Insert the tip of the right needle into the next stitch on the left needle as if to knit it, but instead slip it off the left needle without working it. Repeat for the next stitch.

02 Knit them together
Guide the tip of the left needle into the front loops of the two slipped stitches. Wind the yarn anticlockwise around the tip of the right needle and knit the stitches together.

03 Decrease
You have now decreased by one stitch, notice how it slants to the left; this decrease is often used on the right hand edge of knitted pieces.

Slip, slip, purl (ssp)
Not commonly used for decreases, usually used in lace

01 Slip two stitches
Slip the next two stitches, individually, knitwise (insert needle as if to knit the stitch, but without working slip it from left to right needle). Insert the left needle into the front loops of both the slipped stitches and transfer them back to the left needle.

02 Pick up both stitches
With the right needle at the back of the work, insert it first from left to right into the second stitch, then into first stitch. Bring right-hand needle tip to the front of work.

03 Slip them off
Wrap yarn anticlockwise around tip of right needle as if to purl, then draw yarn through both loops and slip them off the left needle.

Double decreases
Learn how to decrease two stitches at once

01 Knit three stitches together (k3tog)
This is essentially the same as k2tog. Guide the tip of the right needle into the left side of the third stitch on the left needle, then push it through the second and first stitch. Wind yarn around needle and knit the three stitches together. Two stitches have been decreased.

02 Double slip decrease (sk2p)
Slip the next stitch knitwise from left to right needle, knit the next two stitches together, then using the tip of the left needle, insert it into the slipped stitch and lift it over the worked stitch and off the needle.

03 Slip 2, K1, pass slipped stitch over (s2 K1 psso)
Insert the right needle into the first 2 stitches on the left needle as if to k2tog, but slip them off onto the right needle, K1, then insert the left needle into the two slipped stitches from left to right and lift them over the worked stitch and off the needle

Working on double-pointed needles

Double-pointed needles (DPNs) are used to knit a tubular shape such as socks, and are often used to make the yokes of jumpers

For centuries people have been knitting socks and stockings, and history books suggest that most of this knitting was done on double-pointed needles (DPNs). Whole villages of women, men and children were part of the sock knitting industry until the dawn of mechanisation and knitting machines made the process faster and cheaper.

Now, though, sock knitting has become popular again, and while they can be made on a circular needle, they're just as easy to knit on four or five double-pointed needles. While the prospect of knitting

with more than two needles can be daunting, when you actually get started you'll see that the process makes perfect sense. All you are doing is transferring the stitches of one needle to an empty needle, knitting around and around in a spiral.

Socks are knit on short double-pointed needles (DPNs), but longer ones are available, and these can be used to work jumpers in the round, up to the armholes. The sleeves are then worked separately, in the round, then the yoke and neck can be worked in the round. This is the perfect way to knit for those who dislike seaming.

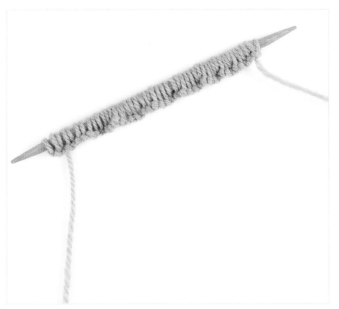

01 Cast (bind) on stitches

Cast (bind) on the number of stitches as specified in your pattern. If you're starting with a rib, you need a nice stretchy cast (bind) on such as the long tail cast (bind) on (page 20).

02 Arrange stitches

Evenly distribute the cast (bind) on stitches across 3 or 4 needles — most sock patterns suggest 3 needles but either way you will work in the same way. Place the needles on a flat surface and arrange as illustrated with the working tail of yarn on the right and all cast (bind) on loops facing inwards. Ensure that there is no twist between the needles, as this will show when you knit your first round.

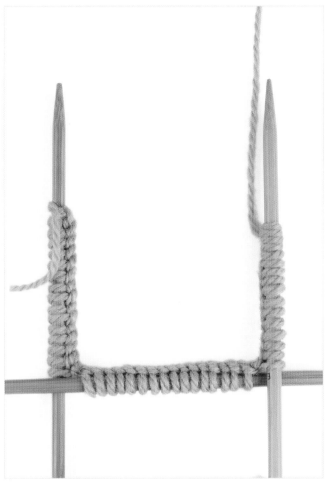

03 Join the round

Slip the first stitch off the left needle, onto the right needle to meet your last cast (bind) on stitch. Now insert the tip of the left needle into the last cast (bind) on stitch and slip it over the stitch you just slipped and onto the left needle. Now you are ready to work. With your fourth needle, start to knit in the round. As you are working in the round, it is difficult to see the beginning and end of each round, so place a stitch marker between the first and second stitch.

TOP TIP

If the stitches become crowded on one needle, use needle stops to prevent stitches falling off or add in a double-pointed needle (DPN) and redistribute the stitches.

Tension (gauge)

When changing needles it is essential to keep an even tension (gauge). If the stitches are too loose at the needle junction, a ladder will appear in your knitting. To avoid this, start knitting with the new needle on top of the old, and pull the first stitch tight.

Picot-topped ankle socks

Learn how to make this pretty project using the below pattern and achieve a decoratively topped sock you can be proud of

Difficulty ★★★☆☆

Skills needed

Decreasing
Lace stitches
Pick up & knit
Knitting in rounds
Seaming
Turning a heel

Finished measurements

The pattern is designed to fit a women's UK size 6 (US size 8) of average width, but the length can be adjusted — see notes in the pattern.

Yarn

For this pattern you will need a 4-ply yarn. For the example, Rowan Fine Art yarn was used in Rowan. You will need roughly 250m (275yd).

Tension (Gauge)

30 stitches and 38 rounds = 10cm (4in) in stocking (stockinette) stitch (st st)

Needles

2.75mm (US 2) 5x double-pointed needles (DPNs)

Other supplies

1 stitch marker
Tapestry needle

Construction notes

Both socks are worked in the same way

Picot-topped ankle socks

Cast (bind) 60 sts.

Arrange over 4 needles as follows:
Needles 1 & 3: 16 sts.
Needles 2 & 4: 14 sts, being careful not to twist the stitches.

Slip the first stitch on the LH needle onto the RH needle, then pass the first stitch on the RH needle over the top of the stitch you just slipped and place it on the LH needle. This will be the first stitch you work.

Place a stitch marker between stitches 1 and 2 to denote the beginning of the round.

Rnd 1: (K1, P1) to end of rnd.
Rep Rnd 1 3 more times.
Next rnd: (K2tog, yo) to end of rnd. This will create the pretty picot edge around the top of the sock.

Rep round 1 4 more times.
Knit 8 rounds.

Next rnd: (K2, k2tog, yo) to end of rnd.
Knit 4 rounds.
Next rnd: (k2tog, yo, K2) to end of rnd.
Knit 8 rounds

Note: For a longer sock cuff, add more knit rounds here.

Divide for heel

Knit the first 30 sts on to one needle, leaving the rem sts on 2 spare needles.

Turn and working in rows on the first 30 sts, work as follows:

Row 1: Sl1, P to end.
Row 2: Sl1, K to end.

Repeat these 2 rows 8 times more. Then work Row 1 again.

Turn heel

Row 1 (RS): Sl1, K16, ssk, K1. Turn work.
Row 2 (WS): Sl1, P5, p2tog, P1. Turn work.
Row 3 (RS): Sl1, K6, ssk, K1. Turn work.
Row 4 (WS): Sl1, P7, p2tog, P1. Turn work.
Cont in this way, working 1 more st each row before dec until 18 sts remain.
Next row: Sl1, K to last 2 sts, ssk.
Next row: Sl 1, P to last 2 sts, p2tog. (16 sts)

Gusset

With RS facing, K8 sts onto one needle.
Needle 1 (next needle): K next 8 sts, then pick up and K 10 sts down side of heel.
Needle 2: Knit across 30 sts that were held on spare needles.
Needle 3: Pick up and K10 sts up side of heel flap, then K the 8 sts on the first needle.

Continue as follows:
Rnd 1:
Needle 1 (dec): K to last 3 sts, k2tog, K1.
Needle 2: K all sts.
Needle 3 (dec): K1, ssk, K to end of needle.

Rnd 2: Knit all sts.

Rep last 2 rnds until:
Needle 1: 15 sts rem.
Needle 2: 30 sts.
Needle 3: 15 sts rem.

Now knit every round until work, from heel to needles, measures 20cm (8in).

Note: Alternatively, to work a shorter or longer foot, measure the wearer's foot from the back of the heel to the base of the big toe.
Use this measurement in place of the measurement above.

Shape toe

Rnd 1:
Needle 1 (dec): K to last 3 sts, k2tog, K1.
Needle 2 (dec): K1, ssk, K to last 3 sts, k2tog, K1.
Needle 3 (dec): K1, ssk, K to end of needle.

Rnd 2: Knit all sts.

Rep last 2 rounds until 40 sts rem.
Rep round 1 until 24 sts rem.

Place stitches from needles 1 and 3 onto one needle. With RS facing, graft the toe using kitchener stitch.

Making up

Darn in ends. Turn sock inside out, and fold the cuff over so that the cast (bind)-on edge is in line with the last row of rib stitching. You will now see that the picot edge is visible. With needle and yarn, join the cast (bind)-off edge to the body of the sock, along the line of the last rib round.

Knitting in the round

Using a circular needle to work garments in the round, means that you won't need to sew up as many seams

We've already looked at knitting in the round using 4 double-pointed needles on page 52, but if you find that method a bit too fiddly, try knitting with a circular needle. Working in this way, you will create a tube of knitting, and because the work is never turned, the right side is always facing you. To create a stocking stitch finish, simply knit every round. For a garter stitch, alternate rounds of knit and purl.

Working in the round is the perfect way to knit for those who don't like to join seams. Circular needles come in a variety of lengths, making them ideal to knit an array of garments from socks to cowls and full-sized sweaters. If you do plan to knit a sweater on a circular needle, be aware that the weight of the garment can be quite cumbersome and heavy, although when working a lot of stitches, most of their weight is distributed on the cable, which is easier on the hands and wrists compared to working the same number of stitches on straight needles.

TOP TIP If the pattern requires shaping via increases and decreases, use stitch markers of a different colour to show where these actions need to take place on the round.

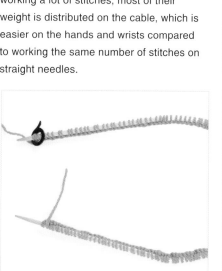

01 Mark the round
Holding the ends of the circular needle in each hand, cast on as you normally would. Once you have cast on the required number of stitches stated in the pattern, slip a stitch marker onto the right-hand needle. This will mark the beginning and end of the round.

02 Join the round
When joining the round, ensure that the stitches haven't twisted around the cable, and all the stitches face into the middle of the cable. When working the first stitch of the first round, pull the yarn with some tension.

03 Work in the round
Continue to work in the round as stated on the pattern. As you are knitting a tube, the right side will always be facing you, and to create a stocking stitch, simply knit every round. Each time you reach the stitch marker, slip it from one needle to the next.

Colourful, cosy cowl

It's now time to practise knitting in the round using a super chunky yarn. This pattern is perfect if you want to knit something cosy, but equally as vibrant and colourful

Difficulty ★★☆☆

Skills needed
Simple lace stitches
Knitting in the round

Finished measurements
Circumference: 77.5cm (30.5in)
Height: 23.5cm (9in)

Yarn
For this particular project you will need a super chunky yarn. In this example, Rowan Big Wool colour has been used in the Carnival shade, kindly provided by Rowan. You shall require 160m (174yd).

Tension (Gauge)
9 sts and 12.5 rows = 10x10cm (4x4in) measured over st st using 10mm (US 15) needles, or the size required to obtain the correct tension.

Needles
10mm (US 15) circular needle, 40cm (16in) long.

Other supplies
Stitch marker
Tapestry needle

Colourful, cosy cowl
Using 10mm (US 15) circular needle cast on 70 sts.
   Being careful not to twist the cast on stitches, place a stitch marker and join to work in rnds as follows:
Rnd 1: Knit the first row.
Rnd 2: Purl.
Rnd 3: Knit.
Rnd 4: Purl.

Knit 4 rounds.

**Rnd 9:* Purl.
Rnd 10: (yon, k2tog) to end of round.
Rnd 11: Purl.

Knit 4 rounds. **

Rep rnds 9 to 15 twice more.

Rnd 30: Purl.
Rnd 31: Knit.
Rnd 32: Purl.

Cast off kwise (knitting the sts).

Making up
Darn in ends. If you prefer you can block the item but it isn't necessary.

TOP TIP
If you don't have a stitchmarker big enough, cut a 4cm(2in) length of yarn in a contrasting colour, tie into a loose loop and thread onto needle.

Twisted stitches

Often worked in knit stitches on a purl background, cable and twisted stitches offer a raised detail

Adding cables to a piece of knitting is one of the easiest ways to add the 'wow factor' to your work. The technique is worked by displacing a set of stitches onto a cable needle, working the next stitch(es), then working the stitches from the cable needle.

The number of stitches involved and the way they are twisted by holding them in front or behind your work will determine the pattern that can be created. From ropes and plaits, to more complicated Celtic knots, all can be worked to produce the archetypal Aran sweater. Going back 2-300 years, not only were twisted patterns used for decorative purposes, but the thick fabric that these stitches produced combined with wool yarn also created some very warm garments for fishermen to wear on their trawlers.

Currently, twisted and cable stitches are very popular for interior design, featuring on cushions, throws and even replicated in porcelain for vases.

Narrowing fabric

When you knit a piece with cable stitches and twists, be aware that it can have a significant effect on the width of your fabric compared to when the same number of stitches are worked over stocking stitch. Sometimes the length is slightly reduced too. So if you're thinking of adding a column or two of cable pattern to your favourite stocking stitch pattern, work up a swatch first to see what difference it will make to the overall width.

2-stitch twists

An easy way to create a twist without needing a cable needle

Right Twist (T2R)

01 Knit the stitch
Ensuring your yarn is at the back of your work insert the tip of the right-hand needle into the second stitch on the left-hand needle. Work as if to knit the stitch without slipping it off the needle.

02 Work the second stitch
Now knit (K) the second stitch on the needle and pull both loops from the left-hand needle.

03 Crossover stitch
You should see a crossover stitch that slants to the right. While the sample shown is worked on a knit background, you could also work a purl stitch either side of the 2 knit stitches, so that it is even more prominent.

Left Twist (T2L)

01 Position the needles

With your yarn at the back of your knitting, insert the tip of your right needle behind the first stitch on the left needle and into the front of the second stitch.

02 Wind the yarn

Wind the yarn around the tip of the needle and draw through behind the first stitch, without slipping the stitch off the needle.

03 Knit the first stitch

Now knit (K) the first stitch of the left needle and pull both loops from the left needle, you should see that the twist slants to the left.

Cables

Master the basic cabling technique

4 stitch, cable front (C4F)

01 The front

Once you have worked the setup rows, work to the knit stitches for the cable. Slip the next 2 stitches onto the cable needle and leave it at the front of your work.

02 Knit 2 stitches

Now you need to knit the 2 stitches from the left-hand needle.

03 Slide the stitches

Without twisting the cable needle, slide the stitches to the right end of the needle and knit them onto the left needle.

4 stitch, cable back (C4B)

01 The back

Once you have worked the setup rows, work to the knit stitches for the cable. Slip the next 2 stitches onto the cable needle and push it to the back of your work.

02 Knit 2 stitches

Now knit (K) the two stitches from the left-hand needle.

03 Slide the stitches

Without twisting the cable needle, slide the stitches to the right end of the needle and knit them onto the left needle.

Cable jumper tea cosy

Add a little bit of rustic style to tea time with this teapot cosy, a great little project to ease you into using cable stitches. You'll also get to practise decrease and picking up stitches

Difficulty ★★★☆☆

Skills needed

Decreasing
Cables
Pick up and knit
Knitting in rows
Cast (bind) off in rib
Seaming

Finished measurements

To fit a standard 2-pint teapot

Yarn

For this pattern you will need an Aran weight yarn. In this example we have used Sirdar Hayfield Bonus Aran in Ivory Cream. You will need approximately 100m (110yd).

Tension (Gauge)

18 sts and 24 rows = 10cm (4in) in stocking stitch

Needles

5mm (US 8)

Other supplies

Cable needle
Stitch holder
Tapestry needle

TOP TIP

Turn to page 82 to learn how to pick up stitches.

Cable jumper tea cosy
Special st instructions:
C6B: Slip the next 3 stitches onto your cable needle and hold at back of work, knit the next 3 stitches on the left-hand needle, then knit the sts from the cable needle.

Cast (bind) on 60 stitches.
Row 1: (K1, P1) to end of row.
Rep Row 1 3 more times.

Cable pattern starts
Row 1 (RS): *P3, (K6, P3) 3 times, rep from * once more.
Row 2 (WS): *K3, (P6, K3) 3 times, rep from * once more.

Split for handle opening
Row 3 (RS): P3, (K6, P3) 3 times, place the last 30 stitches on a stitch holder, these will be worked later.
** *Row 4 (WS):* K3, (P6, K3) 3 times.
Row 5 (RS): P3, (C6B, P3) 3 times.
Row 6 (WS): As row 4.
Row 7 (RS): P3, (K6, P3) 3 times.
Row 8 (WS): As row 4.
Row 9 (RS): As row 7.
Row 10 (WS): As row 4.
Row 11 (RS): As row 7.

Rep pattern from Row 4 a further 4 times. **
    Cut yarn and place the 30 sts just worked on to a stitch holder.
    Move the stitches from the first stitch holder onto a needle with RS facing. Reattach yarn and work Row 11 above.
    Then work from ** to **. Cut the yarn.
    Place the stitches from the holder onto the needle with RS facing to join the stitches just worked, and work as follows across all 60 stitches.

Row 1 (RS): *P3, (C6B, P3) 3 times, rep from * once more.
Row 2 (WS): *K3, (P6, K3) 3 times, rep from * once more.
Row 3 (RS): *P3, (K6, P3) 3 times, rep from * once more.
Row 4 (WS): As row 2.
Row 5 (RS): As row 3.
Row 6 (WS): As row 2.
Row 7 (RS): As row 3.
Row 8 (WS): As row 2.

Start decreases
Row 1 (dec): *P1, p2tog, (C6B, P1, p2tog) 3 times, rep from * once more — 52 sts.
Row 2: *K2, (P6, K2) 3 times, rep from * once more.
Row 3 (dec): *P2tog, (K4, k2tog, p2tog) 3 times, rep from * once more — 38 sts.
Row 4: *K1, (P5, K1) 3 times, rep from * once more.
Row 5 (dec): *P1, (ssk, K1, k2tog, P1) 3 times, rep from * once more — 26 sts.
Row 6: *K1, (P3, K1) 3 times, rep from * once more.
Row 7 (dec): *P1, (ssk, K1, P1) 3 times, rep from * once more — 20 sts.
Row 8: *K1, (P2, K1) 3 times, rep from * once more.
Row 9 (dec): P1, (k2tog, P1) twice, k2tog, p2tog, (k2tog, P1) 3 times — 13 sts.
Row 10 (dec): P2tog 3 times, K1, p2tog 3 times — 7 sts.

Cut the yarn leaving a long tail. Thread this onto a tapestry needle and insert needle into the 7 remaining stitches. Pull stitches off the needle and draw up tightly. Secure yarn on wrong side of cosy.

Making up
With right sides together, join the sides of the rib section and the first 2 rows of the cable section at the bottom of the cosy. Join the sides along the decrease section at the top of the cosy.
    With the RS the of cosy facing, pick up and knit 20 stitches along one side of one opening.
    Work 4 rows in (K1, P1) rib.
    Cast (bind) off in rib.
    Repeat for other side of the opening.
Then repeat on the second opening.
    Darn in all ends.

I-cord

The i-cord is a tubular piece of knitting that is worked using two double-pointed needles (DPNs)

I f you're not used to working on double-pointed needles (DPNs), knitting an i-cord can initially seem quite daunting, however, making one is a great introduction to DPNs. While you can make great-looking things for the home, such as the coasters we've made here, i-cords are also perfect for drawstrings and straps for bags, headbands, belts, tie for a hooded top, and more. I-cords look very effective stitched to the edge of a garment in a contrasting colour and can be added in loops to form button holes for toggles.

I-cords are usually worked over between 3 to 6 stitches, on a needle size that fits the weight of the yarn (for example 4mm for DK yarn). They can be worked in one colour, spiralled for a textured finish, and in 2 colours.

Basic i-cord
Learn how to get started with this technique

01 Knit the first row
For a practise i-cord, cast (bind) on 5 stitches using 2 DPNs and knit the first row. *While turning the needle holding the stitches and the bumps to the back, hold it in your left hand and slide the stitches to the other end of the needle.

02 Continue knitting
The yarn should be in the back, but on the furthest stitch from the end of the tip of the needle. Taking the empty needle, insert it in the first stitch and with a taut tension pull the yarn and knit the stitch. Knit the other 4 stitches.

03 Even out
Repeating from * in step 1, continue to knit the i-cord to the desired length. Every now and again give the cord a little tug to even out the stitches and rows.

Twisted i-cord

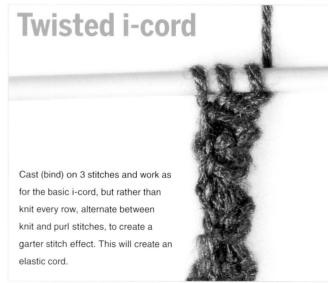

Cast (bind) on 3 stitches and work as for the basic i-cord, but rather than knit every row, alternate between knit and purl stitches, to create a garter stitch effect. This will create an elastic cord.

Striped i-cord
Two simple steps to creating something a bit different

01 Cast (bind) on
Cast (bind) on 5 stitches using yarn shade A and knit the first stitch as normal. Join Yarn shade B then knit the stitch.

02 Start alternating
On the third stitch, swap to yarn A and knit it. Continue to work the i-cord as set in the basic i-cord tutorial, alternating between yarn A and B, working yarn A above yarn A, and yarn B above yarn B stitches.

I-cord coaster

These simple coasters are an easy way of practicing the i-cord technique as well as adding a splash of colour to any surface

Difficulty ★☆☆☆☆

Skills needed
Knitting in rows

Finished measurements
Coaster diameter: 10cm (4in)

Yarn
Oddments of DK yarn. This is a great way to use up yarn left over from other projects

Tension (Gauge)
Tension is not important for this project

Needles
3.5mm (US 4) 2 x DPNs

Other supplies
Tapestry needle

I-cord coaster
Cast (bind) on 4 stitches, leaving a long tail. Following the instructions (page 60), make an i-cord measuring 120cm (47in). Cast (bind) off.

Making up
Starting at the cast (bind) on end of the i-cord, thread the yarn tail onto the tapestry needle. Start to form it into a spiral and start stitching it in place. Gradually spiral and stitch the i-cord until you reach the end. Secure the yarn on the wrong side and tease into a circle shape.

TOP TIP
Why stop at coasters? Make even longer i-cords and create matching teapot stands and place mats.

I-cord cast (bind) off

To try a different way to edge your knitting, work this cast (bind) off in a different colour to add some contrasting detail

Once Elizabeth Zimmermann had discovered the very easy i-cord (or to give it the full title of Idiot Cord), the technique was adapted and used for a variety of different finishes. Here we'll show you how to complete the i-cord cast (bind) off. Practise on a piece of test knitting first, if you're not confident to work it straight onto your knitting. You work it with your stitches on your main needle and two double-pointed needles (DPNs), which can be tricky at first, but you'll soon find your rhythm.

Unlike a ribbed hem or edge, the i-cord cast (bind) off isn't stretchy or close-fitting, so this is best used for edgings of flat pieces of knitting, or the welt and cuffs of loose fitting garments (such as the baby jacket on the following pages). Be careful not to pull your stitches too tightly as this can cause puckering of the fabric. While the tutorial below shows how to cast (bind) off at the end of knitted piece, you could also pick up and knit stitches along the edges of completed pieces, purl (P) 1 row and then work an i-cord cast (bind) off.

Tight tension?

If you find that your tension is a bit too tight and your work is puckering along the cast (bind) off edge, work with a pair of DPNs one size bigger than the needle size you used for the main garment knitting.

I-cord cast (bind) off
End your project with an i-cord

01 Work your pattern

Work the pattern to the cast (bind)-off edge, ending with a knit row. If you are using another colour for the i-cord cast (bind) off, change colours and purl (P) a row. The right side (RS) should be facing you. With the stitches to be cast (bound) off on the needle in your left hand, using the cable cast (bind) on method (see page 19), cast (bind) on 3 stitches at the start of the row with a double-pointed needle (DPN). Knit the first 2 stitches, then separately slip the next 2 stitches knitwise (kwise). Insert the tip of the left needle into the front of the 2 slipped stitches (sl sts) and knit them together. You now have 3 stitches on the right DPN.

02 Work the cast (bind) off

Slide the needle through the stitches so that they are at the other end of the needle, ready to be worked. With the second double-pointed needle (DPN), knit 2 stitches off the first DPN, slip the third stitch knitwise (kwise), then slip the first stitch off the needle holding the stitches to be cast (bound) off. Insert the tip of the left needle into the front of the 2 slipped stitches (sl sts) and knit them together. Repeat this step to the end of the row. You will end up with 3 stitches remaining on the DPN, so cast (bind) these off as normal.

I-cord baby cardigan

Adding an i-cord cast (bind) off to a garment gives it an interesting edge, adding a great finish — perfect for young children's clothes

Difficulty ★★★☆☆

Skills needed

Increasing
Decreasing
Pick up & knit
Knitting in rows
Seaming
I-cord cast (bind) off

Finished measurements

Chest: 48.5 (53.5, 58.5)cm 19 (21, 23)in

Yarn

For this project you will need a DK silk yarn.
In the example Rowan Baby Merino DK Silk
was used in the colours Snow Drop and
Bluebird, kindly provided by Rowan.
Colour 1: Snow drop; 2 (3, 4) x balls
Colour 2: Bluebird; 1 x ball

Tension (Gauge)

21 sts and 30 rows = 10cm (4in) in stocking
(stockinette) stitch

Needles

3.5mm (US 4) circular needle
3.5mm 4x double-pointed needles (DPNs)

Other supplies

4 stitch holders
Stitch markers
Tapestry needle
4 buttons of choice

Construction notes

4 stitch holders
Stitch mark

To fit age (months)	0-6	6-12	12-18
Colour 1 (balls)	2	3	4
Colour 2 (balls)	1	1	1

TOP TIP
This cast (bind) off is best
worked on garments that are
knitted from the top-down (ie
where you start knitting at the
neck line).

I-cord baby cardigan
Back
Cast (bind) on 32, 36, 46 sts using circular needle and col 2.
Row 1: (K1, P1) to end of row.
Rep row 1 3 more times.

Change to col 1.
Row 1 (RS):
Left Front: K4 (4, 5), place marker.
Left Sleeve: K3, (5, 7), place marker.
Back: K18, (18, 22) place marker.
Right Sleeve: K3, (5, 7), place marker.
Right Front: K4 (4, 5).
Row 2 (WS): Purl.

Start increases
Row 1 (inc): K1, kfb, *K to the last st before the first marker, kfb into this st, slip marker, kfb, rep from * for the rest of the row, then K to last 2 sts, kfb, K1.
Row 2: Purl.
Rep these 2 rows 4 more times — 122 (126, 136) sts.

Neck edge increases
Row 1 (inc): K1, kfb, *K to the last st before the first marker, kfb into this st, slip marker, kfb, rep from * for the rest of the row, then K to last 2 sts, kfb, K1.
Row 2: Purl.
Rep these 2 rows 4 more times — 122 (126, 136) sts.

Cont increases
Row 1 (inc): *K to the last st before the first marker, kfb into this st, slip marker, kfb, rep from * for the rest of the row, then knit to the end of the row.
Row 2: Purl.

Work these 2 rows 6, (8, 9) more times.
You should now have a total of: 178 (198, 216) sts on the needle.
This works out as:
Left Front: 26 (28, 30) sts.
Left Sleeve: 37, (43, 47) sts.
Back: 52, (56, 62) sts.
Right Sleeve: 37, (43, 47) sts.
Right Front: 26 (28, 30) sts.

Knit 1 row, Purl 1 row.

Divide for sleeves
On separate holders, place the stitches for the left front, left sleeve, back and right front to work later.

Working on the stitches for the right sleeve continue as follows:
Row 1 (RS): Cast (bind) on 3 sts using the cable method, K to the end of row — 40 (46, 50) sts.

Row 2 (WS): Cast (bind) on 3 sts using the cable method, P to the end of row — 43 (49, 53) sts.

Knit 1 row, Purl 1 row.

Arm decreases
Row 1 (dec): K1, ssk, K to last 3 sts, k2tog, K1.
Row 2: Purl.

Sizes 1 and 2: Rep decrease rows 1 and 2 1 more time — 39 (42) sts.
Sizes 3: Rep decrease rows 1 and 2 2 more times — 47 sts.

Cont in stocking (stockinette) stitch until sleeve is 24 (26.5, 29)cm/9.5 (10.5, 11.5)in from neck edge ending on a K row.
Change to col 2.
Purl 1 row.
Cast (bind) off using the i-cord cast (bind) off.
With right sides (RSs) together join the sleeve seams.
Repeat for left sleeve.

Body
Transfer stitches for left front, back, and right front onto your needle, and with right side facing continue as follows:

Setup row: K across left front and pick up 6 sts along the underside of the left sleeve, K sts for back, pick up 6 sts along the underside of the right sleeve, K across right front — 116 (124, 134) sts.

Work in stocking (stockinette) stitch until back measures 25.5 (28, 30.5)cm/10.5 (11.5, 12.5) in from the cast (bind)-on edge of the neck, ending on a Knit row.

Change to col 2. Purl 1 row.

Cast (bind) off using the i-cord cast (bind) off.

Button band

With right side facing, pick up and K 58 (65, 69) sts along left front edge.

Row 1 (WS): (K1, P1) to end of row.
Repeat 2 more times. Cast (bind) off in rib.

Buttonhole band

With right side (RS) facing, pick up and Knit 58 (62, 66) sts along right front edge.

Row 1 (WS): (K1, P1) to end of row.
Row 2 (RS, buttonholes): (K1, P1) 7 (9, 7) times, *k2tog, yo, (K1, P1) 4 (4, 5) times, K1, rep from * 3 more times.
Row 3: As row 1.
Cast (bind) off in rib.

Making up

Darn in all ends. Block gently on reverse of knitting, avoiding rib and i-cord areas.

Did you know?

The i-cord's full title is '*Idiot Cord*' named by Elizabeth Zimmermann who accidentally discovered this very simple technique.

Working with two colours

Over these two pages we will look at Fair Isle knitting and how to cope with the two different yarns as you knit

F air Isle knitting also goes by the names of Jacquard, stranded, two colour and double knitting. Where intarsia knitting is creating an image or shape via stitches in blocks of colour, Fair Isle knitting carries two or more colours along the row on a repeated pattern and is usually worked in stocking (stockinette) stitch.

Due to the stranding/carrying of the yarns at the back of the work, Fair Isle garments tend to be thick and therefore very warm. Because of this it is usual to work these garments in 4ply or DK weight yarns as anything thicker would result in a very bulky piece of clothing.

As you work across the row, you will carry all the yarns with you, alternating between colours as you follow the chart. The yarns need to be stranded (or woven in) as you knit, other wise the loops (floats) on the back can easily get caught on fingers, buttons and other fastenings. You must also be careful not to pull the floats too tightly, otherwise an uneven tension (gauge) and puckered fabric will result.

TOP TIP
If you are adding a Fair Isle pattern chart to your stocking (stockinette) stitch pattern, note that you will need more yarn than originally stated due to the floats being carried.

Fair Isle
Create fetching repeated patterns

01 Work a knit row
With both colour yarns at the back of your work on the knit row, follow the chart and work the stitches in the first colour, then change when necessary by dropping it and picking up the second colour. When you knit the first colour again do not pull it too tightly. So that you don't carry a colour across a large number of stitches, cross it over with the other yarn every third stitch.

02 On a purl row
On a purl row, bring both yarns to the front. Keep the one you are working in your right hand and let the other fall to your left. When you change the yarn over swap their positions.

03 Keep your yarn even
For best results, make sure that your yarn is evenly tensioned (gauged). This will give you a nice flat fabric. At first this may be tricky, but practice, and learning to hold each yarn in a different hand, will ensure great results in no time.

Holding the yarns

If you're keen to improve your Fair Isle skills, try holding the yarns differently

01 Start stitching

When working two colours, hold one yarn in your right hand (RH) as you would normally do, then in a mirror image of your right hand, hold the second colour in your left hand (LH). On a practice piece, work two stitches in yarn from the right hand.

02 Change colours

Now change colours. Insert the tip of the right needle into the next stitch, with the index finger of the left hand guide the second colour to the front of the tip, wind it over the needles and towards the right.

03 Pull it through

Now pull the new stitch through as you would on a regular knit stitch, keeping tension (gauge) on the left yarn.

Hold both yarns in the right hand

If you don't think you can manage two yarns in different hands, hold the first yarn as you usually would over your index finger, then the second yarn on your middle finger.

In the round

When working Fair Isle, it recommended that you work the project in the round on a circular needle or set of double-pointed needles (DPNs). This is so that every round is worked in knit stitch, and you can see the pattern as it grows. Changing and carrying colours on a purl (P) row can be tricky.

Hold both yarns in the left hand

This method is best to use if you prefer to knit the continental way. Hold one yarn on the index finger, and the second yarn on the middle finger of the left hand. When you knit, the technique is more to 'catch' the yarn with your needle, than 'throwing' it around the needle.

How to weave yarn on the wrong side

As you knit, the floats are caught by the yarn on alternate stitches, or every two or three stitches

Weaving in left yarn

With one yarn in each hand, keep the left yarn above the needles when not weaving it in. On both knit and purl rows, lift the float, insert the right needle into the next stitch ready to work it, and under the float. Simply knit or purl as normal under the float and your yarn will be carried.

Weaving in right yarn

This is a little more tricky than weaving the left yarn. When not weaving in, keep the right yarn to the right of the needle tips. Insert the point of the right needle into the next stitch as if to work it and wind the right float around the needle — on a Knit row wind as if to knit, on a Purl row wind the float under then over the needle. Wind the working yarn of the left hand around the needle as normal. Return your right-hand yarn to the normal position, then draw stitch through with the left yarn.

TOP TIP

If you want longer cuffs you can either add a few rounds in the main colour after the chart in knit stitch, or you can have a longer rib by adding rounds.

Fair Isle boot cuffs

Add flair to your plain boots with these Fair Isle boot cuffs. Once you get the hang of working multiple strands of yarn, you'll never want to stop!

Difficulty ★★★★☆

Skills needed
Colourwork (stranded)
Knitting in rounds
Working from a chart

Finished measurements
Size S/M fits calves up to 34cm (13.5in). L fits up too about 40cm (15.75in).
Total length: 13cm (5in)
Width (when laid flat): For S/M: 15cm (6in) and for L 19cm (7.5in)
As with most knitted accessories the boot cuffs are very stretchy.

Yarn
For this design you will need DK yarn in various colours. In the example shown, Yarn Stories Fine Merino DK has been used in Dove, Raspberry, Primrose, Spring Green, Lilac, Thistle and Leaf.
Colour 1: Dove; 1 x ball
Colour 2: Raspberry; 1 x ball
Colour 3: Primrose; 1 x ball
Colour 4: Spring Green; 1 x ball
Colour 5: Lilac; 1 x ball
Colour 6: Thistle; 1 x ball
Colour 7: Leaf; 1 x ball

Tension (Gauge)
24 sts over 30 rows = 10cm (4in) in Fair Isle pattern using needle 4mm (US 6)

Needles
4mm (US 6) double-pointed needles

Other supplies
2 removable stitch markers
Tapestry needle

Construction notes
There are seven colours at work in the project and that can seem overwhelming. You never use more than two in the same round, so concentrate on that. Cut the main colour yarn when you have finished the upper rib and the first two rounds of the chart. Then you have one less thread

getting in your way. Rejoin to knit the final two rounds of the chart and the lower rib.
The stitches at the beginning/end of the rounds may look untidy. Don't worry as, when you darn in all the ends after knitting, you can always tighten any loose stitches.

Fair Isle boot cuffs
With col 1 and double-pointed needles (DPNs) cast (bind) on 72 (88) sts (18 sts on each needle for S/M, 22 sts on each for L). Join to work in the round and don't twist the cast (bind)-on edge as you do so.

Rnd 1: *K2, P2, rep from * to end.
Next rnd: Work in rib K2, P2.

Continue in K2, p2rib for a further 7 rnds.

Work the chart.

Continuing with col 1 and in K2 P2 rib as set previously, work 16 rnds.
Cast (bind) off loosely in rib.

Making up
Make the other boot cuff the same way.
Weave in loose ends and block carefully by using an iron set on wool with the steam function on. Wear proudly!

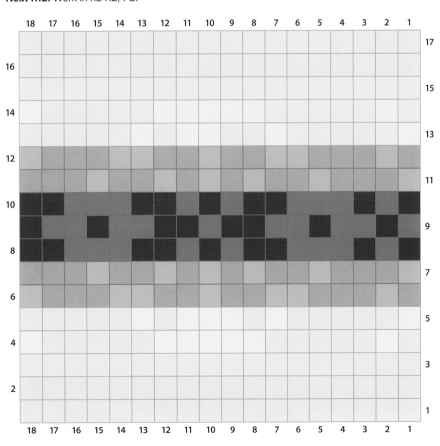

Key:
☐ Colour 1   ☐ Colour 3   ▨ Colour 5   ▨ Colour 7
☐ Colour 2   ▨ Colour 4   ■ Colour 6

Colour work

Adding different colours in horizontal stripes is a fairly easy and simple way to make a plain piece stand out

There are several different ways to add colour to knitting and some are a lot more complicated than others. For example, Fair Isle and intarsia knitting are more advanced techniques that will take a bit of practise and concentration to grasp. However, one fairly easy technique of adding colour is to work in horizontal stripes, which can be added in different sizes and even different fibres to create interesting textures. You can introduce stripes to any single-colour pattern without affecting the tension (gauge) or shape of the knitting. Here are just a few ways to add colour to your knitting. They all have a right side, which is shown in these swatches.

Two-colour garter-stitch stripe

Worked in garter stitch, this stripe pattern uses two colours (A and B) that are alternated every two rows. To work the pattern, knit two rows of A, then two rows of B, and continue until the desired length. When you change colours, drop the yarn not in use at the side of the work and simply pick it up again when needed.

Two-colour knit and purl pinstripe

Working with two colours (A and B), begin by knitting six rows of A in stocking stitch. Then drop A at the side and knit two rows of B. This will create a purl ridge in the second colour on the right side. Repeat this for a pinstripe effect. To avoid loose strands of B at the edge, wrap A around B at the start of every RS row.

Five-colour stocking-stitch stripe

To work stripes in multiple colours and carry the colours up the side of the work, use a circular needle. Work back and forth in rows in stocking stitch, changing colour as and when you like. If a yarn you need to pick up is at the opposite end, push all the stitches to the other end of the circular needle. Then work the next row in the same stitch as the last.

Textured stocking-stitch stripe

To add a different texture as well as colour, use a different type of yarn when you add a stripe. This stripe is worked with a chunky yarn and a 4ply yarn. Work in stocking stitch (st st) on circular needles.

People cushion cover

Impress everyone by creating this fun, detailed cushion cover using the Fair Isle, intarsia and moss (seed) stitching techniques

Difficulty ★★★★☆

Skills needed

Knitting in rows
Fair Isle
Intarsia
Moss (seed) stitch
Seaming
Buttonholes
Working from a chart

Finished measurements

Made to fit a 40x40 cm (16x16 ins) cushion insert

Yarn

For this pattern you will need eight different colours, as listed below, in Aran weight. In this example Drops Alaska and Drops Nepal.
Colour 1: Light Grey; 4 x balls.
Colour 2: Off White; 1 x ball.
Colour 3: Light Olive; 1 x ball.
Colour 4: Dark Turquoise; 1 x ball.
Colour 5: Cerise; 1 x ball.
Colour 6: Baby Cashmerino Peach Melba (yarn used double); 1 x ball.
Colour 7: Goldenrod; 1 x ball.
Colour 8: Orange; 2 x balls.

Tension (Gauge)

18.5 sts and 25 rows = 10cm (4in) in st st using 5mm needles
20.5 sts and 23 rows over Fair Isle.

Needles

5mm (US 8) needles.

Other supplies

40cm (15¾in) x 40cm (15¾in) cushion pad
5 x medium sized buttons

People cushion cover

Make in one piece

Using col 4, cast (bind) on 77 sts.
Row 1: K1, *P1, K1 to end.
Row 2: As row 1.
These 2 rows form moss (seed) st. Cont in moss (seed) st as set for a further 5 rows. Change to col 1.
Work in st st stripes as follows;
Row 1: K with col 1.
Row 2: K1, P to last st, K1 with col 1.
Rows 3 and 4: As rows 1 and 2.
Row 5: K with col 8.
Row 6: K1, P to last st, K1.
Repeat these 6 rows 12 times more.
Change to col 1.
Next 2 rows; with col 1, K, increasing 6 sts evenly across first row. (83 sts)

Start front

With RS facing, and keeping continuity of K1 at beginning and end of each row, work 2 rows st st.

Note: When following charts, work from right to left on RS rows and left to right on WS rows. Charts 1, 2, 3 and 5 are worked in Fair Isle, chart 4 in intarsia.

Start pattern

Row 1: K2 with col 1, following row 1 of Chart 1 work the 18sts 4 times, then rep the first 7 sts once more, K2 with col 1.
Row 2: K1, P1 with col 1, then following row 2 of Chart 1 work the last 7 sts once, then work the 18sts 4 times, with col 1 P1, K1.
Rows 3-10: Continue to follow Chart 1 as set, until 10 rows have been worked.
Rows 11 and 12: Work 2 rows st g st col 1.
Row 13: K1 with col 1, following row 1 of Chart 2 work these 9 sts 9 times, K1 col 1.
Row 14: K1 with col 1, following row 2 of Chart 2 work these 9 sts 9 times, K1 col 1.
Rows 15-17: Continue to follow Chart 2 for a further 3 rows as set.
Rows 18 and 19: st st col 1.
Rows 20-31: as rows 1-12.
Row 32: K1 with col 1, following row 1 of Chart 3 work these 9 sts 9 times, K1 col 1.

Rows 33-36: continue to follow Chart 3 for a further 4 rows, as set.

Rows 37 and 38: With col 2 work 2 rows in st st.

Row 39: K3 with col 2, following row 1 of chart 4, (using intarsia method) work these 22 sts 3 times, then rep the first 11 sts once more, K3 with col 2.

Row 40: K1, P2 with col 2, then following row 2 of Chart 4 work the last 11 sts once, then work the 22 sts 3 times, then P2, K1 with col 2

Rows 41-56: Continue to follow chart 4 as set, until 18 rows have been worked.

Rows 57 and 58: With col 2 work 2 rows in st st.

Row 59: K1 with col 2, following row 1 of chart 5 work these 9 sts 9 times, K1 with col 2.

Rows 60-63: continue to follow chart 5 as set for a further 4 rows.

Rows 64 and 65: With col 1 work 2 rows in st st.

Rows 66- 77: as rows 1-12.

Rows 78-82: as rows 13-17.

Rows 83 and 84: With col 1 work 2 rows in st st.

Rows 85-94: as rows 1-10.

Continuing to work with col 1 only, work 2 rows in st st.

Next row (dec): Knit, decreasing 6 sts evenly across row. (77 sts).

Next Row (WS): Purl to create fold line.

Change to col 4.

Knit 1 row.

Work 3 rows in moss (seed) st.

Buttonhole row: moss (seed) 7 sts *k2tog, yon, moss 13; rep from * to last 10 sts, k2tog, yon, moss (seed) to end.

Work a further 3 rows moss st.

Cast (bind) off.

Making up

Press under a damp cloth, blocking to correct measurements.

   Sew side seams.

   Sew buttons on to correspond with buttonholes.

Chart 1

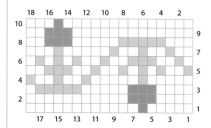

Chart 2

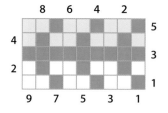

Chart 3

Chart 5

Chart 4

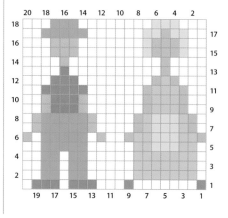

Key:

☐ Colour 1		■ Colour 5	
☐ Colour 2		☐ Colour 6	
■ Colour 3		☐ Colour 7	
■ Colour 4		☐ Colour 8	

Did you know?

Queen Victoria was an avid knitter throughout her life. During her reign the popularity of handcrafts increased significantly.

Short row shaping

Learn how to create definition in garments by adding shape and smoothing edges — all you need to master is the technique of working partial rows

The technique of short row shaping is used in a multitude of patterns to structurally shape knitting. Whether to add more definition to the bust of a sweater, create a rounded shoulder, or add the perfect curve to the heel of a sock, this simple but effective technique will deliver great results. While it is mainly seen on a stocking stitch base, it can also be quite effective when used on a garter stitch.

Also called 'turning', the technique is achieved by working the stitches part way along a row, then turning your work and working back along the stitches just worked. This means that those stitches have been worked for two more rows compared to the rest of the

knitting. Depending on the pattern, you may knit partway and return for many rows, or just work a few short rows at regular intervals. One problem that is caused by working short rows is that a hole will form where the knitting has been turned, depending on the pattern worked. Below are two ways to avoid holes.

> *"Add more definition to the bust of a sweater or create a rounded shoulder"*

Tie or Wrap (and turn, w&t)
Start shaping and wrapping your stitches

01 Short row shaping
Work the number of stitches stated on the pattern for the short row shaping. Take the yarn to the other side of the work through the needles. Slip the next stitch purlwise (pwise), then take the yarn to the original side of the work and turn. Sometimes, slipping the first stitch purlwise gives a smoother finish.

02 Wrapped stitches
Once you have completed the short row, when working across all stitches, the wrap may interfere with your pattern. Work to the stitch that has been wrapped and work it together with the stitch that has been wrapped by inserting the needle into the loop of the wrap from underneath and then into the stitch.

Use 'over' to avoid holes
Make sure it joins up

01 Turn position
Work the number of stitches to the turn position. Take the yarn to the other side of the work though the needles, then bring the yarn back to the original side over the needle (creating an 'over'). Continue to work the short row. On the next long row, if working knit stitches, knit the yarn over and the next stitch together.

On a purl row, drop the 'over', slip the next stitch, pick up the over and place it on the left needle, then purl the over and the slipped stitch together.

Bluebird of happiness

Put the techniques into practice and follow this pattern to make a soft children's toy — perfect for newborn babies

Difficulty ★★★☆☆

Skills needed

Increasing
Decreasing
Pick up and knit
Knitting in rounds
Wrap and turn (short rows)

Finished measurements

10cm (4in) long from beak to tail

Yarn

For this pattern you shall require a DK (worsted) yarn. In the example, Red Heart Super Saver yarn was used. You will need a total of 27m (30 yards).

Tension (Gauge)

Gauge is not important with toys. Changing yarn weight or needle size will only serve to make your finished object smaller or larger.

Needles

3.5mm (US 4) 4x double pointed needles (DPNs)

Other supplies

Tapestry needle
Stuffing

Bluebird of happiness

Note: Work begins at neckline.
Cast (bind) on 18 stitches onto 3 DPNs, join in the round and work the following rounds:
Rnd 1: K all sts.
Rnd 2 (inc): (M1, K6), rep to end of rnd — 21 sts.
Rnd 3: K all sts.
Rnd 4 (inc): (M1, K7) rep to end of rnd — 24 sts.
Rnd 5: K all sts.
Rnd 6 (inc): (M1, K8) rep to end of rnd — 27 sts.
Rnd 7: K all sts.
Rnd 8: K3, w&t, P6, w&t, K3.
Rnd 9: K4, w&t, P8, w&t, K4.
Rnd 10: K5, w&t, P10, w&t, K5.

Rnd 11: K6, w&t, P12, w&t, K6.
Rnd 12: K7, w&t, P14, w&t, K7.
Rnd 13: K8, w&t, P16, w&t, K8.
Rnd 14 (dec): K1, k2tog, K to last 3 sts in rnd, ssk, K1 — 25 sts.
Rnds 15—19: Rep Rnd 14 — 15 sts.
Rnd 20: K all sts.
Rnd 21 (dec): Rep Rnd 14 — 13 sts.
Rnd 22: K all sts.
Rnd 23 (dec): Rep Rnd 14 — 11 sts
Rnd 24: K all sts.
Rnd 25 (dec): Rep Rnd 14 — 9 sts.
Rnd 26: K all sts.
Rnd 27 (dec): Rep Rnd 14 — 7 sts.
Rnd 28: K all sts.

Cut the yarn, thread end into a tapestry needle, and slip through remaining live stitches. Do not pull closed yet.

Head

Beginning just to the right of the first cast (bind) on stitch (centre of the bird's chest), pick up and knit 18 stitches, 1 in each of the original cast (bind) on stitches, then work the rounds below. (Round 3 should be worked exactly as written; 2 of the stitches will be wrapped 3 times each.)
Rnd 1: K all sts.
Rnd 2: K all sts.
Rnd 3: K12, w&t, P6, w&t, K6, w&t, P6, w&t, K12.
Rnd 4: K all sts.

Rnd 5: K all sts.
Rnd 6 (dec): (K1, k2tog) to end of rnd — 12 sts.
Rnd 7 (dec): (K2tog) to end of rnd — 6 sts.
Rnd 8 (dec): (K2tog) to end of rnd — 3 sts.

Making up

Cut yarn, thread end into a tapestry needle, and slip through remaining live stitches. Pull tightly closed and secure.

Using the end of a straight needle, stuff the bluebird's head and body through open end at tail, being mindful of his graceful lines. Do not stuff the tail; rather, flatten it out and bend in an upward direction.

Pull yarn tightly closed and secure.
Darn any holes; weave in loose ends.

Fixing a dropped stitch

It's easy to panic when you drop a stitch, but there's really no need to worry, as it is very simple to fix

If a stitch drops off one of your needles, don't worry. This is called a dropped stitch and there are steps you can take to get it back on the needle. If you see the stitch come off the needle, fix it immediately by picking it up with the tip of whichever needle it has dropped from, being sure to keep the right leg of the stitch on top. However, if the stitch has begun to unravel from the work, secure it with a crochet hook or cable needle as soon as you can to prevent any further damage. If a dropped stitch is left, it can unravel all the way to the cast (bind)-on edge. When this happens, you are left with a vertical column of horizontal strands that used to be stitches — this is called a ladder, as the unravelled stitches look like rungs on a ladder. Follow these steps to get your stitches back where they're supposed to be.

Pick up a dropped stitch
Make it look as though it never dropped off

01 Locate your dropped stitch
If your dropped stitch has only unravelled by one row and you have what looks like one rung on a ladder, the solution is very simple.

02 Pick up the stitch
With the left-hand needle (you can also use the right to help you if it's easier), pick up the dropped stitch, from front to back, leaving the strand at the back of the work.

03 Get the strand
Now move the strand onto the left-hand needle, also from front to back.

04 Fix the stitch
Move the dropped stitch (the first one you picked up) off the needle, making sure you lift it over the strand. This has remade the stitch that was dropped, and you can continue knitting.

Fix a ladder
Get your stitches back on track

01 Crochet hook

If the stitch has unravelled even further and you have a ladder, it is going to be a bit trickier to fix, but uses the same technique as fixing one rung of a dropped stitch. After you have secured the stitch to stop it unravelling further, you'll need to get a crochet hook to fix the error.

02 Grab the stitch

With the right side (RS) of your work facing you, put the crochet hook through the dropped stitch, from front to back. If you need to, pull the knitting apart slightly so that you can better see the ladder of strands.

03 Begin the climb

Put the crochet hook underneath the first strand and hook it.

04 Make the stitch

Pull the strand through the dropped stitch with the crochet hook, making sure the dropped stitch leaves the hook. You have now corrected one row.

05 Continue

Keep hooking the strands through to make new stitches, being sure to work in order. When you have completed the ladder and come to the final stitch, slip it off the crochet hook and onto the left-hand needle. The mistake is corrected.

TOP TIP
Don't forget to work in a pattern. If you're fixing a ladder that has knit and purl stitches, make sure the knit side is facing you as you complete each row.

Finishing

**Complete your
projects in style**

"When choosing which buttonhole to work, consider the stretch of the fabric"

Picking up stitches

To add borders to your finished work, you will first need to pick up the stitches on the edge that you wish to 'finish'

If the pattern you're following calls for a border, you may find that you need to pick up the edges along your finished piece of work. This is a technique that even experienced knitters can find challenging, so careful preparation and lots of practice will help. When picking up stitches, always have the right side (RS) of the yarn facing you, as it creates a ridge on the wrong side (WS). If you're following a pattern, it should specify which size needle to pick up the stitches with and the required number of stitches for you to pick up. In these instructions a contrasting colour yarn has been used to demonstrate the technique, however, picking up stitches in a matching yarn will hide any imperfections. If your pattern calls for a contrasting border, start with the new colour on the first row of the border.

> *"This is a technique that even experienced knitters can find challenging"*

Along a cast (bind) on/off edge
From front to back

Insert a knitting needle into the first stitch from front to back, leaving a long, loose tail. Wrap the working yarn around the tip of the needle and pull it through, as if knitting a stitch. Continue along the edge, picking up and knitting (K) one stitch through every cast (bind)-on or cast (bind)-off stitch.

Along row ends
Mark and pick up stitches

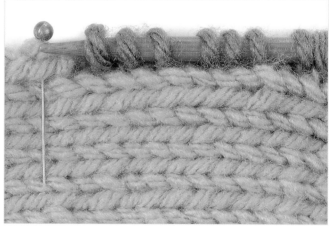

01 Mark stitches
On light-weight or medium-weight yarn, pick up about 3 stitches for every 4 row ends. Mark out which stitches you are going to pick up by placing a pin on the 1st of every 4 row ends. You will only pick up the stitches in between the pins.

02 Pick up stitches
Insert the needle tip through the centre of the edge stitches and pick them up in the same way as for along a cast (bind)-on edge. Make sure you skip each 4th row end.

With a crochet hook
Hook stitches and transfer them

01 Hook stitches
Being sure to use a crochet hook that fits through the stitches, insert the hook through the first stitch. Wrap the hook behind and around the yarn from left to right and pull through.

02 Transfer to needle
When a new loop has been formed on the crochet hook, transfer it onto a knitting needle. Repeat this for all stitches.

Picking up stitches around a curve
You'll most often need to pick up stitches on a curve around armbands and necklines

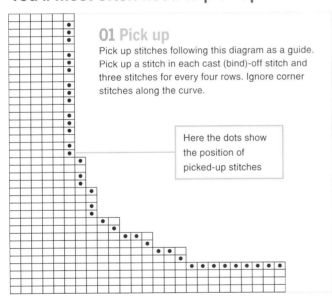

Here the dots show the position of picked-up stitches

01 Pick up
Pick up stitches following this diagram as a guide. Pick up a stitch in each cast (bind)-off stitch and three stitches for every four rows. Ignore corner stitches along the curve.

02 Knit the border
When the number of stitches stated on the pattern have been picked up, knit the border as instructed.

Tips for picking up stitches

- Always catch a whole loop; just working into the edge loop can cause holes and distort knitting, and doesn't hide the edge.

- Try using a knitting needle one or two sizes smaller than the needle used to make the project to pick up stitches.

- When picking up stitches ensure the right side is facing you.

- Be careful not to split the yarn when inserting the needle into the fabric.

- The first row you work after picking up stitches will be a wrong side row.

- If working the border in a contrasting colour to the main piece, pick up stitches in the shade that worked the main piece, as this will hide imperfections.

Buttonholes

It's more important than you might first think to find the best buttonhole for your project. Our guide will talk you through the various options and advantages

Buttons are a very common fastening for hand-knitted projects. Whether on the front of a cardigan, the neckline of a sweater or to close a bag, buttons not only offer a secure closure, but with the myriad of styles available, they can also add a decorative element to the finished piece.

The most popular form of buttonhole is the eyelet hole, usually created by working 2 stitches together (k2tog), then forming a yarn over (yo). This creates an elastic hole to pass a button through. However, over the next six pages, we'll show you how to make the various buttonholes available to knitters and what projects they are best suited to.

When choosing which buttonhole to work, take into account the stretch of the fabric; sometimes knitting a strand of colour-matched sewing thread just on the buttonhole stitches can help to reinforce the hole. Also, if you have worked a horizontal buttonhole, the button will rarely sit in the centre of the hole; instead it will move to the outer side. Often, buttonhole bands and button bands (the part that the buttons are sewn onto) will be added to the garment separately.

Loose-fitting jackets made in thicker yarns will need fewer buttons than a fitted cardigan worked in fine yarn such as 4ply. There are no rules for button placement, but they must be evenly and consistently spaced. Sometimes, groups of buttons can make a great feature.

> *"When choosing which buttonhole to work, consider the stretch of the fabric"*

Spacing buttons
To have a well-balanced closing, it is important to evenly space buttonholes

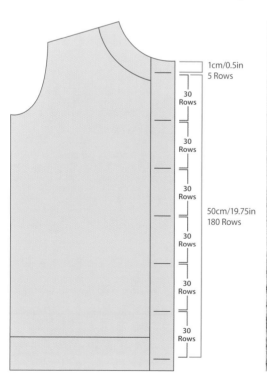

1cm/0.5in
5 Rows

30 Rows

30 Rows

30 Rows

50cm/19.75in
180 Rows

30 Rows

30 Rows

30 Rows

How many buttons?
The majority of patterns you will work, will state exactly how many buttons you will need, and state in the instructions where and how to make the buttonholes. However, you may have a pattern that simply states 'evenly space buttons'. To do this, first work the edge that you will sew the buttons on to, before working the buttonhole band.

On the buttonhole band, place a pin or loose stitch of contrasting yarn 1cm (0.4in) from the top of the band and another 1cm (0.4in) from the bottom — this marks the top and bottom buttons. Now measure the gap between, and evenly space pins to show the other button positions.

Based on the button band, make a note of how many rows and stitches need to be worked between each buttonhole.

Sewn button loops

Use this method to add button loops to a finished piece of knitting

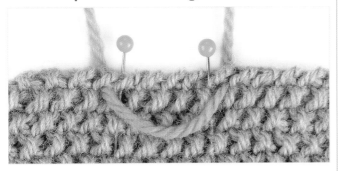

01 Form a loop

Mark the position and width of the loops with pins. Thread a tapestry needle with matching or contrasting yarn, and pass it through the knitting, back to front, pulling it most of the way, but leaving a small tail. Hold the tail in place as you take the needle back through the knitting at the 2nd pin position to form a loop.

02 Create a double loop

Take the needle from back to front through the 1st pin position again to give you a double loop of yarn with a short tail (this tail will be hidden when the loop is worked).

03 Pass the needle through

Pass the needle through the yarn loop, around the back, and through the loop you have just created. Pull tight. Continue to cover the doubled yarn loop and tail. Once finished, pass the needle through a few of the stitches on the loop and cut the yarn.

Knitted button loop

If you can't sew a button loop, knit a loop and attach it with securing stitches

01 Cast (bind) on and off

In the same or contrasting yarn as the knitted piece, cast (bind) on the number of stitches to match the length of loop you wish to create. Now cast (bind) off all stitches.

02 Attach the loops

First, folding the loop in half, attach the ends of the loop to the edge of the reverse side of your knitting.

TOP TIP

Button choice

Match the size of the button to the weight of the yarn. Delicate yarns suit small, pretty patterned buttons, while heavier fabrics, worked in yarns such as Aran or Chunky really complement toggles, leather or wooden buttons.

Simple or chain eyelet
Ideal for making a small buttonhole

01 Wind the yarn over the needle

Work along the row to the position of the buttonhole. Wind the yarn over the needle (yon).

02 Work 2 stitches together

Knit the next 2 stitches together (k2tog). You can see that the yarn over (yo) has created a hole in your knitting and an extra stitch on your needle. By working 2 stitches together you have kept the number of stitches on the needle the same.

03 Purl the yarn over

When you work the next row, simply purl the yarn over (yo) as you would normally. This type of buttonhole is perfect for baby clothes, or when a small button is required.

Open eyelet buttonhole
A variation on the previous buttonhole

01 Wind the yarn

Knit to the position of the buttonhole. Wind the yarn over the needle (yon) from front to back, slip 1 stitch (sl1), knitwise (kwise). Knit the next stitch.

02 Pass over

Pass the slipped stitch over (psso) the knit stitch. (You've added a stitch with the yarn over (yo), but taken one away with the pass slipped stitch over decrease.)

03 Purl the yarn over

When you work the next row, make sure you purl the yarn over (yo) as you would normally.

Reinforced eyelet
This method creates a strong, neat buttonhole

01 Work the row
When working on a stocking stitch (st st) background, knit to the position of the buttonhole and yarn over needle (yon), taking the yarn front to back, then over the needle. Work as stated to the end of the row. On the next row, purl to the yon stitch, slip it purlwise (pwise), then create another yon. Work the rest of the row as stated.

02 Slip the stitch
When you reach the yarn over needles (yons) on the next row, slip the stitch directly before the yons knitwise (kwise). You should knit the 2 yons together, but don't slip them off the needle.

03 Knit 3 stitches together
Pass the slipped stitch over the stitch just made, as you would in a cast (bind) off. Finally knit 3 stitches together (the yarn overs (yos) plus the next stitch on the needle).

04 Stronger eyelet
The eyelet you have created looks just the same as the simple eyelet, but will be stronger. This makes it a great option for children's knits, or garments that will get a lot of wear.

Horizontal one-row buttonhole

Start working this buttonhole on the right side. It is stronger than most holes, with little give

01 Work the yarn through and back

Work to the point in the row for the buttonhole. Bring the yarn through the needles to the front of the work, slip the next stitch purlwise (pwise), and take the yarn back (yb).

02 Slip and pass the stitches

Slip the next stitch purlwise (pwise), then pass over the previously slipped stitch (sl st). Continue to do this until the stated number of stitches have been slipped and passed. Slip the last stitch on the right needle back on to the left needle.

03 Cast (bind) on

Turn your work so that the wrong side is facing, and using the cable cast (bind) on method, cast (bind) on the same number of stitches that were passed over. Cast (bind) on an extra stitch, but before transferring it to the left needle, make sure that you bring the yarn forward (yf), and add a stitch to the left needle.

04 Continue the row

Turn the work and slip the 1st stitch knitwise (kwise). Pass the next stitch over this, and continue to work the rest of the row as stated.

Horizontal buttonhole – buttonhole cast (bind) on
Use a sturdier cast (bind) on to create a sturdy horizontal buttonhole

01 Cast (bind) off

With the right side facing, work to the buttonhole position. Work another 2 stitches, and pass the 1st over the 2nd. Continue to cast off the stated number of stitches. Slip the next stitch knitwise (kwise) onto the right needle and pass over the last cast off loop. Pulling yarn with some tension (gauge), continue the rest of the row as stated.

02 Wind the yarn

On the next row, work to the buttonhole cast (bind) off section. Dropping the left needle, hold the yarn in your right hand, and with your left thumb pointing down, wind the yarn from back to front around thumb. Bringing the thumb to an upright position, you have twisted the loop. Insert the tip of the right needle into the loop.

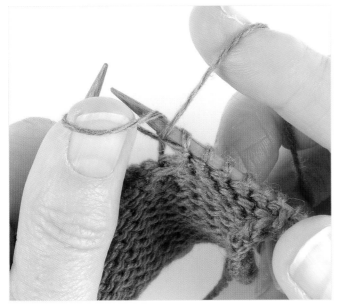

03 Pull the yarn tight

Wind the yarn around the tip of the right needle from back to front, and then moving the thumb, take the loop over the end of the right needle. Remove your thumb and pull the yarn tightly, holding the stitch in place with your finger if necessary.

04 Continue the row

Continue to make stitches in this way until you have replaced the required number of stitches. Work to the end of the row as stated.

Vertical button hole
You will need a stitch holder to help you create this buttonhole

01 Slip onto a stitch holder
For ease, instructions will assume the pattern is worked in stocking stitch (st st). With right side facing, work to the position of the buttonhole. Slip the rest of the stitches from the left-hand needle onto a stitch holder.

02 Work the stitches
Turn the work, slip the 1st stitch purlwise (pwise), then purl the rest of the row. Work the stitches that fall to the right of the buttonhole for the required number of rows as stated on your pattern, ending on a wrongside row, slipping the 1st stitch of all purl rows. Cut the yarn. Slip the stitches from the holder onto the empty needle, then slip the stitches from the right side of the buttonhole onto the stitch holder.

03 Create a make 1
Slip the 1st stitch knitwise (kwise) and create a make 1 increase (m1) (see page 37). Knit to the end of the row. Continue to work in stocking stitch (st st), slipping the 1st stitch of all knit rows, until you have worked the same number of rows as the previous side ending with a wrong side row. Cut the yarn.

04 Restore the correct number of stitches
Transfer all of the stitches to the same needle and in the correct order, ready with the right side facing. Knit to buttonhole, knitting the two hole-edge stitches together in order to restore the correct number of stitches on the needle.

Sloping (diagonal) buttonhole
This buttonhole adds a decorative finish to a project

01 Purl to the end
On a right side row, knit to the buttonhole position. Transfer the stitches left on the left-hand needle to a stitch holder. Turn your knitting and *slip the 1st stitch, purlwise (pwise). Wind the yarn over the needle (yon) from the back to the front and purl to the end of the row.

02 Continue
Turn work and knit to the yarn over (yo) stitch. Knit into the back of the loop, knit the last stitch. Repeating from the * symbol in step 1, continue to work the required number of rows.

03 Transfer the other stitches
Leaving a long tail, cut your yarn, place the stitches just worked on a stitch holder, and transfer the 1st set of stitches back onto your needle. With the right side facing, join in yarn, slip 1 stitch (sl1) knitwise (kwise) and create a make 1 increase (m1). Knit to the end of the row.

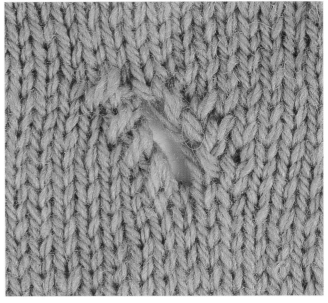

04 Work the two sides together
On the next row, *purl to the last 3 stitches, purl 2 together (p2tog), purl the last stitch. Knit the next row, slipping the 1st stitch. Repeat from * until the same number of rows have been worked. Cut the yarn. Transfer the stitches back to the needles with the right side facing. Rejoin the yarn. Knit across row to the buttonhole, work the two side edges together.

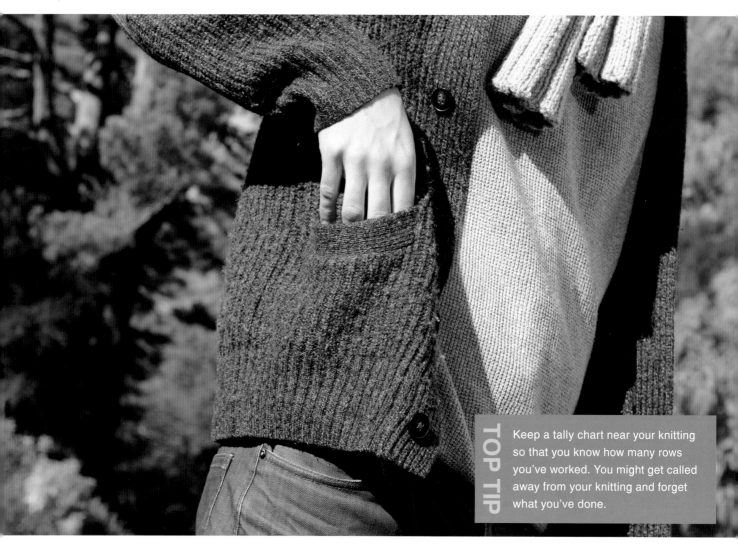

Keep a tally chart near your knitting so that you know how many rows you've worked. You might get called away from your knitting and forget what you've done.

Pockets

Whether practical or decorative, there are several ways you can insert a pocket into your project

Here we will look at three of the most common ways of adding a pocket to a knitted project or garment. First is the patch pocket: this is added to your knitting once you have finished it. You can add lots of fun to sweaters and cushion covers by working the pocket in an outrageously contrasting yarn, or even working an interesting shape such as a hexagon, closing all but the top side. To work this pocket you will pick up the bottom edge of stitches then work the panel, which will be sewn on later.

Second is the horizontal slit pocket — many find this neater than the patch pocket because the lining is worked separately and the opening is more discreet. It is the pocket that most patterns will call for. The example shown here shows the lining worked in a contrast colour to more clearly show you the stitches, but you can also work it in the same colour as the rest of the pattern.

This type of pocket is perfect for a patterned background, such as cable. Make a feature of the pocket and incorporate a cable running up the middle.

Finally, we have a pocket that is perfect for cardigans and hooded projects, the vertical pocket. This is usually inset on the edge of a panel with the pocket lining worked at the same time.

"Add lots of fun by working the pocket in an outrageously contrasting yarn"

Patch pocket
Add these to your garments for a wonderful finishing touch

01 Position the panel
Once you have completed the garment panel, use a contrasting yarn and tapestry needle to 'tack' and outline the pocket position.

02 Secure it
Thread the end of the yarn you are using for the pocket, take it through the right side of the knitted panel, at the bottom-left corner of the pocket position, and secure it on the wrong side. With a crochet hook, insert the point into the centre of the 'v' of the first stitch on the bottom-right corner of the pocket position. Take the point below the top loop, then back out to the front. Catch the yarn with the end of the hook and pull through to make a loop.

03 Work it up
Transfer the loop to a knitting needle, keeping an even tension. Continue to pick up stitches with the crochet hook and transferring them to your needle until you have the required number of stitches on your needle. Turn the work, so that the needle with stitches to be worked is in your left hand, and starting with a wrong side row, work the number of rows required. You can add a garter stitch or ribbed welt to the top of the pocket for a neat finish.

04 Finish it off
Gently block the pocket panel, avoiding the welt, and pin in place on the knitted panel. Remove the tacked stitches. Join the sides to the panel with mattress stitch, darn in ends.

Horizontal slit project
Create this charmingly discreet pocket

01 Work on position
First work the pocket lining as stated in your pattern — this will generally be 2 stitches wider than the cast (bind)-off edge of the pocket. You can leave this panel on a spare needle or stitch holder until you are ready to work it. Now knit to the pocket position and with the right side of the work facing you, cast (bind) off the required number of stitches. Continue to work to the end of the row.

02 Continue the rows
On the next row, work to 1 stitch before the cast (bind) off stitches, and with the wrong side of the pocket lining facing you, work together the last stitch and the first stitch of the pocket lining, then work across all but the last stitch of the pocket. Work this stitch together with the first stitch of the main piece, then work across the rest of main piece stitches.

03 Attach the sides and base
Once you have finished working the garment, attach the sides and base of the pocket to the wrong side of your work.

04 Or try this variation...
Rather than casting (binding) off the stitches on the first step, transfer the pocket top stitches to a stitch holder. Once you have completed the knitted panel, transfer the pocket top stitches to a needle and work a rib or garter stitch welt.

Inset pocket
Learn how to create this final pocket alternative

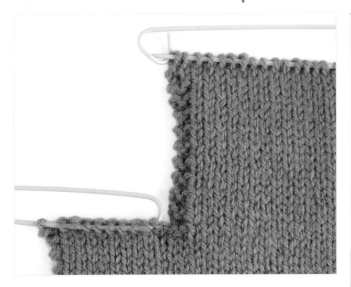

01 Start the pattern

Work your pattern as stated, then on a right-side row, work to the pocket position. Transfer remaining stitches from the left-hand needle to a stitch holder. Turn the work and on the wrong side, knit 2 or 3 stitches to form a garter stitch border, then work to the end of the row. Continue to work the knitted panel until you have worked enough rows for the height of the pocket, keeping the garter stitch edge and ending with a wrong side row. You can keep the stitches worked on a spare needle or transfer them to a stitch holder and cut yarn.

02 Work on the lining

Transfer the stitches from the first stitch holder to a needle ready to work with right side facing. Rejoin yarn and using the cable cast (bind) on method, cast (bind) on the required number of stitches for the pocket lining. Knit across the row, then turn and working on just these stitches, work the same number of rows for the lining as you worked for the front of the pocket. Leave stitches on the needle.

03 Join the lining

To join the pocket lining to the main piece, transfer the stitches from the holder to a needle. With right side facing, work until the same number of stitches that you cast (bound) on for the pocket lining are left on the right needle. With the lining stitches at the back, work together the first 2 stitches of both needles.

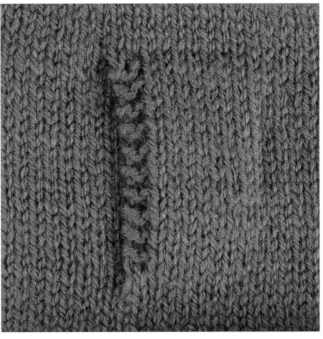

04 Finish up

Continue until all stitches have been worked together. Knit to end of row. Once you have completed your knitted panel, you can pin in place the pocket lining and sew it to the front.

Add a picked up/folded hem

Use this method to create a good thick hem in stocking (stockinette) stitch. It's ideal for smock type sweaters and loose-fitting sleeve cuffs

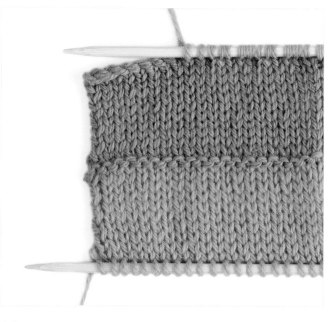

01 Work the hem

Cast (bind) on the number stitches required in the pattern, using a needle one size smaller than you'll use for the main body of the garment. Work the inner hem to the length required, ending on a knit row. If using two colours, change yarn now. Knit the next row (to create a fold line), then change to larger needles and work the same number of rows as worked on the first part of the hem, ending on a purl row.

02 Transfer stitches

With the cast (bind) on edge uppermost, right side (RS) facing and a smaller needle, pick up and knit through the centre of each cast (bind) on stitch using a length of the main body colour yarn. Transfer these stitches so that the point of the needle is facing the opposite direction.

03 Fold the hem

With wrong sides (WS) together, fold the hem and hold both needles in your left hand ready to proceed.

04 Knit stitches together

Rejoin main yarn then insert right needle into the first stitch of both needles. Knit these stitches together. Continue across the row until all stitches have been worked.

05 Finish it

Block hem as per the ballband's instructions.

Picot edge

Use this as an alternative hem for socks, cardigans and more, and you'll get garments with attractive edges

Creating a picot hem is one of knitting's little tricks. Start off by knitting a few rows, be it in rib or stocking (stockinette) stitch, then on 1 row you alternate working 2 stitches together with a yarn over. Carry on working the following rows in your original stitch, then when you fold the hem at the point of the yarn over row with wrong sides together, you'll see you've created an edge of bumps.

Due to the fact that the edge is folded, it lends itself to be used on a stocking (stockinette) stitch border preventing the knitting from rolling. Also if you use this hem on the base of a garment, the fold lends some weight to the piece, helping it to drape nicely. Unless you have used a ribbed picot hem (such as on the sock pattern on page 54), the hem will not be elastic. So only incorporate this style into loose fitting garments.

01 Start your stitches

After having first cast (bind) on an even number of stitches, work between 5 and 7 rows of stocking (stockinette) stitch. The next row will be a right side row. Work the row as follows: *k2tog, yon. Repeat from * to the end of the row.

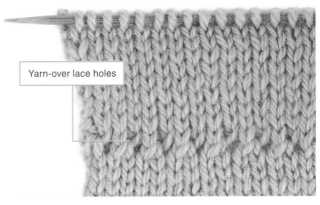

Yarn-over lace holes

02 Purl it

On the next row purl the stitches and the yarn over needles (yon) as you would do normally. Continue to work your pattern as stated.

Tighter hem

Cast (bind) on with a needle size smaller than the pattern suggests to work up to and including the yarn over row. Then change to the recommended needle size.

03 Making up

When you are at the making up stage, fold the picot hem over at the yarn over needle (yon) row, with the wrong sides (WS) together. Pin the hem in place, ensuring that the cast (bind) on edge lines up with a row of knitting. With a tapestry needle thread with yarn, sew the cast (bind) on edge to the row of knitting by inserting the needle into a loop of the stitch, and then into the corresponding stitch on the cast (bind) on edge. Pull yarn through and continue in this way to the end of the hem.

04 Block it

Gently block, being careful to avoid the folded edge.

Blocking

Set your knitting in place and keep it looking its very best by blocking it with steam or water

Once you have spent many hours creating your knitting garment or accessories, you'll want it to look good forever. The way to do this is blocking. Essentially you wet the knitted fabric (before or after) pinning it out to the shape and dimensions given in the measurements and let it dry fully. Sometimes you apply heat but it depends on the fibre you have worked with, so check the yarn label.

There are two processes to blocking: dampening the knitted fabric, and pinning it out to the desired dimensions and shape. If you are making up a garment from separate pieces, block each to the stated size on the measurements table of the pattern by measuring and pinning to size each piece. Once all the pieces are dry you will be able neatly join them all to make up the garment.

Tips for blocking

You don't need specialist equipment to block your knitting.

- **Pins:** You can purchase specific T-pins for blocking your work, but if you're just starting out, regular non-rusting glasshead pins will work just fine.

- **Spray bottle:** The type you use to spray water on plants or to damp hair before cutting.

- **Steam iron:** Not used for all fibres. Please read *'How to treat different fibres'* section for more details.

- **Tape measure:** A metal one is best, as over time fabric tape measures have a tendency to stretch.

- **Blocking mats:** Interlocking foam playmats are ideal, although knitters have been know to block sweater panels over towels pinned to a spare bed.

TOP TIP Place a piece of chequered cloth between the blocking mat and knitting. Use the straight lines to help you pin out straight edges.

How to treat different fibres
Check your yarn's ball band for the fibre content

Wool: This is very forgiving. There are three ways to block this: Wet blocking (do not wring the water, as you will damage the fibres) is ideal for heavy patterns such as cable, Steam Blocking, and Pin and Spritz, which is effective on finer tension (gauge) yarns.

Silk: Once wet, silk becomes very fragile. It is best to Pin and Spritz silk knit fabrics.

Nylon, polyester and other man-made fibres: Avoid the steam iron completely as the heat will damage the fibre structure. It is best to Pin and Spritz.

Cotton: Adding structure during the knitting process is best for cotton. The fibres are inelastic, tend not to hold their shape and have no memory. Steam Blocking is best.

Alpaca and Cashmere: Both of these animal fibres are very delicate indeed. Play it safe with them and Pin and Spritz.

Fibre blends: When there is more than one fibre making up your yarn, again play it safe and Pin and Spritz.

Types of blocking

Here are the three ways to block your knitting. See the opposite page to work out which method would work best for your project

Wet blocking

Immerse your knitted piece into lukewarm or cold water. Gently squeeze out the water, do not wring it as this can damage the connecting fibres. Lay the piece flat on a towel and roll it up like a Swiss roll to squeeze out as much moisture as you can. You may need to repeat this. You can either position your piece on another towel that has been placed on the blocking mat or lay it directly on the mat. Pin it in place and leave it to completely dry.

Steam blocking

Pin your knitted piece out to the dimensions given on the pattern, with your knitted fabric placed right side up. Wet a clean pillowcase or tea towel and wring out any extra moisture. Place this flat on top of your knitting. With your iron on the steam setting, hover it 2cm/0.5in above the knitting; the steam will penetrate the fabric and go through to your knitting. Avoid pressing your iron down, especially on ribbed sections. Once the pillowcase/towel is dry, remove it and leave the knitted piece to cool down and dry out completely overnight.

Pin and Spritz

With the right sides of your pieces facing upwards, pin them into shape and to the dimensions stated on the pattern. With your plant sprayer set to a fine mist, spray your knitting with cold water. You'll find that some fibres will need to be sprayed less than others; wool for example will only need a light mist, while synthetic fibres will require more. Allow the knitting to completely dry away from direct heat and light sources, but preferably in a warm room. This method is perfect for textured knitting, hems and welts.

Pinning out

Take time with this stage for great results

Whether you have wet the fabric first, or will apply moisture after, follow these easy rules. With your pattern to hand place your knitting flat on the blocking mat. Pin all the main points such as top of the shoulders, underarms, neck edges, left and right sides above ribs and cuffs. These should all fit to the measurements given on the pattern. With more pins, secure the fabric between these points at regular intervals. If you are pulling out points, you could be pulling too hard, or don't have enough pins in between. Remember not to put any tension on ribbed sections, as this will cause it to permanently stretch.

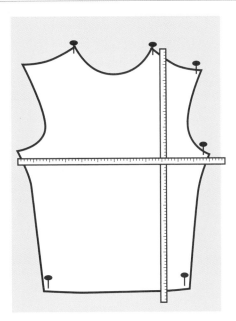

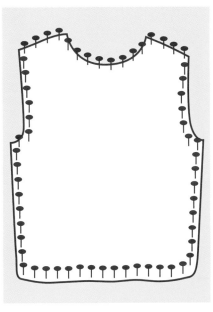

Seaming & edging
Once you've finished knitting the main pieces of your project,
you're going to need to join them together

Figure of eight
Neatly secure your yarn before sewing a seam

01 Get started
With the pieces to be joined, side by side, insert the needle from back to front of the corner of the right piece. Next insert the needle from front to back, on the corner of the left-hand piece and pull through.

02 Secure it
Insert the needle from front to back of the right-hand piece again. Pull through to secure.

03 Be ready to work
For mattress stitch and other joins to be completed with the right side facing, insert the needle into the back of the left piece again so that the yarn is at the front ready to work.

Mattress stitch
Create an invisible seam

01 Use the figure of eight
In order to work this stitch, both pieces must have the same number of rows. To start, place pieces next to each other with right side facing. Attach the yarn you are sewing with using a figure of eight.

02 Join the edges
Insert your needle on the first row between the first and second stitch, pick up the strand and pull the yarn through. Repeat this with the second side. Continue in this way until you have joined the edges. You should have an almost invisible seam.

Edge-to-edge seam
Secure the edges side by side

With the wrong side (WS) facing you, place both pieces to be seamed flat on a surface in front of you. Secure the yarn using the figure of eight at the base, then sew along the edges picking up the little bumps on each edge.

Backstitch
Make a secure seam with a backstitch

This is one of the most popular stitches to use for seam knitting. With right sides facing, pin both pieces together to ensure they don't move. Secure yarn with a figure of eight. Working close to the edge of the knitting, make one stitch by inserting the needle front to back. Bring the needle back through to the front and to the left of the first stitch. Take the needle back to the edge of the previous stitch. Continue in this way until the edge is joined.

Whipped stitch seam
Take the yarn over the top to secure it

With right sides (RS) facing, pin both pieces together to ensure they don't move. Secure the yarn with a figure of eight. Working back to front, insert the needle through the centre of the first stitch of each piece. Take the yarn over and continue to stitch in the same way until the piece is joined.

Hints and tips

- Before you join your knitted pieces, block them to the correct dimensions first. Better stitch definition will ensure a neater finish.

- It is always a good idea to pin the edges of the pieces together at regular intervals so that they don't slip. Use long glass-headed pins for the best results.

- If the yarn you have worked with is too slippery or fluffy, use another yarn of the same colour to join the edges.

- Use a blunt, large-eyed tapestry needle to join knitting. A sharp point will split the yarn, making it difficult to pull yarn through.

"Backstitch is one of the most popular stitches to use for seam knitting"

Grafting
Join your fabric invisibly

01 Secure the yarn

This creates an almost invisible seam, which works particularly well on shoulder seams. With right sides (RS) facing and both cast (bind)-off edges together, secure the yarn with a figure of eight, then on the bottom piece insert the needle under both strands of the 'v' point from left to right. Repeat on the corresponding stitch on the top piece.

02 Create the invisible join

Ensure that you evenly pull the stitches through so that they blend in with the knitted tension (gauge). Once you have finished you should have and almost invisible join.

Grafting open edges together
Create a seamless finish

01 Start grafting

When joining open edges you must have the same number of stitches on both pieces. First remove the waste yarn or stitch holders and place both pieces on a flat surface with the right sides (RS) facing upwards. Thread your needle with the yarn in the same colour as the piece to be grafted (note: for illustrative purposes, we're showing the joining yarn in a contrast colour).

02 Continue the combination

Insert the needle from behind into the middle of the first 'v' stitch on the left piece. Next, insert the needle from bottom to top behind the two legs of the first 'v' stitch on the right piece. Your yarn should be at the front of the work.

Adding an edging
Work a border separately and then sew it on once you've blocked the knitted pieces

01 Place pins
With right sides together, place the knitted edging on top of the main knitted piece. Place pins at regular intervals to prevent either piece moving.

02 Join together
Starting with a figure of eight at the start of the edging, with even overcast stitches, join the two pieces together.

03 Finish up
Once you have sewn all the edging on, unfold it. For a neat finish, you will need to steam block the join using a damp towel and a steam iron (but only if the yarn allows).

03 Close the gap
Take the needle back to the left piece and insert it from bottom to top beneath the two legs of the next 'v', pulling the yarn through to the right side. As you pull the yarn through, gently close the gap between the two pieces, ensuring that the joining stitch is the same size as the stitches in the main knitted pieces. Take the yarn back to the right piece and continue until you have worked all stitches.

04 Secure it
Secure and darn in the end of the yarn on the wrong side (WS) of the work. With the wrong side of the knitting facing you, unravel and discard the contrast waste yarn. Block the piece as recommended.

Fastenings

Once you've finished your knitted piece, it may need to have some closures added. Whether buttons, poppers or a zip, here's how to add them professionally

Once a garment has been knitted and seamed, adding the fastenings can often come as an afterthought. However, choosing the way to close a garment or accessory should be as integral as choosing the yarn and pattern.

Buttons are the most popular way to fasten garments from cardigans and jackets, to open shoulder seams and cushion covers. Choose your buttons before knitting, so that buttonholes can be made the right size, although it is possible to decided on your buttons afterwards so that you can be sure of an good match with the pattern and yarn.

Poppers are a great way to add a fastening if you want an invisible closure and don't have the option in the pattern to add buttonholes. The size of popper needed will be determined by the weight of the yarn worked and the width of the area to be fastened.

Zips can look great on jackets and for easy closures on cushion covers, however their stiffness does not work too well with the elasticity of hand-knitted fabrics. If you are keen to add a zip, choose a yarn that will not shrink or stretch after wearing or washing. Also be aware that zips come in set lengths — purchase your zip before you start knitting and you can work your pattern to the exact zip length. Zips don't tend to come in a variety of shades, so if you don't have an exact match to your yarn colour, adding a zip in a contrasting shade can make a real feature of it

TOP TIP

Drawstrings

Little tote bags can be fastened with a drawstring closure. A row of evenly spaced eyelets can be worked near the top seam of the bag. A drawstring of ribbon, crocheted chain or i-cord can then be threaded through the eyelets.

Sewing buttons
Pick the yarn used for the projects to secure the buttons

01 Secure the yarn

With the yarn/sewing thread doubled, tie a knot at the end. Insert the needle into the right side of the fabric, bring it up from the wrong side and insert into the loop at the end of the yarn by the knot. Pull gently to secure the yarn. On the surface of the fabric, place a cable needle and insert the sewing needle into the hole from the back of the button.

02 Sew the button in place

Sew the button into place in the usual way, keeping the cable needle between the button and the fabric. This ensures that the button isn't sewn on too tightly. Once you have made enough stitches to hold the button do not cut the yarn, but feed the needle through the hole — just don't take it through to the wrong side of the fabric.

03 Strengthen the fastening

With the thread between the fabric surface and the button, lift the button and wind the thread around the connecting stitches several times. This will strengthen the fastening and prevent the button rubbing on the knitted fabric, which could damage it.

Poppers
Place the female side on the outside and the male on the inside

01 The female side

Decide where the poppers is to be placed on the right side (RS) of the inner part of the opening. Evenly space the positions and mark with pins. Taking a needle threaded double with matching thread, secure as for step 1 on attaching buttons. With three or four little stitches, attach the female side popper through the little holes. There is no need to cut the thread between holes, just carry it to the next one.

02 The male side

For the male counterpart of the popper, position them so that they are directly opposite the female side. This time however, when working the little stitches, ensure that the needle and thread do not come through to the right side (RS) of the fabric; instead catch the yarn as you stitch.

Adding a zip
An invisible zip will give the best finish to your knitted garment

01 Choose the right zip

Finding a zip that is the same length as your knitted piece can be hard. Do not be tempted to stretch or bunch your knitted edge to fit the zip length. Instead, choose your zip first and knit to the same length.

02 Pin it

With the zip closed, lay the knitted piece right side (RS) up on a flat surface in position on top of the zip. The knitted edge should cover the teeth of the zip. Pin horizontally at the top, middle and bottom of the zip. Now add pins in the centre of the gaps, then add more pins at the centre of those gaps to ensure even placement. Continue until you have placed enough pins two or three rows apart.

03 Stitch the fabric

With a contrasting yarn or thread, tack the zip to the knitted fabric in a vertical line from top to bottom. Remove pins. Thread a sharp-tipped needle with yarn or matching thread, secure at the bottom hem on the wrong side (WS) and neatly back stitch the fabric to the zip, vertically between the same line of stitches.

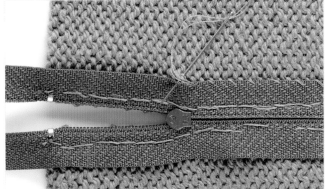

04 Finish it up

Turn the knitted fabric over and using the same yarn or thread, attach the edge of the zip fabric to the wrong side (WS) of the knitting, being careful not to take the needle all the way through the knitted fabric, but following the same vertical line of knitted stitches.

Patterns

Apply your new skills in these patterns

Pretty bunting

Whether for a baby's nursery or an outdoor garden party, this pretty bunting will add a vintage feel. Let your imagination run riot and use many different colours

Difficulty ★★★★★

Skills needed

Decreasing
Colourwork (intarsia)
Knitting in rows
Working from a chart

Finished measurements

Each pennant measures approx 18x14cm (7x5.5in)

Yarn

For this pattern you will need a DK yarn in two colours. In this example, Patons Diploma Gold DK has been used in Cream and Cyclamen.

Colour 1: Cream 1 x ball
Colour 2: Cyclamen; 1 x ball

Tension (Gauge)

22 stitches and 30 rows = 10cm (4in) in stocking stitch (st st)

Needles

4mm (US 6) needles

Other supplies

Stitch holder
Tapestry needle
Ribbon (optional)

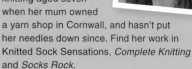

Lou Butt

Lou has been designing knitwear for print and independently for over ten years. She started knitting aged seven when her mum owned a yarn shop in Cornwall, and hasn't put her needles down since. Find her work in Knitted Sock Sensations, *Complete Knitting* and *Socks Rock*.

Pretty bunting

Basic pennant
Cast (bind) on 36 sts
Knit 4 rows.

Start decreases
Row 5 (RS): K3, ssk, K to last 5 sts, k2tog, K3. (2 sts decreased)
Row 6 (WS): K3, P to last 3 sts, K3.
Rep rows 5 and 6 until 8 sts rem.

Next row (RS): K2, ssk, k2tog, K2. (6 sts.)
Next row: Knit.
Next row: K1, ssk, k2tog, K1. (4 sts.)
Next row: Knit.

Next row: ssk, k2tog. (2 sts.)
Next row: k2tog.
Cut yarn and pull through stitch to secure.

Making up
Darn in ends and light block on wrong side by pinning to a triangle shape and placing a damp tea towel on the pennant, then lightly brushing over a steam iron. Leave to cool and dry completely before removing.

Tape
Cast (bind) on 3 sts.
   Knit every row until tape measures 168cm/66in. This is enough to allow you to space out the pennants with approximately 8cm (3in) between them.
   Place sts on a stitch holder, then pin pennants onto knitted tape, leaving 8cm (3in) gaps between each one. You may find that you need to knit more rows, or undo some rows.
   Cast (bind) off and darn in ends.

Note: The bunting would also look great attached to pretty ribbon.

Pennant alternatives

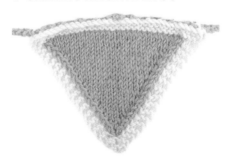

Pennant with coloured border
Work as for **basic pennant** casting (binding) on in col 1, but on first decrease row add in second yarn colour, work as normal to last 3 sts, join in first yarn colour. So that you don't have to purchase a second ball, locate the yarn end from the centre of the ball to work the second border of colour.

Remember to twist yarns at each colour change to avoid holes.

Continue to work with a col 1 garter stitch border, until 8 sts rem, cut second yarn colour and second col 1 strand. Finish with just one strand of col 1.

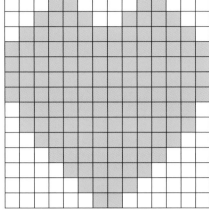

Striped pennant

Work as for **basic pennant** casting (binding) on in col 2, but on first decrease row add in second yarn colour after working the first 3 sts, work as normal to last 3 sts, join in first yarn colour. So that you don't have to purchase a second ball, locate the yarn end from the centre of the ball to work the second border of colour.

Remember to twist yarns at each colour change to avoid holes.

Alternate yarn colours every 2 rows, carrying the col 1 and col 2 yarns at the back of the work. (See intarsia technique).

Continue to work with a col 2 garter stitch border, until 8 sts rem, cut col 1 yarn and second col 2 strand. Finish pennant with just one strand of col 2.

pattern. As you work decreases, the col 1 section of the chart will be decreased away: continue to work the col 2 section as set. Once the chart is complete, continue only in col 1 and complete as per the **basic pennant**.

Moon pennant

Cast (bind) on in col 1 as for basic pennant for 2 sets of decrease rows, until you have 32 sts, ending with a WS row.

In the next row, you add in the second colour and work the chart pattern.

Next row (RS): K3, ssk, K4, work first row of Chart across next 10 sts, K4, k2tog, K3. (2 sts dec)

This sets moon pattern. Follow chart as set and continue with **basic pennant** pattern. As you work decreases, the col 1 section of the chart will be decreased

away: continue to work the col 2 section as set. Once the chart is complete, continue only in col 1 and complete as per the **basic pennant**.

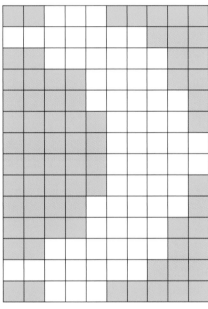

Heart pennant

Cast (bind) on in col 1 as for **basic pennant** for 2 sets of decrease rows, until you have 32 sts, ending with a WS row.

In the next row, you add in the second colour and work the chart pattern.

Next row (RS): K3, ssk, K4, work first row of Heart Chart across next 14 sts, K4, k2tog, K3. (2 sts decreased.)

This sets the Heart pattern. Follow chart as set and continue with **basic pennant**

Garter stitch placemat & coaster

Use several different yarns in various different colours and textures to create this simple yet impressive placemat and coaster set

Difficulty ★☆☆☆☆

Skills needed

Knitting in rows

Finished measurements

Placemat: 32cm (12.5in) deep by 38cm (5in) wide
Coaster: 10cm (4in) by 10cm (4in)

Yarn

For this project you shall require an aran weighted yarn. In the example Texere Wild Silk 8, Crystal Palace Cotton Chenille, Rowan Revive DK (doubled), Yeoman Yarns Cotton Club No. 6 Aran and Yeoman Yarns DK Panama (doubled) were used.

Tension (Gauge)

19 stitches and 30 rows = 10cm (4in) in garter stitch

Needles

4.5mm (US 7) needles

Pattern notes

Any aran weight yarns can be used for this project. Finer yarns can be doubled up. The sample uses several different yarns in various colours and textures.

Sian Brown

After doing a Fashion/ Textiles BA, Sian worked for companies in London supplying to high street retailers on machine knits. Sian has one book to her name, *The Knitted Home*. Visit her at **sianbrown.com**.

Placemat and coaster

Placemat

With colour 1, cast (bind) on 60 stitches. Work in garter stitch until work measures 38cm (15in) from cast (bind) on edge, bringing in colours 2—7 randomly for whole or part rows.

Cast (bind) off.

Neaten off ends, especially at edges of placemat. Press under a cloth, evening out edges while pressing.

Coaster

With colour 1, cast (bind) on 20 stitches. Work in garter stitch as for placemat until work measures 10cm (4in) from cast (bind) on edge.

Finish as for **placemat**.

Diamond cushion cover

Make this cosy looking cushion cover complete with button holes, seaming and a cable pattern

Difficulty ★★★☆☆

Skills needed
Cables
Knitting in rows
Seaming

Finished measurements
41x41 cm (16x16 in) cushion pad.

Yarn
For this project you will need an Aran weight yarn. In this example Wendy Aran in cream. You will need one 400g ball.

Tension (Gauge)
20sts and 24 rows = 10cm (4ins) over patt.

Needles
2—4mm (US 7)

Other supplies
2 buttons
Darning needle

Thomas B Ramsden

This pattern was kindly supplied by Thomas B Ramsden, a family business who are the suppliers of Wendys and Peter Pan, two of the biggest brands of yarn in the UK. You can find them at **www.tbramsden.co.uk**.

Diamond cushion cover

Front

Cast (bind) on 75 sts, work 2 rows in garter stitch.

Row 1: K1, P1, *m1, K2tbl, p2tog, P1 [K1tbl, P2] twice, K1tbl, P1, p2tog, K2tbl, m1, P1 rep from *to last st, K1

Row 2: K1, *K2, P2, [K2, P1] 3 times, K2, P2, K1 rep from *to last 2 sts, K2

Row 3: K1, P1, *P1, m1, K2tbl, P2, sl, K1, psso, P1, K1tbl, P1, k2tog, P2, K2tbl, m1, P2, rep from * to last st, K1

Row 4: K1, *K3, P2, K2, [P1, K1] twice, P1, K2, P2, K2, rep from *to last 2 sts, K2

Row 5: K1, (K1, yf, K1, yf, K1) in next st, *P2, m1, K2tbl, P2, sl, K1, psso, K1tbl, k2tog, P2, K2tbl, m1, P2, (K1, yf, K1, yf, K1) in next st, rep from *to last st, K1

Row 6: K1, *P5, K3, P2, K2, P3, K2, P2, K3, rep from *to last 6 sts, P5, K1

Row 7: K6, *P3, m1, K2tbl, P2, sl, k2tog, psso, P2, K2tbl, m1, P3, K5, rep from *to last st, K1

Row 8: K1 *P5, K4, P2, K2, P1, K2, P2, K4, rep from *to last 6 sts, P5, K1

Row 9: K1, sl, K1, psso, K1, k2tog, *P2, (K1, yf, K1, yf, K1) in next st, P1, m1, K2tbl, p2tog, K1tbl, p2tog, K2tbl, m1, P1, (K1, yf, K1, yf, K1) in next st, P2 sl, K1, psso, K1, k2tog, rep from *to last st, K1

Row 10: K1, *p3tog, K2, P5, K2, P2, K1, P1, K1, P2, K2, P5, K2, rep from *to last 4 sts, P3tog, K1

Row 11: K1, K1tbl, *P2, K5, P2, m1, K2tbl, p3tog, K2tbl, m1, P2, K5, P2, K1tbl, rep from *to last st, K1

Row 12: K1, *P1, K2, P5, K3, P2, K1, P2, K3, P5, K2, rep from *to last 2 sts, P1, K1

Row 13: K1, K1tbl, *P2, sl, K1, psso, K1, k2tog, P3, K2tbl, P1, K1tbl, P3, sl, K1, psso, K1, k2tog, P2, K1tbl, rep from *to last st, K1

Row 14: K1, *P1, K2, p3tog, K3, P2, K1, P2, K3, P3tog, K2, rep from *to last 2 sts, P1, K1

Row 15: K1, K1tbl, *P2, K1tbl, P1, p2tog, K2tbl, m1, P1, m1, K2tbl, p2tog, P1, K1tbl, P2, K1tbl, rep from *to last st, K1

Row 16: K1, *[P1, K2] twice, P2, K3, P2, K2, P1, K2, rep from *to last 2 sts, P1 K1

Row 17: K1, K1tbl, *P1, k2tog, P2, K2tbl, m1, P3, M1, K2tbl, P2, sl, K1, psso, P1, K1tbl, rep from *to last st, K1

Row 18: K1, *P1, K1, P1, K2, P2, K5, P2, K2, P1, K1, rep from *to last 2 sts, P1, K1

Row 19: K1, K1tbl, *k2tog, P2, K2tbl, m1, P2, (K1, yf, K1, yf, K1) in next st, P2, M1, K2tbl, P2, sl, K1, psso, K1tbl, rep from *to last st, K1

Row 20: K1, *P2, K2, P2, K3, P5, K3, P2, K2, P1, rep from *to last 2 sts, P1, K1

Row 21: K1, k2tog, *P2, K2tbl, m1, P3, K5, P3, m1, K2tbl, P2, sl, k2tog, psso, rep from *to last 22 sts, P2, K2tbl, m1, P3, K5, P3, m1, K2tbl, P2, sl, K1, psso, K1

Row 22: K1, *P1, K2, P2, K4, P5, K4, P2, K2, rep from *to last 2 sts, P1, K1

Row 23: K1, K1tbl, *p2tog, K2tbl, m1, P1, (K1, yf, K1, yf, K1) in next st, P2, sl, K1, psso, K1, k2tog, P2, (K1, yf, K1, yf, K1) in next st, P1, m1, K2tbl, p2tog, K1tbl, rep from *to last st, K1

Row 24: K1, *P1, K1, P2, K2, P5, K2, P3tog, K2, P5, K2, P2, K1, rep from *to last 2 sts, P1, K1

Row 25: K1, p2tog, *K2tbl, m1, P2, K5, P2, K1tbl, P2, K5, P2, m1, K2tbl, p3tog, rep from *to last 26 sts, K2tbl, m1, P2, K5, P2, K1tbl, P2, K5, P2, m1, K2tbl, p2tog, K1,

Row 26: K1 *K1, P2, K3, P5, K2, P1, K2, P5, K3, P2, rep from *to last 2 sts, K2

Row 27: K1, P1, *K2tbl, P3, sl, K1, psso, K1, k2tog, P2, K1tbl, P2, sl, K1, psso, K1, k2tog, P3, K2tbl, P1, rep from *to last st, K1

Row 28: K1, *K1, P2, K3, p3tog, K2, P1, K2, p3tog, K3, P2, rep from *to last 2 sts, K2
From Row 1 to 28th row (inclusive) forms patt. Keeping continuity of patt (throughout) cont until work measures approximately 41 cm (16 ins), ending with 14th row of patt. Cast (bind) off in patt.

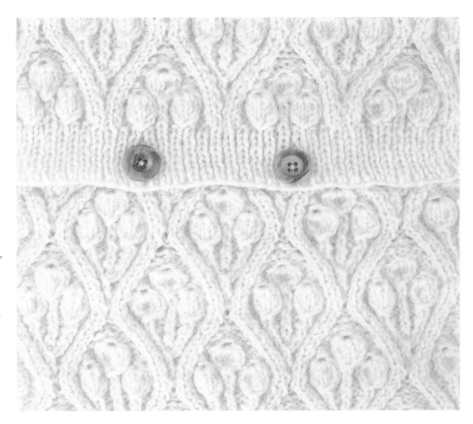

Back (in 2 pieces)

Cast (bind) on 75 sts Work 2 rows in garter stitch.

  Work rows 1 - 28 twice.
  Change to K1, P1 rib and work 4 rows.

Next Row (Buttonhole row): Rib 25, yo, rib 2tog, rib 21, yo, rib 2tog, rib 25.

Work 3 more rows in rib.
Cast (bind) off.

2nd Piece

sing 4mm Needles cast (bind) on 75 sts
Work 8 rows in K1, P1 rib

Cont in patt, starting with row 5 to 28. Rep rows 1-28 until the two pieces of the Back when overlap rib section are put together match the Front, ending with a 14th patt row Cast (bind) off in patt.

Making up

Overlap the rib sections of Back cushion cover together and tack in place. Sew Front and Back together by top sewing. Remove tacking sts.
Sew on buttons. Block.

Hearts Fair Isle tea cosy & hot water bottle cover

Now it's time to really put your skills to the test and practise some of the harder techniques you've learned by creating a fetching tea cosy and hot water bottle cover

"For this pattern you will need 7 different colours"

Difficulty ★★★★★

Skills needed

Knitting in rows
Fair Isle
Seaming

Finished measurements

Tea Cosy: 23cm (9ins) wide x 20.5cm (8ins) deep.
Hot Water Bottle Cover:
20.5cm (8ins) wide x 30.5cm (12ins) deep.

Yarn

For this pattern you will need 7 different colours, as listed below, in Aran weight. In this example Drops Alaska and Drops Nepal. Amounts are the same for both projects unless otherwise stated.
Colour 1: Nepal; Light Grey Green; 1 x ball. (You will need 2 x balls for the Hot Water Bottle.)
Colour 2: Alaska; Mid Purple; 1 x ball.
Colour 3: Nepal; Light Olive; 1 x ball.
Colour 4: Alaska; Red; 1 x ball.
Colour 5: Alaska; Turquoise; 1 x ball.
Colour 6: Alaska; Deep Purple; 1 x ball.
Colour 7: Nepal; Goldenrod; 1 x ball.

Tension (Gauge)

Work 18 sts and 24 rows in st st to measure 10x10cm (4x4in) using 5mm (US 8) needles, or size required to obtain correct tension.

Needles

5mm (US 8).

TOP TIP
If there is an even amount of stitches per row, you will start with alternate knit and purl stitches each row.

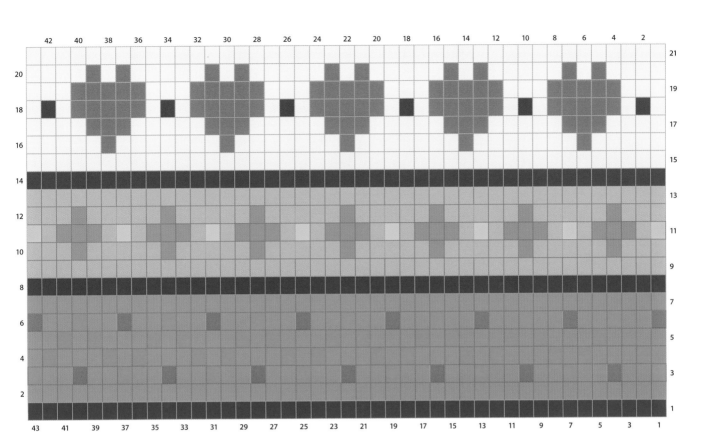

Hearts Fair Isle tea cosy

Front

With col 6, cast (bind) on 45 sts.
Knit 4 rows.

Row 1 (WS): K1 col 3, P43 sts of chart 1 for front, K1.

Rows 2-20; Cont to follow 43 sts chart as set, until 21 rows of the chart have been completed, keeping K1 at each end of every row.

Rows 21-34; Starting with a P row, work rows 1 to 14 once more.

*Row 35; Join col 1, and P 1 row.
Cont with col 1, as follows:
Knit 2 rows.

Eyelet row (RS): K3, *K2tog, yo, K4* rep between * 7 times.
Knit 7 rows.
Break off col 1.
Change to col 6. K 1 row.
Cast (bind) off kwise.*

Back

With col 6, cast (bind) on 45 sts.
Knit 4 rows.

Row 1 (WS): K1, P across 43 sts chart 2, K 1 col 6.

Rows 2-34; Cont to follow chart for back until 34 rows have been worked, keeping K1 at each end of every row.
Complete as for front * to *.

Making up

Press pieces under a damp cloth.
Sew side seams, leaving gaps for handle and spout.

Tie

Cut 6 lengths of yarn in cols 1, 2 and 3, 75cm (30in) long. Plait to form a tie, and thread through eyelets.

Key:

☐ Colour 1
☐ Colour 2
☐ Colour 3
☐ Colour 4
☐ Colour 5
■ Colour 6
☐ Colour 7

Note

As you work through the charts, join colours as you need them. Knit the first and last stitch of each row in the background colour that you used for that row.

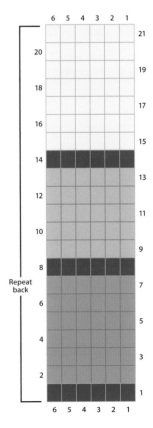

Hearts Fair Isle hot water bottle cover

Front

With col 3, cast (bind) on 45 sts.
　Knit 2 rows.

Row 1 (WS): K1, P across 43 sts chart 1, K1.
Rows 2-20: Starting with row 3, K1, work 43 sts across chart 1, K1.
Cont to follow chart until 21 rows of the chart have been worked
Rows 21-41: Starting with a P row, and col 6, work rows 1-21 of chart again, keeping K1 at start and end of each row.
Rows 42-63: Starting with a K row, and col 6, work rows 1-21 of chart again, keeping K1 at start and end of each row. Row 63 (WS): P 1 row col 6. Break off col 6.
Continue with col 1 only as follows:

Eyelet row (RS): K3, *K2tog, yo, K4* rep between * 7 times.
　Knit 9 rows.
　Change to col 6.
　Knit 1 row.
　Cast (bind) off kwise.

Back

With col 3, cast (bind) on 45 sts.
Knit 2 rows.

Row 2 (WS): K1, P across 43 sts chart 2, repeating the chart across all sts, K 1 col 3.
Rows 3-63: Continue to follow chart 2 for stripe sequence, working K1 st at each end of every row, until 62 rows of the chart have been worked.
　Complete as for front from * to *.

Making up

Press both sides under a damp cloth.
　Sew side and bottom seams.

Tie

Cut 6 strands of yarn, 2 each in cols 1, 2 and 3, 75cm (30in) long. Plait to form a tie, and thread through eyelets.

Sian Brown

After doing a Fashion/ Textiles BA, Sian worked for companies in London supplying to high street retailers on machine knits. She became interested in handknits and have designed these since, working for magazines, publishers and yarn companies. Sian has a book, *The Knitted Home*, and have designed on several others. Visit her website at **sianbrown.com**.

Weekender hat

Knit in rounds to discover this easy, casual, yet elegant style — perfect for protecting against cold weather

Difficulty ★★☆☆☆

Skills needed

Increasing
Decreasing
Lace stitches
Knitting in rounds
Specialist cast-on

Finished measurements

To fit sizes: 18 (21, 23) in
                    45.75 (53.5, 58.5) cm
Finished size: 14.75 (17.25, 19.75) in
                   37 (43, 49.25) cm

Yarn

For this project we have used one ball of Rowan Cocoon yarn, which is made up of 80 per cent Merino, 20 per cent Kid Mohair. You will need a total of 76 (94, 114) metres, 83 (103, 125) yards.

Tension (Gauge)

14 sts and 20 rows = 10cm (4in) in stocking (stockinette) stitch using 6mm (US 10) needles.

Needles

5.5mm (US 9) circular needle, 40cm (16in) long
6mm (US 10) circular needle, 40cm (16in) long
6mm (US 10) DPNs

Other supplies

1 stitch marker
Tapestry needle

Woolly Wormhead

Woolly is a Hat Architect. With a flair for unusual construction, Woolly is a designer whose patterns are celebrated by knitters all over the world. **www.woollywormhead.com**.

Weekender hat

Pattern recommends the Alternate Cable cast-on method — any suitable rib cast-on method will work.

Using 5.5mm needles and alternate cable cast-on method, cast (bind) on 48 (56, 64) sts.

Join in the round, being careful not to twist sts.

Place stitch marker to indicate start of round.

Brim

Rnd 1: *K1, P1; rep from * to end.
Repeat this round for 5cm (2in) (or desired length).
Inc Rnd: *K2, M1; rep from * to end. (72, 84, 96 sts.)

Body

Change to 6mm (US 10) needles for the remainder of the hat, changing to the DPNs for the crown when the hat becomes too small to work comfortably on the circular needle.
Rnd 1: *Yo, K2tog; rep from * to end.

Repeat this round to form the bias eyelet rib pattern until the body of the hat (excluding the brim) measures 9.5 (10.25, 10.75) cm, 3.75 (4, 4.25) in.

Crown

Foundation Rnd: Knit all sts.
45.75cm (18in) size jump to Rnd 5, 53.5cm (21in) size jump to Rnd 3, 58.5cm (23in) size start at Rnd 1, decreasing on every round as follows:

Rnd 1: *K14, ssk; rep from * to end. (90 sts.)
Rnd 2: *K13, ssk; rep from * to end. (84 sts.)
Rnd 3: *K12, ssk; rep from * to end. (78 sts.)
Rnd 4: *K11, ssk; rep from * to end. (72 sts.)
Rnd 5: *K10, ssk; rep from * to end. (66 sts.)
Rnd 6: *K9, ssk; rep from * to end. (60 sts.)
Rnd 7: *K8, ssk; rep from * to end. (54 sts.)
Rnd 8: *K7, ssk; rep from * to end. (48 sts.)
Rnd 9: *K6, ssk; rep from * to end. (42 sts.)
Rnd 10: *K5, ssk; rep from * to end. (36 sts.)
Rnd 11: *K4, ssk; rep from * to end. (30 sts.)
Rnd 12: *K3, ssk; rep from * to end. (24 sts.)
Rnd 13: *K2, ssk; rep from * to end. (18 sts.)
Rnd 14: *K1, ssk; rep from * to end. (12 sts.)
Rnd 15: *Ssk; rep from * to end. (6 sts.)

Break yarn and draw through remaining 6 sts. Tighten to close.

Making up

Weave in all ends. A gentle wash and blocking is required to help the decrease lines settle in and lay flat.

Basketweave fingerless mitts

Sometimes fingered gloves just aren't practical. Have a go at making some funky fingerless mitts that will keep your hands warm but still enable you to carry out everyday tasks

Difficulty ★★☆☆☆

Skills needed
Increasing
Knitting in rows
Seaming

Finished measurements
Sizes approximate around palm or hand.
Small: 15cm (6 in)
Medium: 18cm (7 inches)
Large: 19 cm (7.5 inches)

Yarn
For this pattern you will need a 4 ply yarn. For this example, Wendy Roam Fusion in Force (above) and Heath (right) was used. You will need one ball.

Tension (Gauge)
37 sts and 52 rows = 10 cm (4 ins) over basket weave stitch

Needles
2¾ mm (US 2) knitting needles

Other supplies
Safety pin to hold 20 sts.

Construction notes
There is a lot of counting involved in the pattern. When reaching the thumb, remember to count the 35 stitches across before breaking the basket weave in order to do the thumb stitches.

Thomas B Ramsden

This pattern was kindly supplied by Thomas B Ramsden, a family business who are the suppliers of Wendys and Peter Pan, two of the biggest brands of yarn in the UK. You can find them at **www.tbramsden.co.uk**.

Be wary when following the 'patt to end' in order to match it up to continue the basketweave effect.

Basketweave fingerless mitts

Using 2¾ mm needles, cast (bind) on 57 (65, 73) sts.

Ribbed cuff

1st Row: K3, P2, * K2, P2 rep from * to end.
2nd Row: * K2, P2, rep from * to last st, P1
These two rows form rib. Continue in rib as set until work measures 7cm, 2¾ ins.

Commence basket weave pattern

Row 1: (rs) K1, * K2, P6, rep from * to end.
Row 2: (ws) * K6, P2, rep from * to last st, P1.
Row 3: As row 1.
Row 4: Purl.
Row 5: P5, * K2, P6, rep from * to last 4 stitches, K2, P2.
Row 6: K2, P2, *K6, P2, rep from * to last 5 sts, K5.
Row 7: As row 5.
Row 8: Purl.

These rows form basket weave pattern. Work rows 1 to 8 once and then work rows 1 to 4.

Thumb

Row 13: Keeping basket weave pattern

correct, and starting from 5th row of pattern, patt 28 (32, 36) sts, M1, K2, M1, patt to end.
Row 14: Patt 27 (31, 35) sts, P4, patt to end.
Row 15: Patt 28 (32, 36) sts, K4, patt to end.
Row 16: Patt 27 (31, 35) sts, M1 pwise, P4, M1 pwise, patt to end.
Row 17: Patt 28 (32, 36) sts, K6, patt to end.
Row 18: Patt 27 (31, 35) sts, P6, patt to end.
Row 19: Patt 28 (32, 36) sts, M1, K6, M1, patt to end.
Row 20: Patt 27 (31, 35) sts, P8, patt to end.
Row 21: Patt 28 (32, 36) sts, K8, patt to end.
Row 22: Patt 27 (31, 35) sts, M1 pwise, P8, M1 pwise, patt to end.
Row 23: Patt 28 (32, 36) sts, K10, patt to end.
Row 24: Patt 27 (31, 35) sts, P10, patt to end.
Row 25: Patt 28 (32, 36) sts, M1, K10, M1, patt to end.
Row 26: Patt 27 (31, 35) sts, P12, patt to end.
Row 27: Patt 28 (32, 36) sts, K12, patt to end.
Row 28: Patt 27 (31, 35) sts, M1 pwise, P12, M1 pwise, patt to end.
Row 29: Patt 28 (32, 36) sts, K14, patt to end.
Row 30: Patt 27 (31, 35) sts, P14, patt to end.
Row 31: Patt 28 (32, 36) sts, M1, K14, M1, patt to end.
Row 32: Patt 27 (31, 35) sts, P16, patt to end.
Row 33: Patt 28 (32, 36) sts, K16, patt to end.
Row 34: Patt 27 (31, 35) sts, M1 pwise, P16,

M1 pwise, patt to end.
Row 35: Patt 28 (32, 36) sts, K18, patt to end.
Row 36: Patt 27 (31, 35) sts, P18, patt to end.
Row 37: Patt 28 (32, 36) sts, M1, K18, M1, patt to end.
Row 38: Patt 27 (31, 35) sts, P20, patt to end.
Row 39: Patt 28 (32, 36) sts, K20, patt to end.

1st size only

Row 40: Patt 27 (31, 35) sts, slip next 20 sts onto a safety pin, cast (bind) on 2 sts, patt to end.

2nd and 3rd sizes only

Row 40: Patt (31, 35) sts, M1 pwise, P20, M1 pwise, patt to end.
Row 41: Patt (32, 36) sts, K22, patt to end.
Row 42: Patt (31, 35) sts, M1 pwise, P22, M1 pwise, patt to end.
Row 43: Patt (32, 36) sts, K 24, patt to end.
Row 44: Patt (31, 35) sts, slip next 24 sts onto a safety pin, cast (bind) on 2 sts, patt to end.

All sizes

Work 16 (18, 20) more rows in basket weave pattern over all 57 (65, 73) sts on needle.
Work 8 rows in rib, as worked for ribbed cuff.
Cast (bind) off.

Thumb

Return to sts left on safety pin, rejoin yarn with wrong side facing and P across 20 (24, 24) sts, pick up and P 4 sts over the 2 cast (bind) on sts.

Next Row: K1, M1, K1, P2, * K2, P2, rep from * to end.
Next Row: * K2, P2, rep from * to last st, P1.
Next Row: K3, P2, *K2, P2, rep from * to end.

Rep last 2 rows 4 times more, and then cast (bind) off in rib.

Making up

Join side seam and thumb seam by top sewing
Repeat for the other mitt.

Staggered beanie

Create this fantastic beanie with a staggered block pattern by knitting in the round, perfect as a gift for anyone

Difficulty ★★☆☆☆

Skills needed

Increasing
Decreasing
Knitting in rounds

Finished measurements

To fit sizes: 15 (18, 20, 22, 24) in
38 (45.75, 50.75, 56, 61) cm
Finished size: 13 (15.25, 17.5, 19.75,
21.75) in
33.25 (38.75, 44.25, 50,
55.5) cm

Yarn

For this project you will need a DK yarn.
In this example, Debbie Bliss Blue Faces
Leicester DK was used in Chestnut. You will
need 45 (60, 78, 98, 120) m/49 (66, 85, 107,
131) yd.

Tension (Gauge)

22 sts and 35 rounds = 10cm (4in) in
stocking (stockinette) stitch

Needles

3.25mm (US 3) circular needle, 40cm
(16in) long
3.25mm (US 3) DPNs

Other supplies

1 stitch marker
Tapestry needle

**Woolly
Wormhead**

Woolly is a Hat Architect.
With a flair for unusual
construction, Woolly is
a designer whose patterns are
celebrated by knitters all over the world.
www.woollywormhead.com.

Staggered beanie

Using cast (bind) on method of your choice, cast (bind) on 72 (84, 96, 108, 120) sts onto the circular needle. Join in the round, being careful not to twist sts. Place stitch marker to indicate start of round.

Brim

Rnd 1: *K3, P3; repeat from * to end
Repeat this round until brim measures 1 (1.25, 1.5, 1.75, 2) in/2.5 (3.25, 3.75, 4.5, 5) cm.

Body

Rnd 1: *K3, P9; repeat from * to end

Repeat this round for a further 1 (1.25, 1.5, 1.75, 2) in/2.5 (3.25, 3.75, 4.5, 5) cm until work measures 2 (2.5, 3, 3.5, 4) in/5 (6.25, 7.5, 9, 10.25) cm from cast (bind)-on edge. Work as follows:

Next rnd: Purl all sts

Repeat this round, forming reverse stocking (stockinette) stitch, for a further 1.5in/3.75cm until work measures 3.5 (4, 4.5, 5, 5.5) in/9 (10.25, 11.5, 12.75, 14) cm from cast (bind)-on edge.

Crown preparation

18in size only: *p2tog, P19; repeat from * to end. 80 sts.
22in size only: *P12, p2tog, P13; repeat from * to end. 104 sts.

Crown

15in/38cm size jump to Rnd 13; 18in/45cm size jump to Rnd 11; 20in/50.75cm size jump to Rnd 7; 22in/56cm size jump to Rnd 5; 24in/61cm size start at Rnd 1.

As you work through these instructions, as the hat gets too small to work comfortably on the circular needle, change to the DPNs.

Rnd 1: *(ssp, P26, p2tog); repeat from * to end. 112 sts.
Rnd 2 & all even rounds: Purl all sts
Rnd 3: P12, p2tog, (ssp, P24, p2tog) 3 times, ssp, P12. 104 sts.
Rnd 5: *(ssp, P22, p2tog); repeat from * to end. 96 sts.
Rnd 7: P10, p2tog, (ssp, P20, p2tog) 3 times, ssp, P10/ 88 sts.
Rnd 9: *(ssp, P18, p2tog); repeat from * to end. 80 sts.

Rnd 11: P8, p2tog, (ssp, P16, p2tog) 3 times, ssp, P8/ 72 sts.
Rnd 13: *(ssp, P14, p2tog); repeat from * to end. 64 sts.
Rnd 15: P6, p2tog, (ssp, P12, p2tog) 3 times, ssp, P6. 56 sts.
Rnd 17: *(ssp, P10, p2tog); repeat from * to end. 48 sts.
Rnd 19: P4, p2tog, (ssp, P8, p2tog) 3 times, ssp, P4. 40 sts.
Rnd 21: *(ssp, P6, p2tog); repeat from * to end. 32 sts.
Rnd 23: P2, p2tog, (ssp, P4, p2tog) 3 times, ssp, P2. 24 sts.
Rnd 25: *(ssp, P2, p2tog); repeat from * to end. 16 sts.
Rnd 27: *(p2tog, ssp); repeat from * to end. 8 sts.

Break yarn and draw through remaining 8 sts, tighten to close.

Making up

Weave in all ends. A gentle wash and blocking is required to help the decreases settle in and lay flat.

2x3 rib scarf

Now that you have mastered rib stitch, have a go at this quick to knit scarf. Perfect to keep anyone cosy, as the 2x3 rib stitch causes ripples in the fabric, which will hold in warm air

Difficulty ★★★★★

Skills needed
Knitting in rows
Rib stitches
Cast (bind) off in rib

Finished measurements
140cm (55in) x 18cm (7in)

Yarn
For this project you will need an Aran weight yarn. In this example we have used Sirdar Hayfield Bonus Aran in Denim. You will need approximately 420m (459yd).

Tension (Gauge)
28sts and 22 rows = 10cm (4in) in 2x3 rib stitch using 5mm (US 8) needles.

Needles
5mm (US 8) needles

Other supplies
Tapestry needle

2x3 rib scarf
Cast on 50 sts using 5mm needles
Row 1: *K3, P2; rep from * to end.
Row 2: *K2, P2; rep from * to end.

These 2 rows form 2x3 rib pattern. Continue in pattern until your knitting measures 140cm (55in), or your desired length, from the cast (bind) on edge.
     Cast (bind) off.

Making up
Darn in ends and gently block.

Did you know?
You can use different combinations of knit and purl stitches to create a different looking rib pattern. A 2x2 rib is common for a good stretchy cuff on knitted hats.

Lou Butt

Lou has been designing knitwear for print and independently for over ten years. She started knitting aged seven when her mum owned a yarn shop in Cornwall, and hasn't put her needles down since. Find her work in Knitted Sock Sensations, *Complete Knitting* and *Socks Rock*.

Cosy welly socks

Whether you're on a dog walk, splashing in puddles or pottering in the garden, keep your feet cosy with these thick welly socks

Difficulty ★★★★☆

Skills needed

Decreasing
Cable
Pick up & knit
Knitting in rounds
Kitchener stitch
Turning a heel

Finished measurements

They are thick, so if your wellies are snug, make them a little shorter. The measurements in this pattern are designed to fit a women's size 6 foot of average width. The length of foot can be adjusted for a better fit; see notes in the pattern.

Yarn

For this pattern you will require a super chunky yarn to keep your toes nice and toasty. In this example Wendy Serenity Super Chunky has been used, which is made up of 10 per cent wool, 20 per cent alpaca and 70 per cent acrylic. The shade used is 1711 Peony. You will need 2 balls.

Tension (Gauge)

10 stitches and 14 rounds = 10cm (4in) in stocking stitch

Needles

10mm (US 15) 4x double pointed needles

Lou Butt

Lou has been designing knitwear for print and independently for over ten years. She started knitting aged seven when her mum owned a yarn shop in Cornwall, and hasn't put her needles down since. Find her work in Knitted Sock Sensations, *Complete Knitting* and *Socks Rock*.

Other supplies

1 stitch marker
Cable needle
Tapestry needle

Construction notes

Both socks are worked in the same way, except for the cable stitch. On one sock the cable is turned left, on the other the cable is turned right.

Special st instructions:

C4B: Slip the next 2 sts onto your cable needle and hold at **back** of work, K the next 2 sts on the left-hand needle, then K the sts from the cable needle.

C4F: Slip the next 2 sts onto your cable needle and hold at **front** of work, K the next 2 sts on the left-hand needle, then K the sts from the cable needle.

Right sock cable pattern

Worked over 11 sts, in the round
Rnds 1 & 2: K3, P2, K4, P2.
Rnd 3: K3, P2, C4B, P2.
Rnd 4: K3, P2, K4, P2.

Left sock cable pattern

Worked over 11 sts, in the round
Rnds 1 & 2: K3, P2, K4, P2.
Rnd 3: K3, P2, C4F, P2.
Rnd 4: K3, P2, K4, P2.

Cosy welly socks

Cast 30 sts onto a single needle.
Arrange stitches evenly over 3 needles being careful not to twist the stitches.
Slip the first st of the left-hand needle, onto the right needle, next lift the first st on the right needle over the top of the st you just slipped and place it on the left-hand needle.
This will be the first st you work.
Place a stitch marker between stitches 1 and 2 to denote the beginning of the round.

Rnd 1 (establish ribbing): (K1, P1) to end. Rep rnd 1 8 more times.
Next rnd (establish cable pattern): Work appropriate Cable pattern over first 11 sts of round, K to end.

Work 8 rounds in pattern as set, until 2 full repeats of the Cable pattern have been worked.

Next rnd (dec): Work Cable pattern as set, K2, K2tog, K to last 2 sts, K2tog. (28 sts.) Work 7 rounds even as set.
Next rnd (dec): Work Cable pattern as set, K1, K2tog, K to last 2 sts, K2tog. (26 sts.)

Continue even in pattern until piece from cast-on edge measures 43cm (17in), ending with Rnd 4 of the cable pattern.

Divide for heel

Arrange your stitches so that there are 14 on the first needle of the round. The heel is worked on these stitches only.
Row 1 (RS): Sl1, K2, P2, K4, P2, K3. Turn.
Row 2 (WS): Sl1, P2, K2, P4, K2, P3. Turn.
Repeat these 2 rows twice more.

Turn heel

Row 1 (RS): Sl1, K7, SSK, K1. Turn.
Row 2 (WS): Sl 1, P3, P2tog, P1. Turn.
Row 3: Sl 1, K4, SSK, K1. Turn.
Row 4: Sl 1, P5, P2tog, P1. Turn.
Row 5: Sl 1, K6, SSK. Turn.
Row 6: Sl 1, P6, P2tog. Turn. 8 sts rem on heel.

Rnd 1 (gusset setup):
Needle 1: Knit 8 heel sts, then pick up and knit 4 sts along first side of heel, using the slipped sts as a guide.
Needle 2: Knit all 12 sts.
Needle 3: Pick up and knit 4 sts along second side of heel flap using the slipped sts as a guide, then K4 sts from the first needle.

Gusset rnd 2:
Needle 1: K to last 3 sts, k2tog, K1.
Needle 2: K.
Needle 3: K1, SSK, k to end of needle. (2 sts decreased)

Gusset rnd 3: Knit all sts.

Repeat gusset round 2 once more. 24 sts rem.

Now knit every round until work from heel to needles measures 19cm (7.5in), or 5cm (2in) short of full foot length.

Shape toe

Rnd 1:
Needle 1: K to last 3 sts, K2tog, K1.
Needle 2: K1, SSK, K to last 3 sts, K2tog, K1.
Needle 3: K1, SSK, K to end of needle. (4 sts decreased.)

Rnd 2: Knit.

Rep Rnd 1 and 2 once more. 16 sts. Work Rnd 1 twice. (8 sts)

Knit the sts from needle 1 onto needle 3. With right side facing, graft the toe using a kitchener stitch.

Making up

Darn in ends.

Nordic winter hat

Keep yourself warm when the temperatures begin to drop with this fun Nordic-style hat

Difficulty ★★★☆☆

Skills needed

Decreasing
Colourwork (stranded)
Knitting in rounds
Working from a chart

Finished measurements

One size fits most people
Circumference: 55cm (22in)
Length: 34cm (13.5in)

Yarn

For this pattern you will need a super chunky yarn. In this example Drops Eskimo has been used. You will need approximately 100m (108 yd).
Colour 1: Red; 2 x balls
Colour 2: White; 1 x ball
Colour 3: Grey; 1 x ball

Tension (Gauge)

13 stitches and 16 rounds = 10cm (4in) in stocking (stockinette) stitch

Needles

8mm (US 11) 40cm (16in) circular needle
8mm (US 11) DPNs

Other supplies

1 stitch marker
Tapestry needle

Nordic winter hat

With contrast colour 2, cast (bind) on 72 stitches on circular needles. Join to work in the round and take care so you don't to twist the cast (bind)on edge as you do so. Place a stitch marker in order to indicate the beginning of the round

Work rib (K2, P2) for 4 rounds.

Start working the chart, joining main colour on round 1 of chart and joining contrast colour 1 on round 8 of chart.

When you have finished working the chart, knit 1 round in main colour, and continue in main colour as follows:

Change to double-pointed needles when the stitches do not go easily around the needle.
Rnd 1 (dec): *K7, k2tog* around — 64 sts.
Rnd 2: K
Rnd 3 (dec): *K2, k2tog* around — 48 sts.
Rnd 4: K
Rnd 5 (dec): *K1, k2tog* around — 32 sts.

Cut the yarn about 40cm (16in) from the work.
Pass the yarn through the live stitches on the needles.
Pass the thread at the top through the hole in the middle and turn the hat inside out. Pull the loose end tight (make sure you don't pull so hard you break it!).
With a tapestry needle, secure the end and make a few stitches to cover up the hole that is left at the top

Making up

Weave in loose ends.
With an iron set on Wool and the steam function on, gently press the hat.

Eline Oftedal

Eline is a Norwegian knitting designer who lives and works in Oslo. She has a deep affinity for traditional Scandinavian knitting, and her heritage can often be seen in her designs. She sells individual patterns online and teaches classes in knitting in several countries. You can see more from Eline at **byeline.no**.

Key: ☐ White ☐ Light grey ■ Red

Owl hat and mitts

Learn how to make these adorable items for children, just perfect for a bright and colourful gift on a birthday or as a baby shower present

Difficulty ★★☆☆☆

Skills needed
Increasing
Decreasing
Knitting in rows

Finished measurements
Owl Hat:
Width around head (when slightly stretched)

33	35.5	38	41	43	*cm*
13	14	15	16	17	*ins*

Mitts to fit corresponding age:
Age (approximate)

Prem	0	6	12	24	*months*

Yarn
For this pattern you shall require DK yarn.
In the example, Peter Pan DK was used in
Blue Jeans, Jade and White, kindly supplied
by Thomas B Ramsden.
Colour 1: Blue Jeans; 1 x ball
Colour 2: Jade; 1 x ball
Colour 3: White; 1 x ball

Tension (Gauge)
24 sts and 32 rows = 10cm (4in) in stocking
(stockinette) stitch on 4mm needles

Needles
2 - 3¼mm (US 3)

Other supplies
Tapestry needle

Thomas B Ramsden
This pattern was kindly
supplied by Thomas
B Ramsden, a family
business who are the
suppliers of Wendys and Peter Pan, two
of the biggest brands of yarn in the UK. You
can find them at **www.tbramsden.co.uk**.

Hat

Using 3¼mm needles and col 2, cast (bind) on 73 (79, 85, 91, 97) sts.

Row 1: K1, * P1, K1, rept from * to end.

Row 2: P1, * K1, P1, rept from * to end.

These two rows form rib, repeat 1st and 2nd row three times more.

Change to 4mm needles and join in A. Now, working in st st throughout, and commencing with a K row, work 2 rows in col 1 then 2 rows in col 2.

Last 4 rows set stripe pattern, repeat these 4 rows 3 (3, 4, 5, 5) times more. Break off col 2, and continue in col 1 only.

Continue in st st until hat measures 12 (12, 13, 14, 14)cm, 4¾ (4¾, 5¼, 5½, 5½)ins from cast (bind)-on edge ending on a P row.

Cast (bind) off.

Eyes

Using 4mm needles and col 3, cast (bind) on 3 sts.

Row 1: [Inc in next st], rept in each st to end. 6 sts.

Row 2: [Inc in next st], rept in each st to end. 12 sts.

Row 3: K1, * inc in next st , K1 rept from * to last st, K1. 17 sts.

Row 4: K1, * inc in next st , K1 rept from * to end. 25 sts.

Cast (bind) off.

Join row end edges, work will then form a circle.

Inner eyes (Make 2)

Using 4mm needles and col 2, cast (bind) on 5 sts.

Row 1: Sl 1, P3, sl 1.

Row 2: K5

Row 3: Sl 1, P3, sl 1

Row 4: K5

Cast (bind) off pwise.

Run a gathering stitch around outer edge, and gather up to form a small berry shape.

Beak

Using 4mm needles and col 2, cast (bind) on 2 sts.

Row 1: Purl.

Row 2: K1, m1, K1.

Row 3: P3.

Row 4: K1, m1, K1, m1, K1.

Row 5: P5.

Cast (bind) off.

Making up

Using the photograph as a guide, and placing the beak at centre of work, attach eyes and beak as shown.

Fold in side edges of hat so that they meet at centre back. Join back seam and top seam by top sewing.

Mitts

Using 4mm needles and col 1, cast (bind) on 26(26, 28, 28, 30) sts.

Row 1: * K1, P1, rept from * to end

Repeat this row 5 times more.

Row 7: (Make eyelet holes) K1, * yo, K2tog, rept from * to last st, K1.

Next row: Purl to end.

Continue in st st for a further 20 (22, 24, 28, 30) rows, ending with a purl row.

Cast (bind) off loosely.

Eyes (Make 2)

Using 4mm needles and col 3, cast (bind) on 3 sts.

Row 1: [Inc in next st], rept in each st to end. 6 sts.

Row 2: [Inc in next st], rept in each st to end. 12sts.

Row 3: K1, * inc in next st, K1 rept from * to last st, K1. (18sts)

Cast (bind) off.

Join row end edges, work will then form a circle.

Inner eyes (Make 2)

Work as given for inner eyes of hat.

Beak

Work as given for beak of hat.

Making up

Fold mitten in half, so the seam is at one side.

Using the photograph as a guide, attach eyes and beak as shown.

Join side and top seam by top sewing.

Using col 2 and col 3, make a twisted cord and thread through eyelet holes.

Parlour cat

Make your very own feline friend and apply your knitting skills to this cuddly creation that will make the perfect gift for any animal lover

Difficulty ★★★★★

Skills needed

Increasing
Decreasing
Pick up & knit
Knitting in rounds
Wrap and turn (short rows)

Finished measurements

25cm (10in) long

Yarn

For this project you will need a DK yarn. In the example, Red Heart Super Saver was used. You shall need a total of 155m (170yd) in your chosen colour.

Tension (Gauge)

22 sts and 30 rounds = 10cm (4in) in st st
Note that tension is not very important with toys. Changing yarn weight or needle size will make your finished object smaller or larger. You should work the fabric more densely than you would for a scarf or a garment, so that it holds the stuffing in.

Needles

3.5mm (US 4) DPNs

Other supplies

2 stitch markers
Buttons for eyes (optional)
Length of scrap yarn
Tapestry needle
Stuffing

Did you know?

Hazel Tindall currently holds the title of World's Fastest Knitter, completing 262 stitches in 3 minutes.

Sara Elizabeth Kellner

Sara Elizabeth Kellner is a knitting designer who combines her love of art, animals, and children to create charming and whimsical toy patterns. See more from Sara on her website: **www.rabbitholeknits.com**.

Parlour cat

Body

Cast (bind) on 52 sts onto a single needle.
Distribute across 3 DPNs, placing 18
stitches on the first two needles, and 16 on
the third, and join for working in the round.

Rounds 1-2: Knit.
Round 2: K1, m1, K2, m1, K to last 3 sts,
m1, K2, m1, K1. (4 sts increased.)
Round 4-7: Knit
Round 8-17: Repeat rounds 2-7 twice more.
(64 sts.)
Round 18: K1, m1, K2, m1, K2, m1, K to
last 5 sts, m1, K2, m1, K2, m1, K1. (6 sts
increased).
Rounds 19-22: Knit.
Round 23-27: Repeat rounds 18-22 once
more.
Round 28: Repeat round 18. (82 sts.)
Rounds 29-44: Knit.

Measure off about 25 yards of yarn for
finishing the rear and tail later and then cut.
Thread a darning needle with a piece of
scrap yarn and slip all of the live sts onto it.

Chest

Stitches are now picked up in the original
cast (bind) on sts to form the cat's chest.
Count 10 sts to the left of the first cast (bind)
on st, rejoin yarn and pick up and knit 15
sts in the cast on edge with the first needle;
using a second needle, pick up and knit the
following 15 sts.

Purl back across all sts on the second
DPNs only. This will leave your working yarn
in between the first and second DPNs, and
you are ready to work the short rows.

Short rows are now worked back and forth
across these two DPNs:

Row 1: K3, w&t,
Row 2 (WS): P6, w&t,
Row 3: K7, w&t,
Row 4: P8, w&t,
Row 5: K9, w&t,
Row 6: P10, w&t,
Row 7: K11, w&t,
Row 8: P12, w&t,

Continue like this, working one more st
before the turn each row, until all but four
sts on each end have been worked (3 sts

unwrapped on each side). You will end with
a Purl row.
Cut yarn

Head

Additional sts are now picked up between
the end of the second DPN and beginning
of the first. Rejoin yarn and with your third
DPN, pick up 22 sts, one in each of the
remaining cast (bind) on sts. (52 sts.)

Round 1: Knit.
Round 2: k2tog, K21, ssk, K1, k2tog, K to
last 2 sts, ssk. (48 sts.)
Round 3: k2tog, K19, ssk, K1, k2tog, K to
last 2 sts, ssk. (44 sts.)
Rounds 4-5: Knit.
Round 6: k2tog, K17, ssk, K1, k2tog, K to
last 2 sts, ssk. (40 sts.)
Rounds 7-8: Knit.
Round 9: K1, m1, K17, m1, K3, m1, K to last
2 sts, m1, K2. (44 sts.)
Rounds 10-11: Knit.
Round 12: K1, m1, K19, m1, K3, m1, K to
last 2 sts, m1, K2. (48 sts.)
Rounds 13-14: Knit.
Round 15: K1, m1, K21, m1, K3, m1, K to

last 2 sts, m1, K2. (52 sts.)
Rounds 16-17: Knit.
Round 18: K1, m1, K23, m1, K3, m1, K to last 2 sts, m1, K2. (56 sts.)
Rounds 19-20: Knit.
Round 21: K1, k2tog, K22, ssk, K2, k2tog, K to last 3 sts, ssk, K1. (52 sts.)
Rounds 22-23: Knit.
Round 24: K1, k2tog, K20, ssk, K2, k2tog, K to last 3 sts, ssk, K1. (48 sts.)
Rounds 25-26: Knit.
Round 27: K1, k2tog, K18, ssk, K2, k2tog, K to last 3 sts, SSK, K1. (44 sts.)
Rounds 28-29: Knit.
Slip the first 7 sts onto your working DPN without knitting them. Thread a darning needle with a piece of scrap yarn, and slip the next 30 sts onto it for working later. You now have 14 sts remaining on 2 DPNs. Transfer some of them to a third DPN for working in the round. With RS facing, rejoin yarn at the first original st on the outer right side of the head.

Rounds 1-3: Knit.
Round 4: ssk, K3, k2tog, ssk, K3, k2tog. (10 sts.)
Round 5-6: Knit.
Round 7: ssk, K1, k2tog, ssk, K1, k2tog. (6 sts.)
Round 8: Knit.

Cut yarn and thread through a darning needle; thread yarn through remaining sts and pull tight to close. Insert needle down through center of ear and secure to inside.

Place the next 8 sts from scrap yarn at the front of the head onto a DPN. Place last 8 sts from the scrap yarn at the back of the head onto a 2nd DPN. Using Kitchener stitch, graft these 16 sts together to form the area between the ears. Arrange the 14 remaining live sts onto 3 DPNs. The first stitch should be the innermost stitch on the right side of the ear. Repeat all rounds (1-8) for this ear as with the first one.

Sew up any holes, weave in any loose ends, and stuff the head and front half of body. Be sure to stuff the entire chest area very firmly. This will ensure the proper posture for your Parlour Cat.

Rear and tail
Return the 82 held sts from the scrap yarn back onto 3 DPNs.

Round 1: (K7, k2tog) 4 times, .K10, (K7, k2tog) 4 times. (74 sts.)
Round 2: Knit.
Round 3: (K6, k2tog) 4 times, K10, (K6, k2tog) 4 times. (66 sts.)
Round 4: Knit.
Round 5: (K5, k2tog) 4 times, K10, (K5, k2tog) 4 times. (58 sts.)
Round 6: Knit.
Round 7: (K4, k2tog) 4 times, K10, (K4, k2tog) 4 times. (50 sts.)
Round 8: Knit.
Round 9: (K3, k2tog) 4 times, K10, (K3, k2tog) 4 times. (42 sts.)

Round 10: Knit.
Round 11: (K2, k2tog) 4 times, K10, (K2, k2tog) 4 times. (34 sts.)
Round 12: Knit.
Round 13: (K1, k2tog) 4 times, K10, (K1, k2tog) 4 times. (26 sts.)
Round 14: Knit.
Round 15: k2tog 4 times, K10, k2tog 4 times. (18 sts.)

The 18 remaining sts will form the tail. Finish stuffing the cat's body. Knit all sts for 3 inches, working a k2tog at the start of the round every inch or so, until 15 sts rem. Knit all 15 sts for approximately 12.5cm (5in).

Next round: k2tog, k to end of round.
Following round: Knit.

Repeat the last 2 rounds twice more. (12 sts)

Knit all sts for 1 inch. Cut yarn, thread through remaining live sts. Stuff tail, pull tightly closed, and secure. Hold the tail alongside of the body and seam together at bottom.

Front legs

Cast on 15 sts onto a single needle. Distribute across 3 DPNs, placing 5 on each needle, and join for working in the round. Knit all sts for 12.5cm (5 in).

Cut yarn, thread through live sts, pull tightly closed and secure. Stuff all but about 1 inch at open end.

Fold the closed end of paw inward and stitch to hold in place. Seam leg to bottom of cat's body.

Finishing
Create the face

Eyes, nose, mouth and whiskers can be embroidered, painted or appliqueed. Make your Parlour Cat as unique as you like!

Plumley the penguin

Work with different colours to make this bright and fun design — a cute addition to any home

Difficulty ★★★★☆

Skills needed

Increasing
Decreasing
Colourwork (stranded)
Colourwork (intarsia)
Knitting in rows
Working from a chart
Seaming

Finished measurements

Height (excluding hat): approximately 19cm (7.5in)
Width (around widest part of penguin): 33.5cm (17in)
Width (around head): 21.5cm (8.5in)

Yarn

For this pattern you will need a DK yarn. In the example, Hayfield Bonus DK was used in Black, Cream, Sunflower and Signal red.
Colour 1: Black; 1 x ball
Colour 2: Cream; 1 x ball
Colour 3: Sunflower; 1 x ball
Colour 4: Signal red; 1 x ball

Tension (Gauge)

Tension is not important as it's a toy.

Needles

3.5mm (US 4) needles

Other supplies

Wool needle
2 x 8mm toy safety eyes (note: for safety reasons, use yarn eyes for under 3's)

Lynne Rowe

Lynne is a knitting and crochet designer, writer and tutor from Cheshire. Her aim is to encourage as many people as possible to knit and crochet. To read more about Lynne, visit her website at **lynnerowe.weebly.com**.

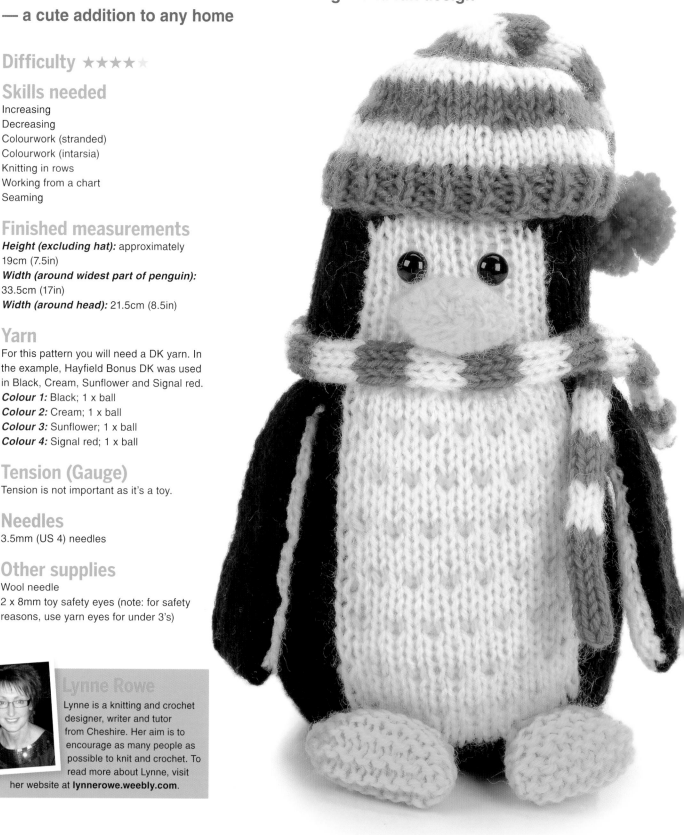

Pattern notes

When working the stranded colourwork rows in col 3 (Rows 5, 9, 13, 17, 21, 25, 29), cut yarn after each row, leaving a 15cm (6in) tail end for weaving in later.

Split black into 2 balls ready for the intarsia rows on body and head. Always twist yarns at colour change to avoid making holes.

Plumley the penguin

Penguin base

Using col 1, cast (bind) on 10 sts.
Row 1 (WS): Purl.
Row 2 (RS): kfb in every st. (20 sts.)
Row 3 and every alternate row: Purl.
Row 4: [K1, kfb] to end. (30 sts.)
Row 6: [K2, kfb] to end. (40 sts.)
Row 8: [K3, kfb] to end. (50 sts.)
Row 10: [K4, kfb] to end. (60 sts.)
Rows 12-13: Knit.

Penguin body

The penguin body uses intarsia, working a section of cream (col 2) in the centre of the two col 1 sections. Use a separate ball of col 1 for each section and always twist yarns at colour change on every row to avoid holes.

Rows 5, 9, 13, 17, 21, 25 and 29 also used stranded colourwork. See the 'Pattern notes' section.

Row 1 (RS): K25 with col 1, K9 with col 2, K26 with col 1.
Row 2: P25 with col 1, P11 with col 2, P24 with col 1.
Row 3: K23 with col 1, K13 with col 2, K24 with col 1.
Row 4: P23 with col 1, P15 with col 2, P22 with col 1.
Row 5: With col 1 [K4, m1] 5 times, K2, [K1 with col 2, K1 with col 3] 7 times, K1 with col 2, with col 1 K3, [m1, K4] 5 times. (70 sts.)
Rows 6, 8, 10, 12: P28 with col 1, P15 with col 2, P27 with col 1.
Row 7: K27 with col 1, K15 with col 2, K28 with col 1.
Row 9: K27 with col 1, K2 with col 2, [K1 with col 3, K1 with col 2] 6 times, K1 with col 2, K28 with col 1.
Row 11: Rep Row 7
Row 13: With col 1 K2, [k2tog, K3] 5 times, [K1 with col 2, K1 with col 3] 7 times, K1 with

col 2, with col 1 [K3, k2tog] 5 times, K3. (60 sts.)
Rows 14, 16, 18, 20: P23 with col 1, P15 with col 2, P22 with col 1.
Row 15: K22 with col 1, K15 with col 2, K23 with col 1.
Row 17: K22 with col 1, K2 with col 2, [K1 with col 3, K1 with col 2] 6 times, K1 with col 2, K23 with col 1.
Row 19: Rep Row 15.
Row 21: With col 1 K2, [k2tog, K2] 5 times, [K1 with col 2, K1 with col 3] 7 times, K1 with col 2, with col 1 [K2, k2tog] 5 times, K3. (50 sts.)
Rows 22, 24, 26, 28: P18 with col 1, P15 with col 2, P17 with col 1.
Row 23: K17 with col 1, K15 with col 2, K18 with col 1.
Row 25: K17 with col 1, K2 with col 2, [K1 with col 3, K1 with col 2] 6 times, K1 with col

2, K18 with col 1.
Row 27: Rep Row 23.
Row 29: With col 1 [K2, k2tog] 4 times, K1, [K1 with col 2, K1 with col 3] 7 times, K1 with col 2, with col 1 [K2, k2tog] 4 times, K2. (42 sts.)
Row 30: P14 with col 1, P15 with col 2, P13 with col 1.
Row 31: K13 with col 1, K15 with col 2, K14 with col 1.
Row 32: Rep Row 30.
Row 33: K13 with col 1, with col 2 K2, skpo, K1, skpo, K1, k2tog, K1, k2tog, K2, K14 with col 1. (38 sts.)
Row 34: P14 with col 1, P11 with col 2, P13 with col 1.
Row 35: K13 with col 1, with col 2, K2, skpo, K3, k2tog, K2, K14 with col 1. (36 sts.)
Row 36: P14 with col 1, P9 with col 2, P13 with col 1.

Head

Row 37: K13 with col 1, K9 with col 2, K14 with col 1.

Row 38: P14 with col 1, P9 with col 2, P13 with col 1.

Rows 39-46: Rep Rows 37-38 4 more times.

Row 47: K14 with col 1, K7 with col 2, K15 with col 1.

Row 48: P16 with col 1, P5 with col 2, P15 with col 1. From here, continue with one ball of col 1 and cut all other yarns.

Rows 49-56: With col 1, starting with a K row, work in st st for 8 rows.

Row 57: K1, [K1, k2tog] to the last 2 sts, K2. (25 sts.)

Row 58: Purl.

Row 59: [K1, k2tog] to the last st, K1. (17 sts.)

Row 60: P1, [p2tog] to end. (9 sts.)

Cut yarn, leaving a long tail of approximately 45cm (18in) for sewing up. Using a darning needle, thread tail end through the 9 rem sts. Pull tight to gather and tie off yarn to secure gathers. Tie off and trim all other yarn ends (except for the long tail end, which you will use to sew the back seam.)

If you are using toy safety eyes, attach them now at approximately Row 45, leaving a gap of approximately 1.5cm (.5in) between the eyes. If the penguin is for a small child, stitch the eyes by hand, using black yarn. Use the long tail end of yarn to stitch the back seam of the penguin, until you reach the last row of the Penguin base. Fill the head and body with toy filling until nice and plump (note, the bottom half of the penguin back is wider than the top half, to make the roly-poly shape). Cont to stitch the base until you reach the cast (bind) on sts. Gather the cast (bind) on sts and pull tightly to close the hole. Tie off yarn and weave end into the penguin body.

Beak (Make 1)

Using col 3, cast (bind) on 10 sts.

Rows 1-2: Starting with a K row, work in st st for 2 rows.

Row 3: K1, skpo, K to last 3 sts, k2tog, K1. (2 sts decreased).

Rows 4-6: Starting with a P row, work in st st for 3 rows.

Row 7: Rep Row 3. (6 sts.)

Row 8: Purl.

Row 9: K1, skpo, k2tog, K1. (4 sts.)

Row 10: Purl.

Row 11: k2tog twice. (2 sts.)

Rows 12-14: Starting with a P row, work in st st for 3 rows.

Row 15: kfb twice. (4 sts.)

Row 16: Purl.

Row 17: K1, m1, K to the last st, m1, K1. (2 sts increased.)

Row 18: Purl.

Row 19: Rep Row 17. (8 sts.)

Rows 20-22: Starting with a P row, work in st st for 3 rows.

Row 23: Rep Row 17. (10 sts.)

Rows 24-26: Starting with a P row, work in st st for 3 rows.

Cast (bind) off (RS is facing). Fold beak in half with right sides facing and stitch the two sides, either by mattress stitch or by a simple whip stitch. Fill the beak lightly and stitch the top seam. Stitch the longest edge of the beak to the centre face of the penguin, below the eyes.

Feet (Make 2)

Using col 3, cast (bind) on 6 sts.

Rows 1-4: Knit.

Row 5: K1, kfb, K to the last 2 sts, kfb, K1. (2 sts increased.)

Rows 6-8: K all sts.

Rows 9-12: Rep Rows 5-8. (10 sts.)

Rows 13-16: Knit.

Row 17: K1, k2tog, K to the last 3 sts, k2tog, K1. (2 sts decreased.)

Rows 18-20: Knit.

Rows 21-24: Rep Rows 17-20 (6 sts.)

Cast (bind) off (RS is facing when you are casting (binding) off). Fold foot in half with WS together and RS facing outwards and stitch the two sides, either by mattress stitch or by a simple whip stitch. Fill the foot lightly and stitch the top seam. Stitch the shortest edge of the foot to the front of the penguin, at the edge of the base.

Flippers (Make 2)

Using col 1, cast (bind) on 6 sts (starting at the top of the flipper).

Rows 1-6: Starting with a K row, work in st st for 6 rows.

Row 7: K1, m1, K to the last st, m1, K1. (2 sts increased.)

Rows 8-12: Starting with a P row, work in st st for 5 rows.

Row 13-24: Rep Rows 7-12 twice more. (12 sts.)

Row 25: K1, skpo, K to last 3 sts, k2tog, K1. (2 sts decreased.)

Row 26: P

Row 27: Rep Row 25. (8 sts.)

Row 28: Purl.

Change to col 2.

Row 29: K1, m1, K to the last st, m1, K1. (2 sts increased.)

Row 30: Purl.

Row 31: Rep Row 29. (12 sts.)

Rows 32-36: Starting with a P row, work in st st for 5 rows.

Row 37: K1, skpo, K to the last 3 sts, k2tog K1. (2 sts decreased.)

Rows 38-42: Starting with a P row, work in st st for 5 rows.

Rows 43-54: Rep Rows 37-42 twice more (6 sts.)

Cast (bind) off (RS is facing when you are casting (binding) off). Fold flipper in half with right sides facing and stitch the two sides and top edge, using mattress stitch. Stitch the top edge of each flipper to each side of the penguin body, just below the head.

Scarf

Using col 4 cast (bind) on 6 sts.

Rows 1-8: Starting with a K row, work in st st for 8 rows.

Join col 2, do not cut col 4.

Rows 9-116: Starting with a K row, work st st in stripes of 4 rows col 2 followed by 4 rows col 4, ending with 4 rows col 2.

Rows 117-124: In col 4, Rep Rows 1-8. Cast (bind) off. The row ends of the scarf will naturally curl inwards. Tie off and trim all loose yarn ends. Place scarf around neck and stitch in place.

Hat

Using col 4, cast (bind) on 44 sts.

Rows 1-4: With col 4 [K1, P1] to the end. Join col 2, do not cut col 4.

Row 5: With col 2, K3, [m1, K7] 5 times, m1, K6. (50 sts.)

Rows 6-8: With col 2, starting with a P row, work in st st for 3 rows.

Rows 9-10: With col 4, starting with a K row, work in st st for 2 rows.

Row 11: With col 4, [K3, k2tog] 10 times. (40 sts.)

Row 12: With col 4, P all sts.

Rows 13-14: With col 1, starting with a K row, work in st st for 2 rows.

Row 15: With col 2, [K2, k2tog] 10 times. (30 sts.)

Row 16: With col 2, P all sts.

Rows 17-18: With col 4, starting with a K row, work in st st for 2 rows.

Row 19: With col 4, [K1, k2tog] 10 times. (20 sts.)

Row 20: With col 4, P all sts.

Rows 21-22: With col 2, starting with a K row, work in st st for 2 rows.

Row 23: With col 2, k2tog 10 times. (10 sts.)

Row 24: With col 2, P all sts.

Rows 25-44: Starting with a K row, work in st st for 20 rows, working in stripes of 4 rows in col 4 followed by 4 rows in col 2, ending with 4 rows in col 4.

Row 45: k2tog 5 times. (5 sts.)

Rows 46-48: Starting with a P row, work in st st for 3 rows.

Cut yarn and pull through final sts to secure, leaving a long tail for sewing up.

Making up

Stitch the hat seam using mattress stitch. Tie off all loose yarns ends and trim.

Make a bobble as follows: Using col 4, wrap yarn around two fingers, approximately 40 times. Carefully remove yarn from fingers. Tie a separate length of yarn around the middle of the wrapped yarn and tie tightly. Cut folded ends of yarn then trim the bobble to make a nice round shape. Stitch the bobble to the top of the hat and stitch the hat to the head.

Lace shawl

A beautiful look to create using this easy-to-follow pattern, this lace shawl could make for the perfect personal present

Difficulty ★★☆☆☆

Skills needed

Increasing
Decreasing
Lace stitches
Knitting in rows
Working from a chart
Short rows

Finished measurements

Width: 183cm (72in) after blocking
Depth: 33cm (13in) after blocking

Yarn

For this pattern you will need a 3- or 4-ply yarn. In this example Claudia's Hand Painted Yarn was used in Mudslide. You will need approximately 365m (400yd).

Tension (Gauge)

18sts and 28 rows = 10cm (4in) in horseshoe lace stitch using 4mm needles after blocking

Needles

4mm (US #6) 91cm/36in circular needle

Other supplies

2 stitch markers (Marker 1)
26 stitch markers in a different colour or style (Marker 2)
Tapestry needle

Pattern notes

A crescent-shaped shawl that is constructed using short rows on a garter stitch base. The beauty of these is that you do not need to wrap the stitches to avoid gaps. The shawl is finished off with a deep edging of horseshoe lace, a traditional Shetland stitch pattern.

Janine Le Cras

Janine is a lifelong knitter who learned to knit at her grandmother's knee. After a break she discovered the world of knitting on the web, which had a new and vibrant image, and was re-inspired to pick up her needles.

Lace shawl

Cast (bind) on 277 sts, placing the sts markers as follows:

Cast (bind) on 3, PM1, (cast (bind) on 10 sts, PM1) 12 times, (cast (bind) on 10 sts, PM2) twice, (cast (bind) on 10 sts, PM1) 13 times, cast (bind) on 4.

The first part of the shawl is worked in garter st (knit every row), but with short rows to give it a curved shape. When working short rows in garter st it is not necessary to wrap the sts to prevent holes.

The stitch markers you have added to the cast (bind) on row help you keep count when casting (binding) on, mark where you will be turning on the short rows and highlight the central 10 sts. They will also serve to mark the placing of repeats of the lace charts later on in the pattern.

Section 1

Row 1: Knit until you reach the furthest marker. With the marker still on the LH needle, turn your work around ready to knit back the other way.

Next row: As row 1.

Row 3: Knit until you reach the next marker in from the one that you previously turned at. With the marker still on the LH needle, turn. Repeat row 3, turning one marker in from the previous one on every row until you reach the middle 20 sts of the shawl. Turn.

Next row: Knit to end of row, turn.

Knit back across all the sts.

This is the first set of short row shaping complete.

Lace Shawl

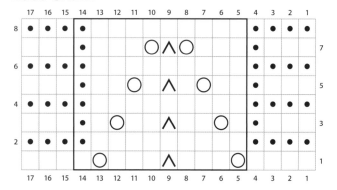

Lace border

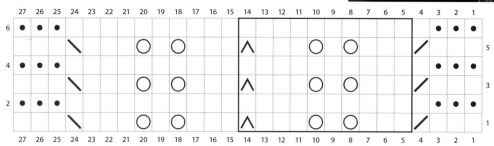

Key: = knit = purl = yo = RS: k2tog / WS: p2tog 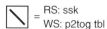 = RS: ssk / WS: p2tog tbl 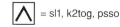 = sl1, k2tog, psso  = name of repeat

Section 2

Row 1: Knit across the sts until you reach the 4th marker from the end of the row. With the marker still on the LH needle, turn your work around ready to knit back the other way.

Row 2: Repeat row 1.

Row 3: Knit across the sts until you reach the next marker in from the one that you previously turned at. With the marker still on the RH needle, turn your work around ready to knit back the other way.

Continue to work in short rows, turning one marker in from the previous row until you have worked only the 10 sts between the 2 markers at the middle of the row. Turn.

Next row: Knit to end of row, turn.

Knit back across all the sts. This is the second set of short row shaping completed.

Lace section

Work rows 1-8 of the Lace Pattern chart, repeating the 10 sts within the red border 27 times in all.

Rep these 8 rows a further 4 times. Work rows 1-8, 5 times in all.

Work rows 1-6 of the Lace Border chart, repeating the 10 sts within the red border 27 times in all. Work rows 1-6 once.

Cast (bind) off all sts using a lace cast (bind) off.

Note: Using a lace cast (bind) off is best as it is stretchy and will allow you to block the shawl to open the lace up and show it off.

Lace cast (bind) off

K2 sts, slip sts back onto LH needle, *k2tog tbl, K1, sl sts back onto LH needle* rep from * to end. Cut yarn, slip end through the last st and tighten.

Making up

Soak the shawl in a wool wash and rinse. Squeeze out as much water as possible, wrap in a towel and press hard to remove more without agitating, which can cause the yarn to felt. Pin out the damp shawl on a flat surface to the shape and dimensions given in the schematic. Pin out the points of each repeat. Leave until dry, unpin and sew in any ends.

Prefer it written?

If you find charts difficult to work with, don't despair. Many designers usually provide written versions of stitch patterns for those knitters who prefer to use them. If not it is very easy to create your own. All you need to do is to write down the sts in each row, remembering to read RS rows from right to left, and WS rows from left to right.

Lace pattern chart (written version)

Row 1 (RS): K4, *yo, K3, sl1, k2tog, psso, K3, yo, K1; rep from * to last 3 sts, K3.

Row 2 (WS): *K1, P9; rep from * to last 4 sts, K4.

Row 3 (RS): K3, P1, (K1, yo, K2, sl1, k2tog, psso, K2, yo, K1, P1) repeat 27 times in all, K3.

Row 4 (WS): As row 2.

Row 5 (RS): K3, P1, (K2, yo, K1, sl1, k2tog, psso, K1, yo, K2, P1) repeat 27 times in all, K3.

Row 6 (WS): As row 2.

Row 7 (RS): K3, P1, (K3, yo, sl1, k2tog, psso, yo, K3, P1) repeat 27 times in all, K3.

Row 8 (WS): As row 2.

Lace border chart (written version)

Row 1 (RS): K3, k2tog, *K3, yo, K1, yo, K3, sl1, k2tog, psso; rep from * to last 12 sts, K3, yo, K1, yo, K3, ssk, K3.

Row 2 (WS): K3, P to last 3 sts, K3.

Row 3 (RS): As row 1.

Row 4 (WS): As row 2.

Row 5 (RS): As row 1.

Row 6 (WS): K3, P to last 3 sts, K3.

Staggered eyelet cardigan

Use lacing techniques to create this beautiful two-tone cardigan, perfect for autumn and spring months

Difficulty ★★★☆☆

Skills needed

Increasing
Decreasing
Lace stitches (eyelets)
Pick up & knit
Knitting in rows
Seaming
Ribbing

Finished measurements

Finished bust

85	90	95	100	106	cm
33.5	35.5	37.5	39.5	41.75	in

Length

56	57	59	61	64	cm
22	22.5	23.25	24	25.25	in

Colour 1

7	7	8	8	9	Balls

Colour 2

2	3	3	4	4	Balls

Yarn

For this pattern you will require a DK yarn in two colours. In this example Debbie Bliss Rialto DK has been used in Coral and Teal. Refer to **finished measurements** for ball amounts.

Tension (Gauge)

20 stitches and 20 rows = 10cm (4in) in staggered eyelet stitch

Needles

4mm (US 6) needles

Other supplies

1 stitch holder

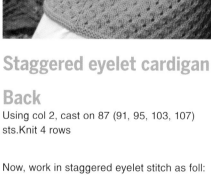

Emma Wright

Emma is a fashion hand-knit and crochet designer. She spends most days tucked away designing, knitting and drinking lots of tea. You can find her at **www.emmaknitted.co.uk**.

Staggered eyelet cardigan

Back

Using col 2, cast on 87 (91, 95, 103, 107) sts.Knit 4 rows

Now, work in staggered eyelet stitch as foll:
Row 1 (RS): Knit.
Row 2 (WS): Purl.
Row 3: *K2, k2tog, yo; rep from * to last 3 sts, K3.
Row 4: Purl.
Row 5: Knit.
Row 6: Purl.
Row 7:*k2tog, yo, K2; rep from * to last 3 sts, k2tog, yo, K1.
Row 8: Purl.

These 8 rows form staggered eyelet stitch. Repeat these 8 rows until work measures 34 (35, 36, 38, 40)cm/13.5 (14, 14.25, 15, 15.75)in, ending with RS facing.
  Change to col 1.
Keeping in staggered eyelet stitch, continue for a further 4cm/1.5in until work measures 38 (39, 40, 42, 44)cm/15 (15.75, 16.5, 17.25) in, ending with RS facing.

Armhole Shaping

Keeping staggered eyelet stitch correct, shape armhole as foll:

Cast off 8 sts at beg of next 2 rows — 71 (75, 79, 87, 91) sts.

Cast off 4 sts at beg of next 2 rows — 63 (67, 71, 79, 83) sts.

Cast off 2 sts at beg of next 2 rows — 59 (63, 67, 75, 79) sts.

Now, continue without shaping in staggered eyelet stitch until armhole measures 18 (18, 19, 19, 20)cm/7 (7, 7.5, 7.5, 8)in from beginning of armhole shaping.

Now, work in staggered eyelet stitch as foll:'

Shoulders

Cast off 10 (12, 14, 18, 20) sts at beg of next 2 rows.

Leave remaining 39 sts on a holder for back neck.

Front

Right

Using col 2, cast on 43 (47, 51, 55, 59) sts. Knit 4 rows.

Now, work in staggered eyelet stitch as foll:
Row 1: Knit.
Row 2: Purl.
Row 3: *K2, k2tog, yo; rep from * to last 3 sts, K3.
Row 4: Purl.
Row 5: Knit.
Row 6: Purl.
Row 7: *k2tog, yo, K2; rep from * to last 3 sts, k2tog, yo, K1.
Row 8: Purl.

These 8 rows form staggered eyelet stitch. Repeat these 8 rows until work measures 34 (35, 36, 38, 40)cm/13.5 (14, 14.25, 15, 15.75)in, ending with RS facing.**

Change to col 1.
Keeping in staggered eyelet stitch, continue for a further 4cm/1.5in until work measures 38 (39, 40, 42, 44)cm/15 (15.5, 16.75, 17.25) in, ending with WS facing.
Next row (dec): Cast off 8 sts, P to end — 35 (39, 43, 47, 51) sts.

Next row: Work in patt.
Next row (dec): Cast off 4 sts, P to end — 31 (35, 39, 43, 47) sts.
Next row: Work in patt.
Next row (dec): Cast off 2 sts, P to end — 29 (33, 37, 41, 45) sts.

Now, continue without shaping in staggered eyelet stitch until armhole measures 13 (13, 14, 14, 15)cm/5 (5, 5.5, 5.5, 6)in from beginning of armhole shaping, ending with RS facing.

Shape Front Neck

Next row (dec): Cast off 10 (12, 14, 14, 16) sts, work in patt to end — 19 (21, 23, 27, 29) sts.
Next row: Work in patt.
Next row (dec): Cast off 5 sts, work in patt to end — 14 (16, 18, 22, 24) sts.
Next row: Work in patt.
Next row (dec): Cast off 3 sts, work in patt to end — 11 (13, 15, 19, 21) sts.
Next row: Work in patt.
Next row (dec): k2tog, work in patt to end — 10 (12, 14, 18, 20) sts.

Now, continue without shaping in staggered eyelet stitch until armhole measures 18 (18, 19, 19, 20)cm/7 (7, 7.5, 7.5, 8)in from beginning of armhole shaping, ending with RS facing.
Cast off remaining 10 (12, 14, 18, 20) sts.

Left

Work as for **Right Front** to **
Change to col 1.
Keeping in staggered eyelet stitch, continue for a further 4cm/1.5in until work measures 38 (39, 40, 42, 44)cm/15 (15.5, 16.75, 17.25)in, ending with RS facing.

Next row (dec): Cast off 8 sts, work in patt to end.
Next row: Work in patt.
Next row (dec): Cast off 4 sts, work in patt to end.
Next row: Work in patt.
Next row (dec): Cast off 2 sts, work in patt to end.

Now, continue without shaping in staggered eyelet stitch until armhole measures 13 (13, 14, 14, 15)cm/5 (5, 5.5, 5.5, 6)in from beginning of armhole shaping, ending with WS facing.

Shape Front Neck

Next row (dec): Cast off 10 (12, 14, 14, 16) sts, work in patt to end — 19 (21, 23, 27, 29) sts.
Next row: Work in patt.
Next row (dec): Cast off 5 sts, work in patt to end — 14 (16, 18, 22, 24) sts.
Next row: Work in patt.
Next row (dec): Cast off 3 sts, work in patt to end — 11 (13, 15, 19, 21) sts.

Next row: Work in patt.
Next row (dec): k2tog, work in patt to end —
10 (12, 14, 18, 20) sts.

Now, continue without shaping in staggered eyelet stitch until armhole measures 18 (18, 19, 19, 20)cm/7 (7, 7.5, 7.5, 8)in from beginning of armhole shaping, ending with RS facing. Cast off remaining 10 (12, 14, 18, 20) sts.

Sleeves (make two)

Using col 2, cast on 36 (36, 38, 38, 40) sts.

Knit 4 rows.
Now, work in staggered eyelet stitch as foll:

Row 1 (inc): K1, m1, K to last 2 sts, m1, K1.
Row 2: Purl.
Row 3: *K2, k2tog, yo; rep from * to last 3 sts, K3.
Row 4: Purl.
Row 5: Knit.
Row 6: Purl.
Row 7: *k2tog, yo, K2; rep from * to last 3 sts, k2tog, yo, K1.
Row 8: Purl.

These 8 rows form staggered eyelet stitch with sleeve inc.
Repeat these 8 rows a further 13 (13, 14, 14, 15) times — 64 (64, 68, 68, 72) sts.
Keeping in staggered eyelet stitch, continue straight until sleeve measures 39 (39, 41, 41, 43)cm/15.5 (15.5, 16, 16, 17)in, ending with RS facing.
Change to col 1.
Keeping in staggered eyelet stitch, continue straight until sleeve measures 43 (43, 45, 45, 47)cm/17 (17, 17.75, 17.75, 18.5)in, ending with RS facing.

Keeping in staggered eyelet stitch, shape armhole and sleeve head as foll:
Cast off 8 sts at beg of next 2 rows — 48 (48, 52, 52, 56) sts.
Cast off 4 sts at beg of next 2 rows — 40 (40, 44, 44, 48) sts.
Cast off 2 sts at beg of next 2 rows — 36 (36, 40, 40, 44) sts.
Dec 1 st at each end of next row — 34 (34, 38, 38, 42) sts.
Work 3 rows, ending with RS facing.
Repeat the last 4 rows four times more — 26 (26, 30, 30, 34) sts.
Dec 1 st at each end of next row and then every alt row twice more.

Dec 1 st at each end of next 3 rows, ending with RS facing.
Cast off 3 sts at beg of next 2 rows — 8 (8, 12, 12, 16) sts.
Cast off rem 8 (8, 12, 12, 16) sts.

Making up

Neck band

Join both shoulder seams.
Using col 1, with RS facing and beg at right front neck, pick up and K 29 (31, 32, 32, 33) sts evenly to right shoulder and then rejoin yarn to 39 sts left on holder for back neck. Next, pick up and knit 29 (31, 32, 32, 33) sts evenly to left front neck — 97 (101, 103, 103, 105) sts.
Beginning on a WS row, knit 4 rows.
Cast off knit-wise on a WS row.

Button band

Using col 2, with RS facing of left front and beg at neck edge, pick up and knit 102 (104, 108, 112, 118) sts evenly to garment hem. Beginning on a WS row, knit 4 rows. Cast off knitwise on a WS row.

Buttonhole band

Using col 2, with RS facing of right front and beg at garment hem, pick up and knit 102 (102, 108, 114, 114) sts evenly to front neck. Row 1 (WS): Knit.

1st, 2nd, 4th and 5th sizes only:
Row 2 (RS; eyelets): (K2, yo, k2tog, K4 [4, 5, 5]) x 12, yo, k2tog, K1, yo, k2tog, K1.

3rd size only:
Row 2 (RS; eyelets): (K2, yo, k2tog, K6) x 10, yo, k2tog, K2, yo, k2tog, K2.

All sizes:
Knit 2 more rows.
Cast off knitwise on a WS row.
Join sleeve and side seams using preferred sewing method. Join cast off of sleeve head to shoulder each and ease sleeve head into armhole neatly. Fasten off any loose ends and block/press as instructed on ball band.

Reference

All the references you need in one place

"When choosing a yarn colour for your project, you may want to think about more than just what it will look like"

Yarn labels

Everything you need to know about the yarn you're using can be found on the label, from weight and thickness to washing instructions

When you buy yarn, it will almost always come with a label around it. This label, which is sometimes also called a ball band, tells you everything you need to know about the yarn, from what size needles to use with it to washing and care instructions. If you think your project will need to use more than one ball of yarn, don't throw this label away, as it will help you ensure you get the exact matching yarn to continue working with.

Symbols

Most yarn manufacturers will use symbols to indicate the properties of yarn and give further details about it. These will often include care instructions and tension (gauge). It will also include the dye lot. When using more than one ball of yarn in the same colour in a single project, ensure that all balls of yarn have the same dye lot. This way, there will be no variation in colour when you switch yarns.

Yarn weight and thickness

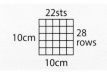
Tension (gauge) over a 10cm (4in) test square

Dye lot number

Hand-wash cold

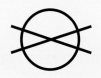
Do not dry clean

Recommended needle size

Shade/colour number

Hand-wash warm

Do not tumble dry

Weight and length of yarn in ball

Do not bleach

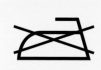
Do not iron

100% WOOL
Fibre content

Machine-wash cold

Machine-wash cold, gentle cycle

Dry-cleanable in any solvent

Dry-cleanable in certain solvents

Iron on a low heat

Iron on a medium heat

TOP TIP
If you're making a garment with more than one ball of wool in the same colour, check that all the balls have the same dye lot (DL), which can be found on the label. This will ensure there won't be any colour variation.

Choosing yarn colours

You can find yarn in almost any colour you can think of, but how do you choose which one to use?

You've finally picked the garment you want to make and a pattern that you like, so the next step is choosing your yarn. Patterns will suggest yarn weight and maybe even fibre, but rarely colour. This decision is up to you. When choosing a yarn colour for your project, you may want to think about more than just what it will look like. For example, as a knitting beginner, you may find black and other darker colours difficult to work with as you won't be able to spot mistakes as easily or see what stitch you just worked. When you're using more than one colour to create a pattern, it is also important to choose colours that complement each other as well as stand out to make the pattern distinctive. A good place to start for choosing colours is to look at a colour wheel.

Using a colour wheel

This is used to see how colours work together. Each segment shows the hue (the pure, bright colour), shade (the colour mixed with black), tone (the colour mixed with grey) and tint (the colour mixed with white) of a colour. Blue, red and yellow are primary colours; green, orange and purple are secondary colours; and all the others are tertiary colours. Colours that are side-by-side harmonise with each other and those that are opposite on the wheel complement each other, and provide bold contrast.

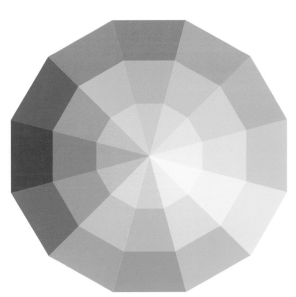

Black and white

These are not included on the colour wheel as they are not classified as colours (black being an absence of all colour and white a combination of all the colours in the spectrum). When using black yarn to knit with, remember that your work will be more difficult to see and any complex details like cabling will not show up as well in the finished piece. When using white yarn, although every stitch will be clear to see, remember that this is not the most practical colour for wearable garments as any stains or dirt will easily show up.

Warm shades

Consisting of mainly red and yellow tones, the colours at the warm end of the colour spectrum can be used to bring richness and depth to a garment. Browns, oranges and purple are also a part of this group. A blend of warm shades can create a flattering garment.

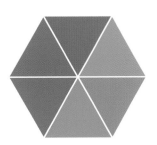

Cool shades

At the cool end of the spectrum are blue, green and violet. Generally darker in tone than warm colours, their impact is lessened when mixed with these. If you need to balance a warm mixture in a project, you will need more cool colours than warm ones to do so.

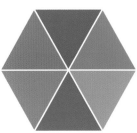

Pastels

These very pale colours are extremely popular for babies' and small children's garments, and as such you will find a high proportion of soft yarns for babies are available in these colours. Pastels also feature strongly in spring/summer knitting patterns for adults.

Brights

Vivid and fluorescent shades can really liven up a piece, especially one that so far consists of muted shades. These colours make eye-catching accessories and intarsia motifs, and also look great when used to add a bright edging or set of buttons.

Knitting abbreviations

Here is a list of the most frequently used knitting abbreviations. Any special abbreviation will be explained within a pattern

alt
Alternate

beg
Begin(ning)

cm
Centimetre(s)

cont
Continu(e)(ing)

dec
Decreas(e)(ing)

foll
Follow(s)(ing)

g
Gram(s)

g st
Garter stitch

in
Inch(es)

inc
Increase(e)(ing)

K
Knit

K1 tbl
Knit 1 stitch through the back of the loop

k2tog (or dec 1)
Knit next 2 stitches together (see page 42)

kfb (o inc 1)
Knit into front and back of next stitch (see page 38)

LH
Left hand

M1 (or M1k)
Make one stitch (see page 39)

mm
Millimetre(s)

oz
Ounce(s)

p
Purl

p2tog (or dec 1)
Purl next two stitches together (see page 42)

patt
Pattern, or work in pattern

pfb (or inc 1)
Purl into front and back of next stitch

psso
Pass slipped stitch over

rem
Remain(s)(ing)

rep
Repeat(ing)

rev st st
Reverse stocking stitch

RH
Right hand

RS
Right side (of work)

Sk k1 psso (skp)
Slip 1, knit 1, pass slipped stitch over (see page 50)

s1 k2tog psso (sk2p)
Slip 1, knit 2 stitches together, pass slipped stitch over

ssk
Slip slip knit (see page 51)

S
Slip stitch

s2 K1 p2sso
Slip 2, knit 1, pass slipped stitches over

st(s)
Stitch(es)

st st
Stocking stitch

tbl
Through back of loop(s)

tog
Together

WS
Wrong side (of work)

yd
Yard(s)

yo (yfwd)
Yarn over

wyib
With yarn in back

wyif
With yarn in front

[ ] *
Repeat instructions between brackets, or after or between asterisks, as many times as instructed

Understanding stitch symbol charts

Sometimes knitting patterns are given as a stitch symbol chart instead of a written pattern. Don't panic. These are easy to follow if you know what you're looking at

Stitch symbol charts provide a knitting pattern in much the same way as a written pattern — each symbol represents a stitch, and you follow it to make the pattern. Some knitters prefer them to written patterns, as they offer a visual representation of what a pattern should look like when it's knitted up and can be easier to memorise. When you come across a charted pattern, the amount of stitches to cast (bind) on will normally be provided, however, if it is not, you can easily work it out from the number of stitches in the pattern 'repeat'. Cast (bind) on a multiple of this number and any extras for edge stitches outside the repeat and you're ready to go.

In a stitch symbol chart, each square represents a stitch and each horizontal line of squares represents a row. After casting (binding) on, work from the bottom of the chart upwards, reading odd-numbered rows, which are usually RS rows, from right to left and even-numbered rows from left to right. After knitting any edge stitches, work the stitches inside the repeat as many times as required. When you have worked all the rows on the chart, start again at the bottom of the chart.

Stitch symbols

These are some of the most commonly used stitch symbols. However, different pattern providers may use different symbols, so always follow the explanations given in a pattern.

☐ = k on RS rows, p on WS rows

⬤ = p on RS rows, k on WS rows

○ = yo

╱ = k2tog

╲ = ssk

⋀ = sk2p

⋀ = s2k k1 p2sso

> **TOP TIP**
> Some symbols mean one thing on an RS row and another on a WS row. For example, a blank square often means knit on an RS row and purl on a WS row.

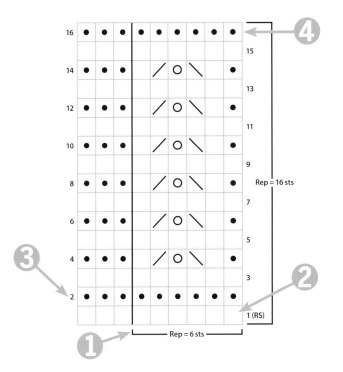

01 Cast (bind) on
The number of stitches you cast on must be a multiple of this repeat plus any edge stitches.

02 Right to left
Read row 1 and all other odd-numbered rows from right to left.

03 Left to right
Read row 2 and all other even-numbered rows from left to right.

04 Repeat
When you have finished the last row of the stitch symbol chart, begin again at row 1. Repeat the pattern until you reach the desired length.

Stitch patterns

Follow this fantastic guide to the different stitches that are available to you, and use them in your amazing creations

After learning the basic techniques of knitting, you now have the ability to create a large variety of stitches. These can be used to start making your own original designs and adapting other patterns to suit your tastes. You may recognise some of the more common stitches, such as moss (seed) and single rib, but there are a wide variety that will enable you to create any number of attractive items. There are just a few examples showcased in this chapter, so take a look through to see which appeal to you most.

> *"Start making your own designs and adapting patterns to suit your tastes"*

TOP TIP

If you lose your place while following a stitch pattern, start by looking at the tail of your work. If it is towards the bottom of your needle, you are about to knit an odd row (3, 5, 7 etc); if it is towards the top, you are about to knit an even row (4, 6, 8 etc).

Knit and purl stitch patterns

There are many stitches that you can create using just these two techniques, and most are simple to work and easy to remember. Although the majority of these will create a pattern that looks the same on both sides, those with a right side (RS) will have the pictured stitch on the front and a different texture on the back. These simple stitches are ideal for making scarves and blankets.

Moss (seed) stitch

For an even number of sts:
Row 1: *K1, P1, rep from *
Row 2: *P1, K1, rep from *
Rep rows 1-2 to form pattern

For an odd number of sts:

Row 1: *K1, P1, rep from *
to last st, K1
Rep row 1 to form pattern

Half moss (seed) stitch

Cast (bind) on an odd number of sts
Row 1 (RS): *P1, K1, rep from * to last st, K1
Row 2: K
Rep rows 1-2 to form pattern

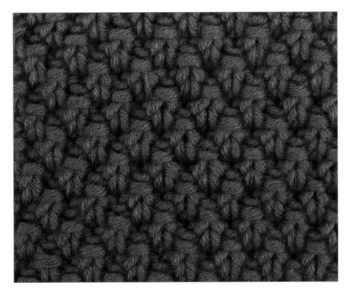

Double moss (seed) stitch

Cast (bind) on an odd number of sts
Row 1 (RS): *K1, P1, rep from *to last st, K1
Row 2: *P1, K1, rep from * to last st, K1
Row 3: As row 2
Row 4: As row 1
Rep rows 1-4 to form pattern

Broken moss (seed) stitch

Cast (bind) on an odd number of sts
Row 1 (RS): K
Row 2: *P1, K1, rep from * to last st, K1
Rep rows 1-2 to form pattern

Single rib

For an even number of sts:
Row 1: *K1, P1, rep from *
Rep row 1 to form pattern

For an odd number of sts:

Row 1: *K1, P1, rep from * to last st, K1
Row 2: *P1, K1, rep from * to last st, P1
Rep rows 1-2 to form pattern

Double rib

Cast (bind) on a multiple of 4 sts
Row 1: *K2, P2, rep from *
Rep row 1 to form pattern

English rib

Cast (bind) on an odd number of sts
Row 1: s1, *P1, K1, rep from *
Row 2: s1 *K1b, P1, rep from *
Rep rows 1-2 to form pattern

Fisherman's rib

Cast (bind) on an odd number of sts and knit 1 row
Row 1 (RS): s1, *K1b, P1, rep from *
Row 2: s1, *P1, K1b, rep from * to last 2 sts, P1, K1
Rep rows 1-2 to form pattern

Garter rib

Cast (bind) on a multiple of 8 sts + 4
Row 1 (RS): K4, *P4, K4, rep from *
Row 2: Purl.
Rep rows 1-2 to form pattern

Basketweave stitch

Cast (bind) on a multiple of 8 sts
Rows 1-5: *K4, P4, rep from *
Rows 6-10: *P4, K4, rep from *
Rep rows 1-10 to form pattern

Little check stitch

Cast (bind) on a multiple of 10 sts + 5
Row 1: K5, *P5, K5, rep from *
Row 2: Purl.
Rep 1-2 twice more, then row 1 again
Row 8: K5, *P5, K5, rep from *
Row 9: Knit.
Rep rows 8-9 twice more, then row 8 again
Rep rows 1-14 to form pattern

Little ladder stitch

Cast (bind) on a multiple of 6 sts + 2
Row 1 (RS): K
Row 2: K2, *P4, K2, rep from *
Row 3: Knit.
Row 4: P3, *K2, P4, rep from * to last 3 sts, P3
Rep rows 1-4 to form pattern

Increasing and decreasing

Using slightly more advanced techniques such as yarn over (yo) and knit/purl two together (k2tog/p2tog), you can create stitches with even greater detail and texture. These form more intricate designs that look great on their own or when combined with other stitches in larger pieces.

Basic chevron

Cast (bind) on a multiple of 12 sts
Row 1 (RS): *k2tog, K3, [inc in next st] twice, K3, s1 K1 psso, rep from *
Row 2: Purl.
Rep rows 1-2 to form pattern

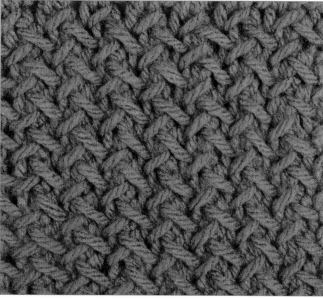

Herringbone stitch

Cast (bind) on a multiple of 3 sts + 1
Row 1 (RS): K1, *yo, s1wyib K2 psso 2 sts, rep from *
Row 2: P1, *yo, s1wyif P2 psso 2 sts, rep from *
Rep rows 1-2 to form pattern

Diagonal rib

Cast (bind) on a multiple of 2 sts
Row 1: *K1, P1, rep from *
Row 2: s1 P1 psso, *K1, P1, rep from *
Row 3: *P1, K1, rep from * to last 2 sts, P2
Row 4: s1 K1 psso, *P1, K1 rep from * to last 2 sts, P1, [K1 P1] into next stitch
Rep rows 1-4 to form pattern

Blackberry stitch

Cast (bind) on a multiple of 4 sts + 2
Row 1 (RS): Purl.
Row 2: K1, *[K1 P1 K1] into next st, p3tog, rep from * to last st, K1
Row 3: Purl.
Row 4: K1, *p3tog, [K1 P1 K1] into next st, rep from * to last st, K1
Rep rows 1-4 to form pattern

Glossary

All of the key terminology you need to learn to follow patterns and get to grips with the skills and techniques you need for knitting

As established, as set
An instruction in knitting patterns that means to continue working as previously established after an interruption in the texture or shaping. For example, an established pattern might be interrupted to work a buttonhole and then continue 'as set'

Bar increase
See knit front and back (kfb)

Blanket stitch
A decorative sewing technique worked along the edge of fabric

Block
A finishing technique in which the knitted piece is set with steam or water. Blocking smooths stitches and straightens edges

Blocking wire
A long, straight wire used for anchoring the edge of knitting during blocking, most often for lace

Cable
A texture in knitting that resembles knitted rope, made by crossing stitches

Cable cast (bind) on
A firm cast (bind)-on edge made by putting the tip of the needle between the first two stitches on the left needle, working a stitch and placing it on the left needle. Although called cable, it is not related to making cables

Cable needle (cn)
A short knitting needle with a point at each end used to temporarily hold a small number of stitches while you make cables. Cable needles are often curved or bent to prevent stitches from sliding off

Cast (bind) on (CO)
To put the first row of stitches on the needles. This row is simply called the cast (bind)-on edge

Cast (bind) off (BO)
Secure the final row of stitches and remove them from your knitting needles

Circular knitting
When you knit fabric in a tube by working the stitches in a spiral. Unlike flat knitting, which is worked back and forth

Circular needle
A needle with a point at each end and a flexible cable in between. Circulars can be used in circular or flat knitting

Decrease
To decrease the number of stitches in a row

Dropped stitch
A stitch that has fallen off the needle and is not secured. A column of dropped stitches is called a ladder

Double-pointed needles (DPNs)
A knitting needle with a point at each end, usually used in a set of four or five to work in the round

Duplicate stitch
Made by running a strand of yarn along the same path as existing knitted stitches. Duplicate stitch can be used on the wrong side to conceal yarn ends or on the right side as a decorative element

Ease
The difference between the garment's measurements and wearer's measurements. A garment with larger measurements has positive ease and one with smaller measurements has negative ease

Eyelet
A single hole in knitted fabric, usually made with a yarn over increase

Fair Isle
Refers to both the motifs and the technique derived from the colour knitting from the Shetland Islands and Fair Isle, north of Scotland. Generally, in Fair Isle knitting, two colours are used in each row, with the colour not being used carried along the wrong side of the work. Sometimes it can be used to refer to stranded colourwork in general

Felt
Made from finished knitting by agitating animal fibre to lock the strands together

Finishing
At the end of a knitted project, when final details are added, such as weaving in ends, sewing pieces together and adding buttons. Can also include blocking

Flat knitting
When you knit fabric as a flat piece by working the stitches back and forth (unlike circular knitting, which is worked in a spiral)

Garter stitch
A reversible, ridged pattern made of alternating knit and purl rows. In flat knitting, garter stitch is made by knitting every row; in circular knitting, it is made by alternating knit and purl rounds

Gauge (tension)
The size of a stitch, so how many stitches and rows fit in to make a certain size of knitting, usually ten centimetres

"Duplicate stitch can be used on the wrong side to conceal yarn ends or on the right side as a decorative element"

Half-hitch cast (bind) on

A simple single-strand cast (bind) on. Stitches are made by twisting the yarn into a loop and placing them on a needle

I-cord

Short for idiot cord, an i-cord is a narrow tube made by knitting every row on a double-pointed needle (DPN) without turning the work

Increase (inc)

To increase the number of stitches in a row

Intarsia

A technique used for working blocks of colour. The yarn is not carried across the back as in stranded colourwork

Join

Either adding a new ball of yarn, turning a flat row into a tubular round or sewing pieces of knitting together

Knit (k, K)

Specifically, to make a new stitch by working with the yarn at the back and inserting the right needle from left to right under the front loop and through the centre of the next stitch of the left needle

Knit two stitches together (k2tog)

Putting the needle through two stitches and knitting together to decrease by one stitch

Knit three stitches together (k3tog)

Putting the needle through three stitches and knitting them together to decrease by two stitches

Knit front and back (kfb)

Knit first into the front and then into the back of one stitch to increase by one stitch. Also called a bar increase

Knitted cast (bind) on

A cast (bind)-on edge made by working a stitch into the first stitch on the left-hand needle and placing it back on the left needle

Knitwise (kwise)

As if to knit — with the yarn in the back and the right needle going into the front of the stitch

Lace

Knitted fabric with an arrangement of holes

Long tail cast (bind) on

A strong cast (bind) on made by using two strands of yarn: the working yarn and the tail

Marker, stitch marker

A small ring or other tool placed on the needle to mark a location or stitch.

Mattress stitch

A method of sewing knitting together that creates a barely visible seam

Multiple (mult)

The number of stitches or rows that are repeated in a stitch pattern

Needle gauge

A tool used to determine the size of unmarked needles.

Pick up and knit

Draw loops through the edge of the knitting and place them on a needle

Place marker (pm)

An instruction to place a stitch marker on your needle

Plain knitting

Knitting without adding texture or colour, often in garter or stocking (stockinette) stitch

Purl (p, P)

To make a new stitch by working with the yarn at the front and inserting the right needle from right to left through the centre of the next stitch of the left needle

Purlwise (pwise)

As if to purl — with the yarn in the front and the right needle going through the centre of the stitch from left to right

Raglan

A style of sleeve where the upper arm and shoulder are diagonally shaped from the underarm to neck

Repeat (rep)

Repeat all steps between indicated points, usually marked by "rep from * to end")

Reverse stocking (stockinette) stitch (rev st st)

Stocking (stockinette) stitch fabric with the purl side used as the right side

Reversible

A fabric with no right side

Right side (RS)

The side of the work that will be displayed when finished

Round (rnd)

In circular knitting, one horizontal line of stitches

Row

In flat knitting, one horizontal line of stitches

Selvedge, selvage

A decorative or functional edge. For example, a selvedge can be made by knitting the first and last stitch of every row, making them neater and more visible

Set-in sleeve
A style of sleeve where the upper arm and shoulder are curved to fit around the shoulder and sewn into the armhole

Slip slip knit together (ssk)
The mirror of k2tog: slip two stitches, one at a time, knitwise, and knit them together to decrease by one stitch

Slip (sl)
Transfer the next stitch to be worked on the left-hand needle to the right-hand needle. Always done purlwise unless stated

Stitch
A loop, either on a needle or in the fabric — the basic unit of knitting

Stitch holder
A tool used to hold stitches that will be worked at a later date. Often shaped like a large safety pin

Stocking (stockinette) stitch (st st)
A smooth pattern made of knit stitches. In flat knitting, stocking (stockinette) stitch is made by alternating knit and purl rows; in circular knitting, it is made by knitting every round

Straight needle
A knitting needle with a point at one end and a stopper at the other

Stranded
A type of colourwork where all the strands are carried on the wrong side of the work

Swatch
A square or rectangle of knitting used to measure tension (gauge) or test stitch patterns

Tail
The short end of yarn that's not being used

Tapestry needle
See yarn needle

Through back loop (tbl)
When making a stitch, put the needle through the back of the loop instead

Twisted stitch
A type of stitch that's worked through the back loop

Weave in
To hide and secure loose ends and the tail on the finished product

Weight
When referring to yarn, weight is the thickness of the yarn rather than the weight of the ball

Working yarn
The yarn that's coming from the ball of yarn and being used to make new stitches

Wrong side (WS)
The side of the work that will be hidden when finished

Yarn needle
A thick, blunt needle with a large eye that's used for darning yarn. It's also called a tapestry needle

Yarn over (yo)
A strand of yarn placed over the left-hand needle to create a new stitch